SECRET MESA

SECRET MESA

Inside Los Alamos National Laboratory

JO ANN SHROYER

John Wiley & Sons, Inc.
New York • Chichester • Weinheim
Brisbane • Singapore • Toronto

Copyright © 1998 by Jo Ann Shroyer.

Published by John Wiley & Sons, Inc.

Library of Congress Cataloging-in-Publication Data

Shroyer, Jo Ann.
        Secret mesa : inside Los Alamos National Laboratory / Jo Ann Shroyer.
            p.   cm.
    Includes index.
    ISBN 0-471-04063-0 (cloth : alk. paper)
    1. Los Alamos National Laboratory—History.   2. Engineering laboratories—New Mexico—Los Alamos—History.   3. Nuclear weapons—Research—New Mexico—Los Alamos—History.   I. Title.
QC789.2.U62L677   1998
620'.00720789'58—dc21   97-9517
                                                                                                             CIP

Printed in the United States of America

10 9 8 7 6 5 4 3 2 1

To my husband, J. G. Preston

Contents

Acknowledgments

I am grateful to the many people of Los Alamos and Los Alamos National Laboratory who generously took time to talk with me and share their stories, especially Joe and Virginia Martz, James Mercer-Smith, Paul White, Mark Tilden, Karen Brandt, Tom Ribe, and Ed Grothus. Thank you to laboratory archivist Roger Meade, the laboratory public affairs office, the Los Alamos Historical Society, and Mesa Public Library in Los Alamos for their assistance. I also wish to acknowledge my family and friends for their steadfast support and understanding during my work on this book. Thank you to my mother, Frances Shroyer, and my children, Jessy, Katy, Peter, and Claire, for their patience and support, to Nancy Golden and my brother, Beryl L. Shroyer, for their research help, to April Carlson for help with travel, and most especially to my husband, J. G. Preston, for his extraordinary research assistance and insights.

Introduction

It's easy to feel watched in Los Alamos. During my first visit to the town several years ago, I stopped by the side of the road to take a picture of what I thought was just the Santa Fe National Forest. A small pickup truck did a quick U-turn and parked next to me until I left. When this happened again on another public highway in the area, I began to wonder whose woods these really were.

Later I learned that the technical areas of Los Alamos National Laboratory (LANL) extend far beyond the obvious cluster of gray and tan buildings at its center. They are spread out over forty-three square miles of woods and canyons and are hemmed in by national forest and parklands. It turns out I was nowhere near the heavily guarded areas of the lab, where picture taking would be considered a threat to national security. But I was quietly watched, nonetheless.

This experience was an enticing first hint of the secretive aura—part fact and part fable—that still clings to this unusual place.

The town of Los Alamos (Spanish for "the poplars") was born in secrecy in 1943; it was created by the United States government during the Manhattan Project as the final assembly site for the world's first atomic weapon. Until the federal government took over the mesa, it had been sparsely populated by a few ranchers and the boys at a boarding school for the sons of privileged East Coast families.

Wide modern highways climb the flanks of the mesa now, but in the early days, the road to Los Alamos was rocky, prone to muddy washouts, and full of hairpin curves. The roads to the top of the mesa are lined with cliffs of tawny, pockmarked rock that looks like old Swiss cheese but is actually solidified volcanic ash, or tuff. In fact, the creators of the world's first atomic explosion built their weapon on the front porch of an ancient giant—a massive volcano that erupted a million years ago, rolling tons of ash over what is now northern New Mexico and launching it on the wind to as far away as Iowa. The Jemez Mountains that tower above Los Alamos on the west are packed with some one hundred silent volcanoes. Los Alamos scientists have experimented at tapping the heat that still remains deep in the rocks, while hikers bathe in the warmth of the many hot springs that rise from the earth in wooded canyons.

Today Los Alamos is the company town for one of the biggest multidisciplinary scientific research centers in the world, conducting a wide range of basic research that has little to do with weapons development. However, as the nation's premier weapons laboratory, LANL owes its existence and its billion-dollar annual budgets to its central mission, the design of nuclear weapons. Fully 80 percent of the warheads in the U.S. stockpile came from the fertile minds of Los Alamos scientists.

The demographics of Los Alamos are rather strange for a town of its size, fewer than twenty thousand people. The population includes more Ph.D.'s—most of them physicists and engineers—per capita than anywhere else in the world, a recipe that guarantees interesting town government, school politics, and family life. There are children in Los Alamos who do not know what their fathers and mothers do for a living and spouses and neighbors who can't talk to each other about work, held in check by security clearances and long-practiced habits of secrecy.

The work of the laboratory was shut off from the prying eyes of ordinary citizens for many years, existing on a secret mesa that was protected first by the army, later by hired protection services, and always sheltered by the classification system that keeps secret a prodigious amount of the information that lab scientists have collected over the past fifty years. While recent openness initiatives have loosened the tight rein on information, the laboratory is still a secretive place because of the sensitive nature of weapons work.

In New Mexico the town is an anomaly—a predominantly white society in the midst of a multicultural state that is mainly Hispanic and Native American. It is an affluent community in a state that is one of the poorest in the nation. And its lifeblood is data—the concrete, observable information that is science—while it is surrounded by Indian cultural traditions whose roots are held in place by powerful, intuitive mythologies. Santa Fe, a magnet for people who live by art and intuition, lies just thirty-five miles south of Los Alamos, but at least a light-year away in terms of attitude and focus. Santa Fe is alive with antinuclear activists who keep a suspicious watch on their neighbors on the mesa.

During the day Santa Fe and Los Alamos are invisible to each other; but at night when the lights come on, Santa Fe—whose sandy-hued adobe houses seem to have sprung whole from the bones of the earth—reveals itself not as the quaint Hispanic village it wants to be, but as the big town that it really is. And the lights of Los Alamos—a town that shows little organic connection to its place—float in the high distance like primitive campfires that are visible for miles. The two towns, as one Los Alamos scientist put it, are like Sparta and Athens: at war with each other, but at the same time needing each other in some fundamental way in order to be complete.

The spirit of Los Alamos is best understood within the context of its history—a story that is still vividly alive in the memories and the on-going mission of both the town and the laboratory. How a team of scientists and engineers, many of them very young, came there and worked against time to create an atomic bomb has become a twentieth-century legend.

The Manhattan Project began when President Franklin D. Roosevelt learned from scientists about the possibility of a horrific new weapon based upon research that began with an early-twentieth-century prediction by Albert Einstein, who had theorized that immense amounts of energy were bound up in the nuclei of atoms. If the bonds holding the nuclei together could be broken, the energy would be released.

Fission was first recognized in the laboratory by German physicist Otto Hahn and Austrian physicist Lise Meitner. When Meitner fled to Sweden to escape Nazi persecution, German chemist Fritz Strassman became Hahn's partner, and together, with Meitner's advice from afar, they worked in 1932 to identify the particles that emerged when neutrons bombarding uranium atoms caused their nuclei to break apart. The mass of the resulting fragments was less than that of the original atom, and it soon became clear that the missing mass emerged from the interaction as energy. New neutrons were also produced by the fissioning of uranium, and were capable of splitting even more atoms, and thus sustaining a chain reaction. If uncontrolled, that chain reaction might set off an explosion. Italian physicist Enrico Fermi proved it in 1934, showing that the uranium nucleus could capture slow neutrons and split apart, releasing massive amounts of energy.

The world scientific community was aware of these astonishing discoveries, and it was only a matter of time, most thought, before someone learned how to make a fission weapon. Those who understood it assumed that Hitler's scientists would understand it as well, and the possibility that the German dictator could get his hands on such a device was a terrifying prospect. Otto Hahn is said to have considered suicide over the consequences of his research.[1] Hungarian theoretical physicists Leo Szilard, Eugene Wigner, and Edward Teller convinced Einstein to write a letter to President Roosevelt, warning him of this potential danger. Ultimately, that act, which Einstein came to regret, set into motion a giant technical effort that cost two billion wartime dollars, brought the long and bloody war with Japan to an abrupt end, and changed the complexion of world politics forever.

The task was named the Manhattan Project because much of the early work was done in research institutions in New York City and coordinated by the army's Manhattan Engineer District.

By 1942, Fermi, who immigrated to the United States in 1938, had achieved the first controlled chain reaction with a graphite-barricaded reactor underneath the football stadium at the University of Chicago. It was there that the atomic age really began.

The director of the nationwide effort to create a fission weapon was army Major General Leslie R. Groves, a hard-nosed military man with a reputation for bringing off huge, complicated building projects like the construction of the Pentagon, which he had supervised. He was a pragmatist who saw the sense in locating the secret laboratory on the mesa, while J. Robert Oppenheimer, a theoretical physicist from Berkeley and the newly appointed director of the lab, suggested the spot because of its stunning natural beauty. Oppenheimer had summered in the area for years and believed that the forceful and still largely untamed mountains, mesas, and canyons of northern New

Mexico would provide respite and solace during what was sure to be a difficult task. Furthermore, it would be a constant reminder of nature's dominion, an important consideration for scientists who pry so deeply into her secrets.

But there were more practical requirements to satisfy. This was an isolated high plateau in the remote mountains of a sparsely populated state, far removed from either coast and the threat of attack, guarded by high cliffs and a primitive road. A perfect place for keeping secrets.

Oppenheimer accepted Groves's tight external security in exchange for the free flow of information within the laboratory. The military's normal procedure is to protect secret information by restricting a worker's access to only those data that are relevant to his or her work. The physicists, chemists, metallurgists, and engineers at Los Alamos would have to work closely together in free communication, Oppenheimer argued, if this project was going to succeed. The notion of open collaboration among scientists of different disciplines is still celebrated today at the laboratory and is an important part of the Oppenheimer legacy. This principle led to a critical technical breakthrough that made the plutonium bomb possible, and it makes today's laboratory uniquely suited to grand technical challenges, lab spokesmen say.

The researchers hired to work at the wartime lab came from university laboratories all over the country—mainly the University of California at Berkeley, the California Institute of Technology, the University of Chicago, Columbia University, and Cornell University. The nucleus of the group was composed of scientists who had been associates and students of Oppenheimer. At Los Alamos they worked alongside European scientists who had escaped fascism and had a deeply personal interest in preventing Hitler from getting the atomic bomb first. As a result, the atmosphere on "the hill," as it came to be known to its residents, was intense.

There were no guarantees that the job they had been asked to do could be done. It has been said that the youth of the researchers, whose average age was twenty-five, may have contributed to the success of the project; they weren't old enough to know how impossible it really was. They were to study the properties of fissionable materials and figure out precisely how to build this "gadget," as it came to be called. However, the amounts of fissionable materials required for the actual weapon did not yet exist. Reactors were built at Oak Ridge, Tennessee, and Hanford, Washington, to separate the needed and quite rare uranium 235 from the isotopes of uranium that formed the bulk of the element that existed on the planet. The Hanford plant set to work making plutonium—a substance that may have once existed in the earth's crust but was now available only in minute man-made portions.

Meanwhile the muddy inaccessibility of the mesa was an impediment to the work that had to be done. There was no local power company to provide energy for the operation of machinery, for example, so the scientists were forced to use four old diesel generators found at an abandoned mine in Colorado. The resulting power plant, replete with a grizzled old miner who came with the equipment, ran with intermittent success. Power fluctuations were a continuing problem. Water was in short supply and had to be carried in overland pipes from Guaje Canyon seven miles north of Los Alamos. Army engineers built dams there to catch mountain runoff. The water was gritty and smelled of chlorine and leaf mold. It caused in newcomers a three-day illness dubbed "Hillitis." The water tank was equipped with a gauge that the new town's citizens consulted before they allowed themselves the luxury of a bath.

The scientists had been permitted to bring their families to the mesa and, being young, created an inconvenient baby boom that overwhelmed the scarce and hastily built housing. The initial plan for the laboratory had allowed for no more than a hundred scientists, but the working population proceeded to double every nine months. Having been promised a complete community with homes, schools, a hospital, a post office, a library, movies, restaurants, a laundry, and all the other accoutrements of comfortable small-town life, the families were stunned by what they found: a muddy plateau with primitive housing, an inadequate water supply, no telephones, censored mail, and armed guards everywhere. Memoirs of the time paint a picture of muddy streets overrun by children and dogs, with everything surrounded by high barbedwire fences that reminded the Europeans of concentration camps.

The long hours of hard work and the discomforts and privations suffered by the scientists and their families were offset by the conviction that they were doing important scientific work that would affect the outcome of the war. They were sustained by patriotism and the excitement of being involved in such an important secret project. These sentiments are still honored in Los Alamos and continue to motivate many laboratory workers today. Retired Manhattan Project veterans and Cold Warriors, many of whom have chosen to stay in Los Alamos, are mystified by the prevailing attitude in the outside world, as they call it, that they should be ashamed of their history. In contrast to the way Los Alamos is often portrayed, many of its residents would prefer to think of it as a symbol of peace, the place where technology made world war unthinkable. The concept of nuclear weaponeers as peacemakers was well established during the Cold War, when some Strategic Air Command bases boasted billboards that declared, "Peace Is Our Profession"; but the notion originated with Oppenheimer and others involved with the Manhattan Project, who believed at the time that humankind, given this terrible power to destroy itself, would find redemption instead.[2]

Given its dramatic history and its strategic importance to U.S. national defense, Los Alamos makes a disappointing first impression. It's neither formidable nor pretty, looking as it does like something a physicist had designed strictly for function and practicality. This is actually very close to the truth because when the physicists began arriving on the mesa during World War II, the experimentalists—unlike the theoreticians who needed only blackboards and peace in which to think, read, and talk—had nothing to do until their buildings and equipment were in place, so they busied themselves putting up structures.

While most of the wartime buildings are gone now, drab government-issue style dominated Los Alamos during the fifties until residents were allowed to build and own their own homes. The barracks-like buildings left over from the early Cold War years now serve as the town's low-rent district. But out on the fingers of the plateau and perched on the edges of the breathtaking canyons there are woodsy and interesting homes like those you might find in any mountain resort community. Nevertheless, there is an aura remaining of that government-run town that gives no quarter to luxuries not vital to the scientific mission. Still dependent on federal dollars and the unpredictable winds of war and politics, the lab and the community invests in function, not flash.

During the war, Los Alamos was closed to all but the families who worked and lived there, plus a few important government representatives and consulting scientists who were allowed to visit. The town remained closed until 1957, when the fences came down, to the dismay of many of the residents who had grown accustomed to feeling safely shut off from the outside world. They unsuccessfully petitioned to keep the gates closed.

Habits of secrecy still cling to the mesa, where a four-hundred-strong civilian contract security force guards the laboratory and, along with the community's police force, watches over the town. The guards are mostly New Mexicans whose primary job is to prevent plutonium and other dangerous substances from falling into the wrong hands. Technical Area (TA)-55, the plutonium-processing facility at the laboratory, may be one of the most intensely guarded acreages in the United States. It is an awesome place, surrounded by a maze of barriers topped with glinting spirals of razor wire and strings of prickly barbed fencing, while motion detectors and armed guards cast suspicious eyes in every direction. The guards are specially trained to turn back terrorist attacks, the chief security worry at Los Alamos. In one such training exercise during the 1994 Christmas season, a guard was shot to death by a colleague who somehow accidentally loaded his machine gun with live ammunition. Locals will tell you that it's important to respect the laboratory's guards. "If they tell you to halt, you'd better do it," a lifetime resident told me.

In their tan uniforms, black boots, and black-holstered sidearms, the security guards have a vaguely foreign, militaristic appearance. As a result, the process of "going behind the fence"—the laboratory euphemism for visiting secured areas—can be unsettling at best. To its freewheeling Santa Fe neighbors and, indeed, anyone not used to the culture, the tightly buttoned and stern public demeanor of Los Alamos National Laboratory is somewhat distasteful and threatening.

Los Alamos has been described as the world supply of nerds—badly dressed, absent-minded brainiacs who can't manage to wear matching socks. That turns out to be an overstatement; what you're likely to see is merely the sort of eccentricity and casual dress that is common on many college campuses. In winter you'll notice the ruddy faces and telltale goggle marks of the Alpine skier. People rush out to the mountains during their lunch breaks to get in an hour of skiing before they go back to their labs and offices. The ski hill is a privately owned membership club that dates back to the winter of 1944–1945

during the Manhattan Project. Ukrainian chemist George Kistia-
kowsky—who had produced the explosive lenses for Fat Man, the
bomb that destroyed Nagasaki, and later fervently opposed nuclear
weapons—cleared trees for the ski run by detonating necklaces of surplus plastic explosives around the trunks, effectively cutting them in
half. Admiral William "Deak" Parsons, the director of the ordnance division in the wartime laboratory, was quoted as saying, "Isn't it wonderful to see five thousand people intent on a single purpose—skiing!"[3]

On any day you will see people jogging, biking, in-line skating, or
walking to work, if they are not roaring around in the ubiquitous four-
wheel-drive vehicles and pickups, nearly always topped with ski racks.
The sort of driven personality that can labor night and day in a laboratory is capable of applying the same intensity of purpose to recreation.
Los Alamos takes its hobbies very seriously. The lab's cafeteria, like its
Wellness Center, dishes up an inoffensive menu of healthful alternatives for lab employees. You would be hard-pressed to find anyone who
smokes.

Los Alamos is a complex place, not easily understood. It is populated by bright, quirky, and unusual people who continue to do important but sometimes controversial work, much of it completely unrelated to weapons design. And while there are few monuments to
its history in the town, the community is still saturated with the details
and purpose of its origin. That human and technical background is
important to understanding the Los Alamos of today—a community
that has been both a beneficiary and a victim of its own history and
mythology.

But the past is not the subject of this book. Los Alamos, like Hiroshima and Nagasaki, is a living, breathing human community that
survived the dramatic events that put it on the map. The lab was slated
to close after the war ended; many of the scientists who worked on the
bomb went back to their university laboratories, some of them so horrified by what they had created that they spent the rest of their lives opposing nuclear weapons. But LANL thrived and grew fat on the mechanics of the Cold War, and only in recent years, with the fall of the
Berlin Wall and the implosion of the Soviet Union, did the institution
have to worry about its future, justify its existence, and come to grips
with the changing attitude toward its mission. The demand for new

nuclear weapons had already begun to fade in the wake of landmark arms control agreements, and with the halt of underground testing, the laboratory was forced to reexamine its reason for being.

But the lab sensibly seized upon new technical challenges, including the immense task of cleaning up the idle and widely contaminated nuclear weapons production complex and somehow containing or eliminating the tons of plutonium and other radioactive detritus that remain. According to a recent Department of Energy estimate, the cleanup cost could consume hundreds of billions of dollars and take more than sixty years to accomplish. Who is more qualified to clean up the mess, lab managers ask, than the people who understand the materials best?

Furthermore, until the United States decides what to do with its remaining nuclear weapons stockpile, someone has to look after it, lab spokesmen explain. As weapons age, the materials from which they are constructed will surely degrade, as will their performance. So they must be regularly maintained, until such time that they, like the production complex that made them, can all be decommissioned—an unlikely prospect in a world where small nations increasingly see nuclear weapons as the big stick that will guarantee their sovereignty.

Many Los Alamos weapons scientists still advocate limited underground testing, describing the maintenance conundrum this way: just as a car would cease to run if you put it on blocks in a garage for thirty years—the age of the oldest nuclear weapons in the U.S. stockpile—and neglected to maintain or test it, so too would nuclear weapons cease to function. They are, after all, technical beasts made with unstable materials that change over time.

Still other weapons experts at the laboratory are convinced that just as they adapted to the ban on aboveground testing, they can likewise deal with the ban on underground testing, identifying new technical tools for what is now called science-based stockpile stewardship. However it's done, lab spokesmen say, the guarantee that nuclear weapons will work if they are called upon is still at the heart of deterrence theory.

It is an irony of our times, however, that while the United States and the former Soviet republics are decommissioning their nuclear weapons as quickly as possible, there are small countries that can't wait to get nukes of their own. Several nations exist as undeclared but unde-niable nuclear states—Israel being the most notable among them, hav-ing perhaps as many as two hundred nuclear weapons in its secret stockpile.

Stopping the furious proliferation of nuclear weapons has become an important mission for both the United States and Russia. Los Alamos scientists have taken a leading role, claiming that the collapse of the Soviet Union has made the world not safer but more dangerous, because the chaos in the crumbling former Soviet Union has allowed nuclear materials to be smuggled out. Such materials could find their way into the hands of people who might show less restraint than did the world's two superpowers during the Cold War. Indeed, several weapons designers at Los Alamos have predicted that sometime within the next ten years a nuclear weapon will be used in anger somewhere in the world, most likely lobbed over the back fence of small but hostile neighbors in limited but dangerous regional conflicts.

Los Alamos scientists have worked to prevent such developments by assisting the Russians in beefing up security for their nuclear mate-rials, and initiating cooperative research programs with scientists at their sister laboratory in Russia. The purpose for the joint research was not only to engage the Russian scientists in challenging work that might prevent them from taking their skills to proliferant countries, but also to allow U.S. scientists to learn from their formidable former adversaries, who have developed some nuclear technologies that are more advanced than U.S. nuclear research.

In addition to its role in maintaining the U.S. weapons stockpile, cleaning up the contaminated weapons complex, and seeing to the dis-position of surplus plutonium, the laboratory continues to do basic re-search in many other areas of science, concentrating on core compe-tencies in nuclear technology; high-performance computing and modeling; dynamic experimentation; systems engineering and proto-typing; materials technology; laser, particle, and ion beam technolo-gies; and complex systems. Such a list doesn't begin to convey the wide variety of research being done at the laboratory by people who were meticulous about distancing themselves from weapons work when I in-terviewed them. Such compartmentalized thinking is another feature in the complex social structure of Los Alamos National Laboratory.

Meanwhile, a large public affairs department churns out press releases and glossy publications extolling the benefits of LANL research. As the lab's public affairs director, Scott Duncan, bluntly put it, his department's primary purpose is to "attract $1.1 billion of funding."[4] At the same time, lab public affairs tries to communicate meaningfully with the public by way of the press, with whom the laboratory shares a mutual and well-oiled distrust. The results have been mixed.

The problem is, most people aren't willing to trust or believe Los Alamos scientists nowadays. After having worked for years in silence and secrecy, these researchers have more recently been forced to court public understanding and acceptance in order to thrive. But they are not very good at it. And it means swimming upstream against a powerful current of cultural distaste for the work that the laboratory has done these past fifty years. Perhaps they were too arrogant after all, lab spokesmen have told me. Perhaps they should have told the public and Congress more about what they were doing with their generous and largely unsupervised annual budgets.

One feature of this new era of openness for government laboratories has been the unhinging of its tightly bound secrets. Among the legacies of of the Cold War was an increase in government secrecy, with not only a corresponding growth in the size of government but also an accumulation of classified documents that is so large that it surpassed the ability of the Department of Energy (DOE), the federal overseer of the weapons complex, to deal with it. In an attempt to reduce the mass of classified documents, to release information useful to the cleanup and safe disposition of nuclear waste and U.S. plutonium stores, and to clarify what really should be kept secret, the DOE has invested in a multimillion-dollar computer program to mine this data mountain. Its first assignment was to scan some hundred million pages of documents.

It was unfortunate timing for the laboratory that at the very juncture when it most needed public understanding and support for its mission, the institution's trustworthiness was called into question by a particularly disturbing aspect of the new Department of Energy openness policy. Energy Secretary Hazel O'Leary decided to reveal the nature of Cold War plutonium experiments on humans, many of them vulnerable people who had not given their consent. Much of the study results had been published in the scientific literature years ago, but recent newspaper articles attached human faces and stories to the scientific data, and revealed that doctors and scientists at hospitals, universities, and national laboratories were involved in exposing retarded children, terminally ill patients, pregnant women, and their own children to radioactive substances. These revelations served only to reinforce the public suspicion that scientists—and government scientists in particular—may not have the people's best interests at heart.

Some thirty-two million pages of classified documents on human radiation testing—equivalent to twenty-five stacks of paper, each as tall as the Gateway Arch in St. Louis—were pulled out of file drawers, storage rooms, and garages around the country. Some of these documents were at Los Alamos.

LANL responded by creating a human studies committee, made up of current and retired lab scientists, to review the materials and release them to the public. This experience was particularly excruciating for the veteran Cold Warriors at the lab and represented an important sea change in the life of the institution. Closely guarded research notes and the rationale for the experiments they documented were becoming an open book. The idea was deeply disturbing.

Los Alamos researchers have complained that neither the press nor the public understands the nature of research, being undereducated in science and quick to make emotional judgments about technical issues. Radiation has become a modern day bogeyman, they've said, the fear of it totally out of proportion to its danger. They pointed to the fact that the Los Alamos researchers who fed radioactive materials to their children back in the fifties were exposing them to lower levels than those inflicted by today's common diagnostic tests.

A more recent event was cited as a further illustration of this so-called senseless, runaway fear of radiation. Energy Secretary O'Leary asked the laboratory to allow *Good Morning America* host Joan Lunden behind the fence and permit her to hold a protectively sheathed sphere of plutonium on camera. The idea was to educate the public about the substance. Lunden was visibly shaken as she held the plutonium in her gloved hands; LANL's director Sig Hecker reminded the television host that she had been exposed to more radiation by simply flying in an airplane to New Mexico than she was by holding that ball. It was a story that I heard from several lab scientists and engineers who thought it both amusing and rather pathetic.

But what many Los Alamos scientists forget is that, to average people, nuclear physics is densely complex and difficult to understand. And even understanding the science behind radiation does not necessarily erase the profound fear that it inspires. One young plutonium scientist admitted to me that even he, after years of study, was surprisingly frightened the first time he walked into the plutonium facility at Los Alamos. He understood what can happen when hard facts are filtered through a strong cultural bias against their meaning.

Furthermore, the study of nuclear weaponry and deterrence theory is so infused with secrets and arcane knowledge as to be nearly impenetrable. As a result, art and pop culture, in the absence of useful information about Cold War science, have offered up their own explanations for everything that happened after Hiroshima. While these images that have been burned into our imaginations are not always scientifically accurate, they contain an element of truth and have become part of a powerful popular image of nuclear science. Many of the Los Alamos scientists I talked to did not seem to understand this. As much as the average citizen struggles to comprehend the mind-set of scientists, the technical culture often fails to understand the deeply entrenched fears and concerns of the general public.

However, it is important to realize that contrary to the way it is sometimes portrayed, the nuclear weapons culture as it exists at Los Alamos today is not completely devoid of conscience or thoughtful discourse. Many of the researchers I spoke with are insightful souls who reflect carefully upon the meaning of their work. I met weapons designers who also specialized in philosophy, ancient history, and music, and resented their portrayal as mindless technobots who callously churned out endless weapons of destruction. They are not a community of Dr. Strangeloves, as one weapons scientist ruefully put it, but the scientists who made the risk of big wars unthinkable, who forced nations to change the way that they relate to one another. And while they radiate a kind of sadness, they will tell you that they are, nevertheless, idealists: "You have to be if you do this kind of work," a weapons designer told me. "I sure hope I'm not fooling myself about this. It's a terrible thing to know that if you are wrong, you are responsible for killing a lot of people. Then, I promise, the seventh circle of the inferno would be far too good for you."

1

The Witch in the Fairy Tale

The offices of X-2, the thermonuclear weapons design group at Los Alamos National Laboratory, look a lot like any university physics department, except that on the day that I first visited, there were armed guards standing around in the hallway. I was there to meet James "Jas" Mercer-Smith, X-2's group leader at the time and soon to be promoted to deputy program director for nuclear weapons technology. "And a scary interview," my overeager public affairs escort assured me as we went through the security checkpoint at the front door. My ID was examined, my purse searched, and I was asked to walk through a metal detector before gaining access to the building and the people in X-2.

But Mercer-Smith, dressed in a dark blue business suit and white shirt, looked no scarier than a bureaucrat or a teacher. In his early forties, he was pale, wore glasses, and had the molelike concentrated stare of someone who spends his life looking at ciphers on a computer screen. He spoke in a gentle, whispery voice and gestured with long thin hands. He had a surprising flair for drama. "Our job, the role that we play in society, is to be the evil witch in Grimm's fairy tales," Mercer-Smith told me, quickly dispelling any resemblance between him and the typical college professor. "Our job is to scare little children into behaving." He referred to the paradox at the heart of his profession—to guarantee peace by making weapons so horrible that no country would ever be foolish enough to provoke their use. The people who created such killing machines were only buying time for the world's politicians

17

to forge a peaceful resolution to their ideological differences. Nuclear weapons were the ultimate big stick, commanding respect and compliance, Mercer-Smith explained. He and many of his colleagues consider such a deterrent to be still necessary and worthwhile in a world where other nations continue to maintain and even add to their stockpiles. Furthermore, he insisted, it is vitally important that as long as the United States has weapons in its stockpile, the expertise to intelligently maintain them should also exist.

We were seated at a table in his office, a room filled with books, file cabinets, and computers; the sun trickled in through the one window that illuminated the office. "You don't like being every child's nightmare. It's not what I would have chosen for my career," Mercer-Smith explained, adding that he had wanted to be an astrophysicist. "You don't set out to do this. You set out to study stars. But I figured this was probably the only place where there was a real job." He also explained that a position at LANL offered him an opportunity to serve his country. In the Soviet Union all the best young physicists disappeared into the weapons program, Mercer-Smith said, while this wasn't true in the United States. "So, it seemed to me to be an important thing to do, in order to maintain balance. It was a commitment to the idea of deterrence. Of course, it was a different era then. I don't know for sure if I would make the same set of decisions now. Anyway, it turned out that I was not that great an astrophysicist. I was good, but not great. But I'm really good at designing nuclear weapons."

Unlike some of the other weaponeers that I met, Jas Mercer-Smith had chosen to face head-on the dark side of his occupation; but he spent considerable time during our talks discussing the idea that weapons designers are actually peacemakers whose work is misunderstood and widely unappreciated. People like him, Mercer-Smith said, had managed to prevent another world war. "But when were nuclear weapons designers ever heroes?" he asked. "During World War II. In the future when will we be heroes for the American people? When we actually have to use one of these weapons to defend our country, and for us, that will be our greatest failure. It's a no-win situation, and that's a hard life. It's very sad, what we're doing," he told me. He said weapons designers were, in a way, tragic heroes. "Nobody would admit it in public; it's not part of the culture. But maybe we all believe it, deep down in our hearts."

In addition to astrophysics, Mercer-Smith loved Roman and Greek history. He drew upon a favorite story from Herodotus, a Greek historian from the fifth century B.C., to explain the nuclear weapons designer's role in today's society: "The king is going to condemn some merchant to death. The merchant knows that the king has a favorite horse, and he persuades the king that if he is allowed to live for a year, he will teach the horse to sing. The king decides he has nothing to lose, so here's the guy out there teaching the horse to sing by singing to it. And the merchant's friends come over and say, 'This is crazy. You can't teach a horse to sing!' And the guy says, 'Many things can happen in a year. I can die, then I won't care. The king can die and I'll be free. Or the horse could die. Or maybe I could teach the horse to sing.'

"And that's why we're here; for the last forty thousand years, people have been getting more and more efficient at the intraspecies competition that we call war. And what we are doing now is stalling for time, trying to keep people from killing themselves in vast numbers." This interpretation of the laboratory's duty—buying time for peaceful solutions—is the polestar by which weapons designers have navigated the choppy waters of the Cold War for fifty years. The theory is attributed to Norris Bradbury, a former laboratory director and the successor to J. Robert Oppenheimer. But it has its roots in the Manhattan Project, when the developers of the first atomic bomb suggested that a demonstration of their invention would be sufficient to force the Japanese to surrender. Many of them were horrified when they realized that the bomb would actually be used to kill people. They advocated international control of atomic energy and weapons, but to no avail; their invention was now in the hands of politicians and the military.

However, contemporary Los Alamos scientists believe that their theory has been proved by the unprecedented arms reduction agreement signed by the United States and Russia in January 1993. By signing the Strategic Arms Reduction Treaty II (START II), both superpowers agreed to reduce their arsenals to a mere 3,500 weapons by the year 2003. This development provoked a flood of calls from reporters to the laboratory's public affairs office, seeking to gauge the mood on the hill now that an arms drawdown appeared to be putting the nuclear weapons industry out of business. Was the mood bleak? the press wondered. A public affairs spokesman polled a number of the scientists at the laboratory and found that the opposite was true. "People were very proud—jubilant, in fact," he reported. "We won, we did our job. This was a great day in history."

And it was also the proof of deterrence theory—an idea that had evolved over forty to fifty years of serious academic debate and was the object of an almost religious commitment within the weapons community, Mercer-Smith said. Many pages have been written about the intricacies of the strategic balance of power between the United States and the former Soviet Union. In 1948 deterrence against Soviet aggression was adopted as official U.S. policy by the National Security Council.[1] Thereafter, mathematical formulae were devised to describe the probabilities of destruction and survival, while the chest-thumping threats of instantaneous massive retaliation by John Foster Dulles in the early 1950s gave way to a carefully balanced standoff that Henry Kissinger came to describe as essentially a mind game. "And it is based on this really uncivilized principle," Mercer-Smith continued. "You as a potential adversary will behave, or I will kill you, your children, and your children's children to the nth generation. Therefore I hope that, out of your own self-interest, you will behave in a rational fashion. This logic actually has worked very well, but it's not pleasant," he said. "That's why we here at Los Alamos are committed to the idea of somehow avoiding nuclear war—any nuclear war, anywhere."

But now that the Cold War is over, historians are beginning to re-examine this logic that drove the arms race to the point that, at its peak, both the USSR and the United States each had over thirty thousand nuclear weapons. In 1968 Henry Kissinger wrote that while deterrence logic may have prevented nuclear wars by posing unacceptable risks, it also fundamentally changed the meaning of power. "In short, as power has grown more awesome, it has also turned abstract, intangible, elusive," Kissinger wrote. Before the bomb, a nation's strength was measured by its ability to protect its people from invasion. After World War II, however, as the superpowers armed themselves with increasingly destructive weapons, it became clear that thermonuclear devices would not guarantee the safety of the country that chose to use them. In fact, it would likely result in extravagant death and destruction on both sides. Thus military strength became separated from the practical formulation of policy.[2] "Making the world safe for conventional warfare," Mercer-Smith said, with a wry smile. Indeed, some historians suggest that a growing nuclear stockpile gave U.S. leaders the confidence to enter into conventional wars like Korea and Vietnam, wars that might otherwise have been deemed, in General Omar Bradley's words, "the wrong war in the wrong place at the wrong time."[3] Of course, there had still been wars, Mercer-Smith conceded, but they were small—like Vietnam, a minor conflict fought with serfs, as he put it—different by orders of magnitude from the violent conflagrations that would occur if the world's big powers had come to blows with the full force of their nuclear arsenals.

Some historians contend that the nascent American stockpile made possible the otherwise unthinkable rebuilding of the German economy after World War II, something that served to fuel the power struggle between the United States and the Soviet Union. The successful June 1946 atomic tests at the Bikini Atoll in the Pacific were a critical turning point in that struggle. Noting the massive explosion, the Soviet newspaper *Pravda* accused the United States of plotting an atomic war.[4] The arms race picked up speed.

Mercer-Smith's talk about the weighty problems of deterrence and the details of nuclear disaster was infused with a brittle, dark humor, a tendency that he described as essential to the work. There were cartoons tacked up outside office doors, something you also will see in a university physics department. However, in X-2 the cartoons poked fun at nuclear terror. One woman had posted a drawing of a mushroom cloud with a happy face. "Have a nice day!" Mercer-Smith quipped as he described it, adding that another woman in his group had designed a T-shirt that was emblazoned with a rose and the slogan "Ladies Crocheting Circle and Weapons Design Group."

"You will see and hear some wild and crazy things if you walk down this hallway," Mercer-Smith said, chuckling. "It's part of the culture, a way of coping." Now, the focus of the most strenuous coping exercises had to do with all of the changes that had been wrought upon the weapons community. How would weapons designers do their jobs, and, for that matter, what were their jobs going to be? One cartoon that had been passed around at the laboratory depicted nuclear scientists behind a glass door, like fire extinguishers; the caption read, "Break glass in case of emergency."

Merri Wood, one of Mercer-Smith's colleagues, had been particularly annoyed at the way her profession was being portrayed in the press—as self-serving whiners who were only interested in keeping their jobs alive. Wood is a wide-eyed, elfin-looking woman who has been working in the laboratory's Thermonuclear Applications Group since 1979, and unlike Mercer-Smith, she has been interested in weapons science since childhood, having read historical fiction about the making of the atom bomb. "I was impressed," she said. Later, as a physicist with nuclear engineering and astrophysics course work under her belt and a firm understanding of neutronics, she was recruited by Los Alamos National Laboratory. Interviewers had asked Wood if she felt betrayed by her country now that there was a moratorium on new nuclear weapons designs and a ban on further testing. "When they asked me if I felt betrayed, I said I thought the nation had been betrayed in terms of losing its capability to maintain a deterrent. But I wasn't whining," Wood raised her voice, frustrated and angry. "I was screaming!" she almost yelled it, and then quietly added, "figuratively, that is." On this day, she was dressed completely in black and jokingly referred to it as a perfect costume for Mercer-Smith's so-called witch in the fairy tale. "Well, look, we usually come across as baby burners, anyway," Mercer-Smith interjected, smiling slightly. "At least we've moved up to whiners." Wood's anger dissolved into laughter; Mercer-Smith beamed.

Wood believed that as long as the nation was committed to keeping at least some of its nuclear weapons, then the task of ensuring their viability and safety would be difficult without actually testing them. "Why would you want nuclear weapons, at all if they hadn't been tested?" Wood asked. "You wouldn't want a car that hadn't been tested! This is so far beyond logic that it's hard to discuss!" she said. The materials in nuclear weapons, just like those in cars, do not last forever, she explained impatiently, and while all of the designs in the stockpile had been tested at one time, the weapons themselves, some of them thirty-five years old, were aging. "What if you left the gasoline in your tank, the oil in the engine, and the insulation on the spark plug wires for fifty years, and now you are going to try and start it?" she asked sarcastically.

Every weapon as it was built was actually certified as functional, Mercer-Smith calmly explained. But the longer warheads sit around, the more likely they are to suffer degradation. And they rattle around on submarines; they get dropped. Furthermore, the longevity of the materials and their interactions with one another are not fully understood. Nuclear weapons technology is still relatively young; its practitioners have little experience with aging components, since weapons have not been kept in the stockpile for years and years. "Nobody was stupid enough to do that in the past, but we're going to," Mercer-Smith laughed.

However, a surveillance and remanufacturing program has always existed to screen stockpiled nuclear weapons and is capable of solving degradation problems without nuclear tests, wrote J. Carson Mark, a veteran of the Manhattan Project and head of the Theoretical Division at Los Alamos from 1947 to 1973. There is a long series of non-nuclear tests available to detect changes in the components of a weapon. In the past such weapons were sometimes tested because that option was available, but it is by no means necessary to do so.[5]

One result of the continuing ban on testing has been the forging of closer collaborations between designers like Wood and Mercer-Smith and plutonium chemists. "Unfortunately, we don't have any fifty-year-old nuclear weapons in the stockpile, or any understanding of what will happen inside a weapon that old," said Joe Martz, a young plutonium chemist at TA-55, the laboratory's plutonium facility. He had been described to me as a respected expert on plutonium and the problems of aging weapons materials. So I was surprised at how young he looked—like a studious high school boy, with the ramrod posture and penetrating focus of Forrest Gump. And like the movie character, the twenty-nine-year-old was earnest, sincere, and idealistic. However, Martz spoke in a speed train of clipped, precise words and is ferociously bright.

The effects of aging are predicted on the basis of the current understanding of the fundamental properties and chemistry of the substances involved, Martz explained. To that end, old weapons are torn apart and examined in detail in an effort to anticipate how their components might change and thus malfunction. This is critical work, Martz said, in view of the deep reductions in the stockpile that are planned by the new millennium, when major classes of weapons will be reduced from the twenty or so that existed ten years ago to perhaps seven in the end. During the heyday of the Cold War, weapons builders enjoyed the luxury of a vibrant manufacturing capability, as Martz put it. "If something went belly-up and a weapons system went bad, to heck with it. We had plenty more to stand in its place and we could always increase the numbers of those systems. Or we could build a new one," he said. "That's a luxury we don't have today."

Just how to make it all work—maintaining deterrence capability while running the arms race backwards, as lab director Sig Hecker likes to put it—is subject to wide interpretation at LANL. Martz believes that it is possible to reduce the number of weapons in the U.S. stockpile to as few as one hundred without jeopardizing the nation's deterrence capability. This is a radical opinion by lab standards, but one that he shares with Hans Bethe, the former head of the theoretical physics division at Los Alamos during the Manhattan Project and a Nobel laureate. In fact, Martz cited a talk Bethe had given in Los Alamos on the fortieth anniversary of the founding of the lab as the inspiration for his own career choice. Martz was a high school student at the time, listening raptly as Bethe concluded his talk on astrophysics with an admonition to the students present concerning the legacy of nuclear weapons. "He looked at us young people and he seemed to be pointing his finger right at me when he said, 'It's up to you to find a better way to solve these problems,'" Martz said. More recently, Bethe has reasoned that reducing the nation's stockpile to as few as a hundred weapons would above all eliminate the threat of a nuclear holocaust, while at the same time maintain a deterrent against countries like Iraq and North Korea, who "treat the problem lightly," he said. "There have to be nuclear weapons in the hands of more responsible countries to deter such use."[6] But the best way to achieve these goals, Martz said, is to resume testing nuclear weapons. "Now that sounds strange at first," he said, "but just look at this. What do you think happened to the total number of nuclear weapons in the United States arsenal between 1965 and 1987?" Audiences at the talks Martz gives on weapons issues nearly always get the answer to that question wrong, he said. It is one of the misconceptions about weapons science that he would like to dispel. Martz is a dedicated and frequent public spokesman for the laboratory, being both knowedgeable and articulate. And he is able to make friends with cynical reporters and hardened antinuclear activists, a talent that can only help the cause that he espouses with an admittedly religious zeal.

The answer to the question, Martz said, may be surprising. "The number [of nuclear weapons] had been cut nearly in half from 1965 to

1987," he said, explaining that these reductions—during the height of the Cold War and before the arms agreements that would dramatically reduce the stockpile—had been achieved through technical improvements in the reliability and accuracy of the weapons. "And the total destructive power or yield of the weapons in the stockpile has gone down by a factor of four. We've made one bomb that can stand in for ten," he added. "And I argue that as we continue to reduce the number of nuclear weapons and as we rely less and less on large numbers of them in our arsenal, issues of reliability become even more important."

Martz has a favorite analogy to illustrate his opinion: "There's a fire and you have twenty fire extinguishers sitting there. You have a pretty good chance of finding one that works and you're going to put out the flames. But if you have only one fire extinguisher, you're going to want to test that thing, understand how it works, and make sure it's recharged!" he said, adding that most of the weapons in the U.S. arsenal have experienced serious reliability problems at one time or another. Some problems have been so serious that entire weapons systems had to be withdrawn. A prime unclassified example, he said, was the W-80 warhead, designed at Los Alamos. It was created to be attached to a sea or air launch missile, a device that would hang underneath the wing or sit in the belly of a bomber in Alaska, for example. As such, the W-80s were designed to work within a range of temperatures or Stockpile to Target Sequence (STS) conditions, Martz said. The STS, or temperature range, was entered into the design computational codes to make sure that the warhead would function under those conditions. When it was tested in Nevada, the W-80 worked fine at ambient temperatures, Martz said, but when they tried to set it off at the low end of the temperature range, the warhead was a dud. The weapon had to go back to the drawing board so that major parts of the system could be redesigned and then tested again. "Now, all of a sudden, we are downsizing our stockpiles and peace is breaking out all over, thank goodness, " Martz said. "Yet right at this critical juncture, people have the intrinsic assumption that we can get rid of nuclear testing and nuclear weapons laboratories, when, the irony is, just the opposite is true. This is the time when we most need them."

However, Carson Mark has written that weapons systems failures cited by those who oppose a comprehensive test ban occurred because the weapons were not adequately tested in the first place. "A weapon should not be deployed before all tests necessary to certify it for deployment have been made and provided acceptable results." Those predeployment tests should anticipate any changes that might occur because of operational conditions or aging. Furthermore, he contends, a single full-fledged nuclear test does little to confirm the total reliability of a weapons system; dozens of the same device would have to be tested in order to produce a statistically reliable sample, an impractical solution that has never been suggested. Mark also believes that any deterioration problems in the stockpile can be corrected by remanufacturing the weapon according to the original specifications of the design, while at the same time avoiding substitutions that would indeed require a full test.[7]

Most senior weapons scientists at the laboratory would not quibble with the idea that there is still a need for weapons expertise and some kind of testing regime, but Martz's suggestion that the stockpile could safely be reduced to as few as a hundred weapons is not widely accepted at all. Steve Younger, director of the nuclear weapons technology program at LANL, reacted to the idea by suggesting that, in short, talk is cheap. "When people say that, with super technology, a hundred weapons are going to be adequate, well, maybe," he said with cool sarcasm. "And maybe that super technology will even work. But the people actually responsible for doing things have a different perspective than people who just have to talk about them."

Younger is a small-framed man, poker-faced, blond, and pragmatic. He reminded me of the stern-faced, hardworking German farmers of my childhood. They kept their old tractors for years and years, making them work just fine, ignoring the latest, and what they viewed as expensive and wasteful, innovations coming out of the farm equipment industry. Younger referred to the laboratory equivalent of the profligate, equipment-hungry young farmer as a technology enthusiast. "They believe their paper-and-pencil calculations that say 'We can do this! And, boy! It's going to be great! It's not going to cost much money and it's going to exceed what everyone else has done!' Well, a few of those programs succeed, but almost all of them fail because they come up against some insurmountable obstacle, or it costs too much, or there's a surprise from an experiment. The hard part, I've come to realize, being around different parts of the nuclear weapons program, is to actually accomplish something," Younger said, placing special emphasis on those last two words, "and to make it work this year and the next year and the year after that—in a cost-effective manner," he added pointedly. "This requires considerable discipline."

Discipline and a certain number of failures, Mercer-Smith said. "Actually, I think the public gives us more credit than we deserve," he laughed as he said it. "We've had many more failures than I think they would be comfortable with. Why do you think we tested so many?" he asked rhetorically. Merri Wood smiled nearby while Mercer-Smith waited for a couple of beats, like a comic about to deliver the punch line to a good, reliable joke. "Because so many of them didn't work!" they both said in unison, laughing heartily afterward. (There have been over a thousand tests done over the history of the U.S. nuclear weapons program, according to lab representatives. This is more tests than any other country has performed, including the former Soviet Union.) Both physicists contend that even though vast reductions in kilotonnage were accomplished by tactical and technical improvements in nuclear weapons delivery systems, there still remained the unpredictability of nuclear weapons science. The most carefully planned design may look perfect on paper, but when it is deposited at the bottom of a two-thousand-foot hole in the Nevada desert, it might not necessarily go off. "But, you see, we don't bang bombs off just to see if they work," Wood grew serious. "Oh, every once in a while we have to do a stockpile confidence test to keep the military happy. They just want to push the button. But we're after data."

During a test, the data are carried to the surface of the Nevada desert by way of fat cable umbilicals. They are attached to an enormous rack that contains diagnostic experiments specific to each test. The bomb is loaded into the bottom of the rack, a structure that can be as tall as two hundred feet, and is lowered into the finely machined hole, which is then carefully backfilled with a calculated layer cake of materials to keep radioactive gases from leaking out. The firing signal travels down to the weapon along the cable bundle, and when the weapon explodes, information races back out along the cables in front of the broiling wave of heat and pressure.

"You don't go in with a thermometer and take a measurement!" Wood declared. "It happens fast, in less than a millisecond, in a hostile environment where it is extremely difficult to extract data. You don't get to calibrate your equipment postshot because you have just vaporized it. Data is inferred from measurements of current alone, not neutron populations, criticality, reactivity, or temperature. All you can do is look at the radiations coming off and try to determine what it meant." This is not a trivial problem, she said. "It's not like a lab science where you can sit there fiddling with it, trying to get inside and figure out what's going on," she said. "You have to do it right the first time."

Up on the surface, when the weapon explodes, a shock wave moves along the skin of the earth, bellying up the desert floor and shaking dust into the air. The soil and rock around the weapon melt and vaporize, quickly creating a cavity. The molten earth captures the bomb debris and drops to the bottom of the chamber as it cools, creating a radioactive puddle of rare earth elements, while on the surface a crater will often form, as the soil above the cavity collapses down into the hole as a sunken column of rubble. The contents of the glassy pool at the bottom of the cavity are sampled by way of a drill hole angled in under the chamber; this material is then shipped back to Los Alamos to be analyzed for clues to what happened during the explosion.

In a profession where publishing is out of the question, peer review occurs within the closed nuclear weapons community, with what is intended to be a healthy competition with the weapons program at Lawrence Livermore National Laboratory in California. "And that is sometimes almost true," Mercer-Smith stated. "Sometimes it's healthy, and sometimes it's not so healthy. But the real reason they built Livermore is that no one at Los Alamos would talk to Teller." Edward Teller, the brilliant Hungarian physicist who came to the mesa in 1945 to work on the Manhattan Project, and later founded the Livermore laboratory, is still deeply resented by many in Los Alamos. Teller's difficult personality had alienated people in the wartime project, but the thing Los Alamos could not forgive was his damaging testimony against J. Robert Oppenheimer during the dark days of the Communist witch hunts, when the former director's ties to known Communists called into question his loyalty and patriotism. Because of Teller's testimony, Oppy, as he is still affectionately known in Los Alamos, was stripped of his security clearance. The rivalry between these two institutions is rooted in that history, and when Los Alamos scientists tried to define for me what their laboratory represents, they would often invoke Teller's name and his ethos in order to illustrate what Los Alamos is not. Steve Younger, who worked at Livermore before moving to Los Alamos, described the difference between the two institutions thus: "Los Alamos has always had the orientation of doing science and research, while Livermore's orientation has always been to build widgets," Younger said, adding that Teller had wanted to build a widget, the hydrogen bomb, and that's why Livermore was founded. "I don't think much of Teller," Younger concluded, a sharp edge in his voice, "but then, he doesn't think much of me."

One of Mercer-Smith's fondest memories of the test site was his success with a shot that Livermore scientists had failed to bring off. "It was our idea originally, but they got to test it first and failed. So we came back a year later to do what they said was impossible, and we did it. It really was as much fun as I have ever had."

Beyond the personal and institutional coup that such a victory represents, a nuclear test is a deadly serious justification of a designer's ideas and research. Within the closed community it can be a very public success or failure, and a weapons designer's future is built upon a foundation of such test-site wins and losses. "You've spent a year of your life in front of a computer screen, plus you've spent a year of the lives of five hundred other people on your crank idea," Mercer-Smith added. "You get just one try and it had better be good, because the government has just spent forty million dollars on it." The technical pressures include the possibility that some seemingly trivial thing can queer the test, Mercer-Smith said, citing the circumstances of a colleague's failed shot. The designer was sitting with the military generals when the countdown came. When the detonation tone sounded, nothing happened. In analyzing preshot photographs to find out what went wrong, the designer determined that a dangling detonation wire had been taped to the top of a battery "by a tidy technician," Mercer-Smith grimaced, and had severed the current needed to set off the explosion. "That's how it goes," he said. "Something as simple as a bad weld can overcome your best calculations and your best design intent. Even a small change can make it not work at all or work too well. Either result can get you into a lot of trouble."

Given the technical difficulties and the professional pressures associated with nuclear tests, it is not surprising then that weapons scientists are deeply superstitious people. Like baseball players, they are up against powers that are largely beyond their control, and so, to ward off bad luck that can ruin months or years of slogging hard work, they perform little rituals. Mercer-Smith had worn all white on the day of his first successful shot, and so wore white for every one of his tests thereafter. A colleague always went to the wellhead the day before they put the bomb into the hole, picked up two rocks, and put them into his pocket. After the shot he would go back and throw one of the rocks into the hole. Another seemingly ritualistic practice was actually based on hard reality: weapons designers used to make a point of patting the bomb before it was put into the hole. That's because plutonium 240, one of the components of the device, is spontaneously fissionable and so gives off heat. "You patted the bomb just to make sure it was the real thing," Mercer-Smith said, sketching the movement in the air, as though patting a baby's behind.

Truth be told, going to the Nevada test site to prove his weapons designs was something to look forward to, Mercer-Smith admitted, describing the adrenaline rush at countdown and the euphoria of a successful shot. "And it's really weird," he laughed unabashed, "but a nuclear test is a lot of fun." I was taken aback by the remark, but soon realized what it reminded me of. Mercer-Smith wore the happy expression of a curious and inventive youth who had brought off a cunning experiment with cherry bombs. He said he enjoyed driving around the desert to look at his old craters, those depressions in the sand that are the only mark of an underground test. And he fondly recalled the parties on the nights before the shots. "We'd stay up late, have a really nice meal at the steak house at Mercury." An entire town had been built to support the test site, located about eighty-five miles northwest of Las Vegas. In its heyday Mercury was populated by some three thousand scientists and support staff, and boasted a bowling alley and a swimming pool, in addition to the steak house where many a weapons scientist celebrated a successful shot. "Then we'd drive out to the command post forty miles away," Mercer-Smith said. More often than not, he would do the driving on the eerie ride north on the Mercury Highway, "because the guy I went with usually had had too much to drink," he noted.

Beyond the personal and professional satisfaction derived from a successful shot, the real value of testing nuclear weapons, both Mercer-

Smith and Wood explained, has to do with the complexity of the physics involved and the inability of current computational programs to accurately predict outcomes. "There's lots of coupled, nonlinear complex physics," Wood said. "And we still have major difficulties with our calculations. We rely on nuclear testing to compensate for that."

Weapons design involves massive computer programs or codes containing a half million lines or more, calculations that trace the behavior of particles, heat, and radiation in an explosion. During the Manhattan Project, huge problems were worked on tabletop calculating machines; some of the operators were scientists' wives. It wasn't until after the war that the laboratory had the benefit of an electronic digital computer—ENIAC, or electronic numerical integrator and computer—the first machine of its kind in the world. It had been built out of army-navy reject electronic parts.[8] ENIAC was used to work the problems associated with the hydrogen bomb. It might have been completed before World War II if the project had not been put on a back burner by military leaders who did not at the time realize how useful it would be. It was only by chance that a Los Alamos scientist found out about its existence and took measures to have it moved from Pennsylvania to New Mexico. ENIAC serves as an example of how weapons research drives technology, Mercer-Smith said, noting that most of the real advances in computer science have come about because of weapons work.

In October 1996, the DOE ordered for the laboratory a new $110.5 million Cray Research computer—billed as the most powerful on earth—to better determine the safety and reliability of aging nuclear weapons. Nevertheless, even with such powerful machines at their fingertips, weapons experts like Mercer-Smith still cannot get accurate answers. The problems are that complex. "We are using the best physics we know to describe nuclear weapons, and the codes uniformly, consistently, absolutely every time you run them, give you the wrong answer." Therefore, one of the chief functions of a designer is to learn how the computer codes lie so that you can compensate, he said. And, given the vastness of the programs, there are ample opportunities for human error. "And the computer can botch," Wood shrugged. "A cosmic ray can go through and flip a bit in the computer so that you get a completely screwball answer."

But perhaps it is too easy to blame the computer, which is just the integrating mechanism for a large and complex river of information, according to Philip Goldstone, the assistant to the program director for nuclear weapons science and technology. The inability of computer programs to accurately nail the processes of a thermonuclear explosion may have more to do with the science going into the codes, he said. Data are gleaned from a wide range of experimentation that includes materials science, high explosives, high-energy-density physics, hydrodynamic testing, and dynamic experimentation. This work is nothing new; it has gone on concurrently with nuclear testing for years. But now, to the deep consternation of antinuclear activists, aboveground experimentation, or AGEX activity, is being "tweaked up," as a lab spokesman put it, in order to compensate for the loss of nuclear tests. Nuclear tests are probably gone forever, said Steve Younger, who has written that there is "an urgent need to develop laboratory techniques that will allow us to simulate the conditions found in a nuclear explosive both to provide more accurate information on the physics of matter at high-energy density and to provide a vehicle needed for the continued development of the special skills required to maintain an understanding of nuclear weapons."[9] None of the AGEX regimes can duplicate what happens in a real nuclear explosion, however; each is only a window into a process that is not entirely understood.

Hydrodynamic testing, in which explosives are used to implode materials so that the effect can be studied, has been used in weapons research since the Manhattan Project. Under the tremendous pressures exerted by the explosives, metals and other solids appear to flow like liquids, hence the term *hydrodynamic*. The process is measured and sampled by various techniques, such as passing X-ray bursts or shooting laser light through the event.

Pulsed power technology uses devices that can store in a capacitor bank an enormous amount of energy and then release it suddenly into a target with a power flow greater than the entire electrical generating capacity of the United States. The target is usually a metal cylinder that is imploded for the purposes of studying the properties of materials under extreme pressures and temperatures and to generate intense X-ray bursts and study their interaction with matter. High explosives are sometimes used to amplify these bursts of electric power.

Lasers can be used to achieve even higher energy densities in very small target materials, while accelerators like the Los Alamos Meson Physics Facility (LAMPF), the most powerful accelerator in the world, can accelerate charged particles to high energies that model some of the processes in a nuclear explosion.[10]

In addition to expanding the understanding of what happens in nuclear explosions, these technologies will be useful in mining the enormous amount of data that was gathered during the years when full-scale nuclear tests were being done at a grueling pace in the Nevada desert. Because there are questions related to the interpretation of test-site data that cannot be reexamined in future test shots, laser, pulse power, and accelerator experiments can address some of these problems. "Many people will be really looking through those archival data in a more concerted way," said Joe Mack, the group leader for the Laser Matter Interaction and Fusion Physics Group at Los Alamos. "I think there's lots of useful information that hasn't been tapped yet." Furthermore, added Bob Gibson, project leader at the Trident laser facility at Los Alamos, "There are a number of physics issues associated with weapons that are not well understood. We understand them enough empirically to design weapons, but we don't really understand the process very well." Aboveground experimentation offers simpler experiments that can look more closely at the basic physics and deepen the understanding of first principles involved, Gibson said. Today's weapons experiments are part of a cultural change away from function—the more engineering, goal-related, empirical work of the past—and toward the basic science of weapons research.

Because of, and perhaps in spite of, the technical complexity of their business, weapons physicists find comfort in such human strengths as intuition and experience. In fact, both Mercer-Smith and Wood view weapons design as a highly creative and intuitive business. "I don't want to call it art," Wood demurred, saying that art permits a freedom of expression that weapons design, confined within the unforgiving bonds of physics, won't permit. But Mercer-Smith allowed that maybe, in fact, their vocation is a kind of art. "Much more like art than most science," he said, "but it's true that you can try really hard to make nature do things, and she is just going to laugh at you," he added, with a tight-lipped, crescent smile that comes often and easily to his face. Furthermore, Wood added, you can make things happen on the computers that will never happen down in the hole. This is one of the important lessons a weapons designer learns.

Mercer-Smith liked to compare weapons design to performing an organ cantata, but with an unusual twist. "Imagine that someone just walked in and handed you the music for a Bach organ cantata and said, play it. Well, this is an easy problem," he said, because on an organ, every time you play a key, you can expect it to be the same note. The physics of nuclear weapons, on the other hand, is nonlinear. "So, if I hit a key here," he said, acting out this concert on the table, "it changes the meaning of a key over there. You're trying to play an organ that is nonlinear and changing in real time."

He speculated that the high number of women in weapons design could be attributed to the intuitive and nonlinear character of the physics. While only 5 percent of the physicists in the laboratory were women, fully 20 percent of the weapons designers were female. The public affairs escort squirmed in his chair over this remark and tried to impose a politically correct spin on the discussion, but Wood and Mercer-Smith wouldn't have it. Mercer-Smith went on to describe what it was about weapons physics that attracted certain personalities. Most physicists are trained to break a problem into small parts and solve it one piece at a time, he said. "That sort of person would go crazy doing what we do." A weapons designer has to hold the whole idea in his mind at the same time, approaching a problem as a gestalt, mentally visualizing what will happen in the messy, nonlinear heart of an exploding bomb where many things happen at once. "It's beautifully rich," Mercer-Smith said, not afraid to admit that his work is interesting. "Trying to describe it is a satisfying intellectual challenge." And fun, Wood added. "But we're here for a reason well beyond the fact that the physics is interesting," Mercer-Smith insisted. "I can play on my computers and run huge computer problems. That's fine. But we're really here because we have a commitment to deter nuclear war. Nobody is going to be here because they think nuclear war is a good idea. That's silly," Mercer-Smith said. "We try to weed those people out," Wood said, laughing. "We have a far better understanding of just how bad a nuclear war would be, and it's really a commitment to seeing that that doesn't ever happen."

Mercer-Smith had been particularly horrified by an editorial during the Gulf War that seriously suggested using nuclear weapons against Iraq's massed forces. "Let's not mince words here. We're talking about murdering a hundred thousand people. It seemed very flippant and cavalier, and people here were just horrified by it. This was some fool who didn't have any idea what he was doing," Mercer-Smith said.

However, the weaponeers at Los Alamos are not above creating hypothetical nuclear solutions just to let off steam during national crises, such as the Iran hostage crisis in the late 1970s and early '80s. They devised an elegant solution of biblical proportions, as Wood described it. "The Flood!" she crowed. Mercer-Smith tried to explain: "A bunch of us were sitting around one afternoon and decided to figure out how much energy it would take to slosh the Caspian Sea and wash Iran off the face of the earth. What kind of energy device would we have to make? How would we deliver it? It was not a serious exercise, of course, but just cathartic, gallows humor. Would we seriously suggest using nuclear weapons to bomb Teheran? Of course not! It would kill millions of people!"

Because their creations can wipe out entire cultures, said Steve Younger, it is essential that weapons designers be more than physicists. During the bloom of the weapons program, while working at Lawrence Livermore National Laboratory, Younger was in a position to interview prospective weaponeers. The first thing he looked at was what they had studied in school. "If they took science and engineering and then Introduction to Civilization 101, I didn't want them. Because I didn't want machines. I could *buy* machines. I wanted somebody who was capable of thinking about what they were doing and putting it into a historical perspective. We were involved in serious business, dealing with objects that could destroy the world. And I didn't want some dope who was a technology junkie, looking to build superweapons just to show that he could do it. There were people like that; there still are. And they're dangerous."

Younger majored in both physics and philosophy as an undergraduate. "Real philosophy, not the philosophy of physics. Ancient and medieval philosophy are my specialty. I'm in physics for the money," he said matter-of-factly. "I went into physics not really intending to go into the nuclear weapons program. But I went to Livermore and was really impressed at the capabilities they had, and quite honestly, it seemed like a really fun thing. We were running big codes and doing complicated experiments and working with big teams of people on a problem that still, at that time, seemed to be of national importance," he said, playing out a fine thread of irony as he talked. We tend to forget that nuclear weapons protect the homeland, Younger explained. "Nobody is going to cause us a serious problem in the continental United States if we have a significant nuclear arsenal."

Younger had been sitting quite still while he thoughtfully parceled out his words. He is outwardly cool and self-contained, with the intensity of his feelings and the sense of purpose that drives him revealed only in glimmers. We want steady hands at the tiller in this kind of work, he said, speaking of others he admired at the laboratory. But you get the feeling that Younger has that quality himself. I told him that I had met scientists at Los Alamos who insisted that moral considerations were not the purview of physics or physicists, and he shot back: "You'd better believe it is! If we can end the world in an afternoon, it's our responsibility to think about it. We are not just following orders." In the final analysis, Younger mused about the usefulness of his craft, there are other things that are much more important than technology and physics theory. "Oh, it's an amusing way to spend one's time—learning things, finding out about nature," he said. "But frankly, it doesn't make any difference whether or not we know how the sun burns. It will continue to burn, anyway." Physicists today are experimenting with ultrahigh energies that do not even occur in the natural world, he said. The experiments are so far away from nature that the researchers tend to forget what nature really is. "But philosophy, on the other hand, is important because it addresses questions that are vital to human existence," Younger said. "Why am I here? What should I do? Is my life fulfilling? Do I understand why I'm doing what I'm doing? Is there a point to it all? That's what human life is about. So, curiously, I see philosophy as more applied than physics. In fact, the most applied course I ever took was scholastic metaphysics," Younger said, explaining that he was drawn particularly to ancient and medieval philosophies, especially the writings of St. Thomas Aquinas. "Because he had a complete system for looking at everything," Younger said. "You could disagree with parts of it, but it was about as basic as you can get, looking at things at their most elemental level, the properties of being. I was tremendously impressed by that." Philosophy has always been the foundation from which Younger looked at other things—including physics and the weapons program.

✦

The impression one has after listening to the explanations of some of the people in the weapons community at Los Alamos is that they are defending something whose time has passed—like big-band leaders up against rock 'n' roll. Recent polls indicate that a majority of the American public would like to be rid of nuclear weapons, while Mercer-Smith allowed that the military doesn't even want them anymore. Joe Martz expressed concern that along with the reduction in the numbers of weapons and the ban on testing, there would also be a reduction in the confidence military planners and political leaders had in the effectiveness of nuclear weapons.

Too late, said Bob Kelley, the laboratory's program manager for counterproliferation and emergency response. The military has already lost interest in nuclear weapons, he said. "And I am completely convinced that this country's nuclear weapons are unusable, anyway. The weapons we have chosen to keep in the enduring stockpile are some of the poorest that we could have chosen." As a result, Kelley fears that nuclear weapons will be shunted off to the outback of national defense—to a position of unimportance under the care of unimportant people, he said. "There will come a time in the next decade where there will be nobody who was important enough to rise to a position of decision making in the military who ever had anything to do with nuclear weapons, because the guys who were given that job were not the guys you would promote. Why would you have an elite unit in nuclear weapons these days if you know you're not going to use these things." The end result, Kelley fears, is that military leaders will eventually dump all their nuclear weapons. "Maybe that's good," Kelley said. "But it's not good to go to zero in a world where the other guys have hundreds or thousands."

While political and military leaders have contemplated using nuclear weapons in the conflicts that have flared up during the past fifty years, they wisely decided not to step over the nuclear threshold. The uselessness of nuclear weapons was never more apparent than during the most recent war waged by the United States, according to the four-star air force general who commanded the coalition forces during Desert Storm. At a July 15, 1994, breakfast with reporters, General Charles Horner said that nuclear deterrence doesn't even apply outside the Russia-U.S. context. The United States would never use a nuclear weapon in war, he said, unless one of the former Soviet republics used one against us first. Even if North Korea used a nuclear weapon against U.S. forces, the general said, the United States would not respond in kind. "What are nuclear weapons good for?" he asked reporters. "For busting cities. What president of the United States is going to take out Pyongyang?"[11] Kelley put it this way: "If we were given the job right now of attacking something in Iraq as a nuclear target, we would have to take tens of kilotons to the problem. If it's anywhere near the city of Baghdad it would destroy the entire city. That's not a usable deterrent. We're not going to do it," he said, adding that what is really needed against someone like Saddam Hussein is a very small hit that could do some physical damage and send a message.

Merri Wood had pondered this problem. "You're talking about a low-yield earth-penetrator to take out a bunker of high military officials. That's the only way to do it." Such a "bunker buster" would take care of the fifty people you wanted to target, Mercer-Smith conceded, but, small as it was, it would represent a dangerous step over the nuclear line, making the use of nuclear weapons more thinkable. Nukes should remain big, scary, and unthinkable, Mercer-Smith said; this was their real purpose.

Nevertheless, development of a mininuke was under way immediately after the Gulf War. And indeed, by March 1992, the laboratory was developing what its director, Sig Hecker, described to Congress as "special purpose weapons."[12] But Project PLYWD (short for Precision Low-Yield Weapons Design and pronounced "plywood") was stopped when the fiscal 1994 budget forbade the creation of weapons with yields under five kilotons. The mininuke would have been the first new nuclear weapon since 1984's Pershing IIs and ground-launched cruise missiles.[13] During the early 1990s scientists at Los Alamos and Sandia National Laboratory in Albuquerque were working on retrofitting the B61 bomb with laser guidance that would transform the workhorse warhead into a smart weapon that could zero in on the bunker door of someone like Saddam Hussein.[14]

General Horner, who was commander of the U.S. intercontinental ballistic missile fleet at the time he made his astonishing remarks, said he would like the United States to just get rid of nuclear weapons altogether. "Go to zero," he said, adding that if Russia could be convinced to do likewise, nukes would then be superfluous. The Gulf War had proved to him the effectiveness of precise conventional bombs as weapons of terror.[15]

Military leaders distanced themselves from Horner's musings, and defense analysts linked the general's candid remarks to his imminent retirement, but Kelley said it was an important indicator of changing attitudes. "He was able to say what was on his mind because he was retiring, but when a four-star talks like that, boy! You really have to sit up and notice. It's a big deal," Kelley said. Later, retired air force general Lee Butler, the former commander of the U.S. Strategic Command and responsible for all air force and navy strategic nuclear forces, said nuclear deterrents did not make any sense, that they were inefficient militarily, expensive, and immoral. He urged the nations of the world to learn from the excesses of the Cold War. Then, on December 5, 1996, a group of sixty other former military commanders from around the world, including Butler, retired army general and NATO commander Andrew Goodpaster, Russia's Alexander Lebed, and Britain's former defense staff chief Michael Carver, issued statements urging their national leaders to quickly reduce the number of nuclear weapons in their arsenals.

So far, the official air force position is that air-, ground-, and sea-based nuclear weapons are important in maintaining a deterrent. Along with reductions in nuclear weapons, a drawdown of intercontinental ballistic missiles (ICBMs) is to be accomplished by the year 2003. The air force will update the remaining five hundred Minuteman III missiles by adding new parts until the year 2020.[16] "Certainly the feeling that we have, though, is that the ICBMs are dead meat," Kelley said. "They're gone." He added that someday the navy will realize it can save billions of dollars by eliminating the fleet of submarines that carry submarine-launched ballistic missiles, noting that submarines were still being built not because they were needed to fight the Russians, but because of political pressure to support the industry. "So, if you don't have the right congressman from New Haven or Groton on the right committee, you could just end up scrapping the whole fleet," Kelley said, adding that in the end, the United States could be left with an odd collection of tactical weapons and no way to deliver them to their targets. A mindless sort of nuclear disarmament, Kelley called it, instead of a decision that deserves more careful consideration. "What if one day you need them and you allowed that capability to get lost?" he asked.

Nuclear capability is more than just weapons, though, according to Joe Martz, who is uncomfortable with old-style Cold War deterrence, anyway. "It represents a tremendous irony, that the most horrible tools of war are used to keep peace," he said, suggesting that within the deterrence paradigm there are other alternatives. "There's something called deterrence by capability," he said. "If you have the capability to reconstitute and deploy a destructive power in a manner that is both timely and assured, does that capability become a deterrent?" Martz asked. "I think the answer is an unqualified yes," he said, explaining that assuring this timely capability was a technical detail. "But for now, just assume it," he said, forging on. "If an adversary knows I have an assured timely capability to reconstitute a nuclear force, will it deter him? I think the answer, again, is yes." Martz cited China as an example: "When they detonated their first nuclear device, our entire attitude toward them changed. We changed our targeting list, we changed our military posture. We knew that they didn't have an arsenal; we knew that they had not deployed a single nuclear weapon, and yet the mere fact that they had demonstrated a capability was sufficient for us to elevate them to a different and more respected status."

The Gulf War provides another demonstration of the power of capability, Martz said. Saddam Hussein could have used chemical and perhaps biological weapons on Israel, but he didn't. "He gave a half-hearted token thrust at Israel with a couple of Scud missiles against Tel Aviv, but he did not wipe the Jewish state off the face of the earth, as he promised. Why? Because he knew that if he even touched Israel, he was going to get waxed," Martz said. Israel has never announced that they have a nuclear arsenal or even admitted to a nuclear test, he continued. "And yet, the perception that Israel has that capability has acted as a deterrent, even against someone as irrational as Saddam Hussein."

Even no-nonsense weaponeers like Steve Younger will concede that deterrence by capability is a valid idea. "It's not the performance of our weapons that is the critical thing, you realize," Younger said. "Curiously enough, it's what other people think of their performance that matters. It's like playing poker." However, in this game, there should always be something behind the bluff, as Martz explained it. "It's not the products of our work," he said. "It is the work itself." The very existence of a weapons laboratory like Los Alamos and its sister military research labs—Lawrence Livermore in California and Sandia in Albuquerque, New Mexico—and the fearsome creativity that resides within them may be the essence of nuclear deterrence.

Deterrence by capability is hampered, however, Martz suggested, by the ongoing ban on nuclear testing; it has reduced the ability of weapons designers to learn their craft, and in this new regime of test bans, shrinking stockpiles, and shrinking budgets, weapons specialists who retire are not being replaced, so that it's not just the nation's weapons that are aging; so too are its weaponeers. Most of the people in Mercer-Smith's design group are in their forties and fifties, with only two people on staff who are in their thirties. It's a problem, he said, because training is done mainly through oral tradition. In losing senior designers, the lab loses not only practical design experience, but also the teaching ability it represents.

"When people retire, you lose very large chunks of history—what works and what doesn't work—because there is no written record," Mercer-Smith explained. "There's an incredibly long training period that is essentially a classic medieval apprenticeship. We bring people on as Ph.D.'s and their function for the first five years is just to be useful, because they have so much to learn." For obvious reasons, physicists don't learn weapons design in graduate school. It takes as long as fifteen years to develop mastery in the field. And what documentation exists, Mercer-Smith said, is handled by the secretaries, who are the security custodians of weapons design. "Things have changed a bit recently, but over the past forty years it was in the secretary's best interest to destroy documents. Compare that to what we know about Soviet security at Arzamas-16, the secret nuclear weapons design city in the former

Soviet Union. One of the secretaries there didn't properly mark a document to be destroyed and ended up being sent to Siberia. The head of Arzamas security, because of past good service, was allowed to commit suicide. At least that way his family could inherit. We aren't anywhere near as tight on security," Mercer Smith said matter-of-factly, with the hint of an ironic smile.

The truth is, he continued, following his logic all the way to ground zero, the best way to get rid of nuclear weapons would be to get rid of the knowledge and the expertise that created them. "If you could guarantee that every one of your counterparts everywhere in the world would die, it ought to be your moral imperative to go kill yourself. You ought to be willing to do that," he said, leaning back in his chair and gazing at me over the tops of his glasses, his hands poised under his chin fingertip-to-fingertip in professorial speculation. Then he drew a deep breath, sighed, and said: "But the problem with that is that you can't guarantee that every designer in the world would do it. In some real sense, maybe the best thing in the world would be that all my friends and I were taken away and killed," he concluded.

2

Spooks and Cold Warriors

W ere the armed guards stationed in the hallway near Jas Mercer-Smith's office there to
protect him and his colleagues in X-2 from someone with that very
idea, I wondered. Someone who really believed that the world would
be better off without nuclear weapons designers like them? Or maybe
someone interested in kidnapping them for their expertise or simply
stealing their information? This made him laugh.

"We're just people thinking about physics," he said. "Sure, we have
restricted data—nuclear secrets, if you will. But go across the hall into
the central core of this building, and you will find yourself in a large
vault—the spook shop. Spies," he added with a conspiratorial fillip.
"Those activities are protected much more carefully than we are.
They're analyzing information that, if it were traced back to its source,
could get people killed."

Los Alamos has been involved in the surveillance business since the
end of World War II, tracking nuclear developments in the former Soviet Union and China, and later watching the flow of nuclear materials
and technology to countries like Israel and South Africa. The first
satellite systems used to detect the telltale emissions of a nuclear explosion were developed with the help of Los Alamos scientists. For over
thirty years the laboratory's space program has designed detection in-
strumentation for satellites that monitored compliance with the high-
altitude nuclear test ban treaties. The instruments detected X rays,
gamma rays, neutrons, and other emissions from nuclear tests, but they
also monitored the natural space background in order to distinguish

between the two. In the process, Los Alamos detectors first discovered cosmic gamma-ray bursts, opening up a new field of study in astrophysics. This work also marked the laboratory's entrée into a long history of collaboration with NASA. Los Alamos continues to design new satellite systems that combine such basic scientific research with national defense objectives, some of the most recent made specifically to monitor the emissions from tests of cruder proliferant-style weapons.

That changing focus of satellite technology represents an overall change in the focus of nuclear intelligence gathering—away somewhat from the old nemesis, the former Soviet Union, toward an increasingly multipolar nuclear world in which a number of countries are intent upon building their own nuclear weapons programs. As the euphoria began to fade after the end of the Cold War, talk at Los Alamos turned increasingly to this new danger.

By 1990, just after Saddam Hussein's troops had invaded Kuwait, Iraq undertook a frantic attempt to complete its own nuclear device. The effort was largely gutted by Allied bombing raids during the Gulf War, after which United Nations inspectors were responsible for demobilizing what remained of the Iraqi nuclear program.

India and Pakistan, antagonistic neighbors who already have fought three wars with each other, are widely believed to have nuclear weapons capability, although they are not declared nuclear states. India exploded a nuclear device as long ago as 1974—"for funsies," as Steve Younger put it—and now India is reportedly preparing for another test, while at the same time claiming not to possess any nuclear weapons at all. And to the dismay of Pakistan, India is known to have recently conducted tests of medium-range missiles. Analysts suggest that both India and Pakistan could quickly assemble nuclear weapons, if need be, practicing what Joe Martz has described as deterrence by capability. Meanwhile, nearby China, an acknowledged nuclear power with whom India fought a brief war in 1962, has admitted to selling nuclear equipment and know-how to Pakistan, thought to have enough enriched uranium to build at least ten bombs.

Both China and Russia have made deals with Iran, sharing expertise and equipment. Iran is working on some eighty projects in nuclear power plant construction, including a controversial $1 billion aid package from Russia for building as many as four new nuclear reactors. Experts in both the United States and Russia claimed that this would give Iran ready access to recycled nuclear fuel and the plutonium necessary to support its own nuclear weapons program. As a suspected sponsor of terrorism, Iran's having nuclear capability is alarming to the world community.

Meanwhile, Israel continues to cast a long shadow in Middle East politics as an undeclared nuclear state, at the same time insisting that it possesses no nuclear weapons, a claim that no one believes. Analysts suggest that Israel has seven nuclear installations that have produced a rumored two hundred weapons, an estimate that made Bob Kelley smile. "That's probably a little high," said the proliferation expert, who had worked for the International Atomic Energy Agency (IAEA) before coming to Los Alamos. There was no doubt that Israel had nuclear weapons, though, a capability that was worrisome to the entire Middle East, Kelley said, noting that some of the more moderate countries seemed inclined to make some accommodation with the Israelis, but wouldn't want to look soft to their own people or to their allies. "And, frankly, it's hard to convince the Israelis that it is in their own interest to get rid of their nuclear weapons," Kelley said. "This is a country that is five miles wide; that's the fireball for a big one," he put it bluntly.

Another nuclear hot spot has been the Korean Peninsula. Western leaders became convinced that North Korea had extracted plutonium from its Yongbyon nuclear power plant in order to fuel at least one or two bombs. The United States scrambled to forestall such a development and forged an agreement with North Korea whereby that country would stop producing plutonium in exchange for $500 million in fuel oil and some $4 billion to build two light-water nuclear power reactors. Unlike North Korea's old graphite-moderated reactors, fuel from these new facilities would not be so easily converted into weapons-grade plutonium. The United States has been trying to get other countries, especially South Korea and Japan, to foot most of the bill for the plan.

The emergence of this new arms race, Mercer-Smith said, adds an ironic twist to the conclusion of the Cold War. Instead of ending our worries about nuclear weapons, he said, it meant we should be more worried than ever before. "The world is a lot more dangerous than you think. We're faced now with a set of challenges that is far more difficult than anything we've faced in the past because the threat is more diffuse. As a result, policy makers have to figure out how to use this mechanism by which we have been able to avoid a nuclear war in a relatively simple bilateral world, and make it work in a very complicated multilateral world," Mercer-Smith said.

"People want to say that it's a better world now than it was a couple of years ago," said Bob Kelley. "I'm not convinced that it is." The Cold War stalemate, as he described it, had kept the world relatively safe, although the scale of potential destruction was frightening. Nevertheless, he considered the complexity of today's situation to be far worse. As potentially deadly as the balance of power between the former Soviet Union and the United States was, noted Steve Younger, it had provided a strange kind of stability in the world. Each superpower had kept a tight rein on a set of potentially dangerous client states. "The Russians carried lots of little countries and we carried lots of little countries, and we both poured huge amounts of money into them to bribe them to do what we wanted," he said. The race finally ended in a draw in terms of each superpower's influence around the world, and now we could either let all these little countries go their own way or we could try to guide them down some rational path. "You can say that's pretty chauvinistic," he said firmly, "but, the fact of the matter is, we are the richest country in the world; we have some obligation to try and keep them from killing each other." And from killing us, Mercer-Smith warned. One of the gravest dangers in a regional nuclear conflict is that it might escalate beyond the warring countries' borders and suck the rest of the world into a conflagration. Furthermore, he said, once a proliferant country has a nuclear weapon and then acquires a delivery vehicle, it can put it into anybody's backyard.

It is not coincidental that some of these countries are interested in developing space-launch vehicles beyond the type of short-range tactical weapon that we saw demonstrated during the Gulf War. An important implication of the Scud missile was that it could be used for other kinds of payloads, nuclear as well as chemical and biological weapons. The sort of space program required to mount a sophisticated intercontinental ballistic missile system is expensive and capable of bankrupting a country, but a consortium of countries working together might find it within their grasp if each country worked on a piece of the task, according to one proliferation specialist at the laboratory. Because of the national independence of each country involved in such a scheme, he said, it would be difficult to intercede until all of the pieces were in place, at which time it would be too late. Also defense analysts have suggested that even short-range tactical weapons could be cobbled together to make crude long-range ballistic missiles. Another scenario that has worried Pentagon officials is the possibility that a shroud of Scud missiles could deliver clustered munitions that could carry a variety of deadly recipes—including chemical, biological, and nuclear materials—that would destroy populations or render their hometowns uninhabitable. A dusting of such materials as cobalt 60 or strontium 90 would make ghost towns of major cities, useless for hundreds of years.[1]

What all of this means for the laboratory is a repackaged mission. More than just providing the technical options to support national defense, weapons experts are charged with "reducing the global nuclear danger"—government lingo for nuclear nonproliferation. Nuclear weapons specialists will develop advanced forensic tools that can anticipate the behaviors of potential proliferants, detect violations of treaties, and if the worst happens, trace the signature characteristics of an exploded weapon back to its creator. If we are to maintain deterrence and survive in this new multipolar world, Mercer-Smith said, it will be important to have experts playing the game. For those like him who have spent their careers creating quirky and cutting-edge nuclear weapons, it might not be as purely interesting, but it will be a challenge. "I'm starting problems that are orders of magnitude larger than anything that we have tried in the past," he said. "But I feel morally compelled to do it."

Another compelling reason to worry, Mercer-Smith intoned cryptically, is that proliferation is easier than you think, an idea that Bob Kelley disputes, offering instead his belief that after years and years of making bombs, experienced weapons scientists underestimate how difficult it really is. "We used to sit around and talk about whether proliferators knew this or that trick or bit of art," he said. "But it really is more difficult than we thought, and I think that's the good news in all of this. If you take some raw plutonium, you still have a big project ahead of you to build a bomb, with months of work, a lot of testing and really no guarantee of success." Kelley's job with IAEA was to make verification inspections in countries like Iraq and also South Africa, a country that began working on a nuclear weapons program, but now positions itself as a fervent supporter of the Non-proliferation Treaty. His work on inspection teams gave Kelley a chance to observe close-up the difficulties proliferant countries encounter, including, surprisingly, an overabundance of information on how to go about building a nuclear weapon. It was this excess of information, Kelley believes, that led to Iraq's undoing because there was no clearly defined and obvious single approach. "I mean they had no idea how to go about it," Kelley said. "They had so much information that they were almost as blind as if they had none. They didn't know how to set priorities, they didn't know which path to choose, so they explored them all. And that was great, because they really fooled around and took their time," he said, chuckling. The simplest approach for a fledgling program, of course, would be to get a complete design that is simple to build. "Or basically, take a bomb out of Russia. That's really what we're more worried about now," he said. A powerful nuclear weapon can be carried away in a suitcase.

Just as the bomb-building methods of proliferant countries varied, so, too, did their reasons for doing it, Kelley found, and that, he said, is useful information for the nonproliferation community. South Africa's brief foray into the nuclear club had been done mostly as a matter of ego, he thought. They were a mineral-rich country looking for a way to capitalize on their uranium deposits, and began with the intent of just being a nuclear supplier in the civil world, selling uranium and uranium-enrichment services. "But as they proceeded down that path," Kelley said, "they realized, 'Gosh, we could do a bomb, too!'" Only later did they come up with political justifications for their bomb program, he added. The Iraqi program was developed for purely military reasons, Kelley said, and was accelerated during crises such as the Iran/Iraq war and the invasion of Kuwait. North Korea, on the other hand, seemed to be motivated primarily by greed, Kelley asserted. "They're the first people that I've seen who would manufacture plutonium and sell it for dollars. They have no scruples, whatsoever. To them, plutonium is just a cash crop."

◆

It seems ironic that Los Alamos weapons scientists, after fifty years of perfecting instruments of mass destruction, should find themselves in the vanguard of this disarmament and nonproliferation movement. Antinuclear activists question the sincerity of these post–Cold War warnings, calling them self-serving attempts to maintain the big-budget status quo that the weapons culture has enjoyed for years. Meanwhile, non-nuclear countries can legitimately complain that they also have the right to the benefits of nuclear deterrence that the United States, the former Soviet Union, France, China, and Great Britain have enjoyed. "They say, 'You've got 'em! Why can't we have 'em?'" Steve Younger said. "And the answer is, quite frankly, we're a superpower and you ain't. We have global force protection; we've done conflict mitigation, and you can't.' Algeria, for example, is a legitimate country, but it ain't a superpower. We are," he said simply, adding that this doesn't mean the United States has the right to dictate other countries' national interests, particularly their conventional military resources. "But nuclear weapons are special," Younger said coolly. "I still remember seeing the crater made by my first design. I saw the code on my computer screen, I held the parts in my hands, and I went through all the processes to build it. Then I went out to see the crater it made from twelve hundred feet down in the rock and holy moly!" he said, grimly recalling a line from an old joke: "One nuclear weapon can ruin your whole day? Well, one nuclear weapon can ruin civilizations as we know them and can change the course of world history. They are worthy of our respect and we need to keep an eye on them. So, no! It's not okay for lots of little countries to have them."

And, in fact, Younger insisted, the United States has a moral obligation to stop it from happening. While you could argue that little countries have a right to kill each other if they want to, he posed, you must also remember that it wouldn't just be dedicated soldiers getting killed. It would be families and children, and in some cases whole cultures. "Because you are not only killing people who are alive now, you're making meaningless the lives of all those people who came before them—destroying the very fabric of civilization."

Furthermore, Younger, like Mercer-Smith, is certain that weapons scientists can play a valuable role in stopping proliferation because they are the ones who understand nuclear weapons best. "It's the old 'takes one to know one' theory," agreed Paul White, a former weapons designer who now works at the Center for International Security Affairs

(CISA) at LANL; until recently Steve Younger had served as the director of CISA, an organization whose purpose is to coordinate the laboratory's involvement in international programs to reduce the threat of weapons of mass destruction. White coordinates the lab's involvement with the Cooperative Threat Reduction Program (CTR), a Department of Defense initiative that was funded by Nunn-Lugar legislation in 1991 and as of February 1995, had received $1.27 billion in U.S. government support.

"There's only one good proliferation hunter, and that's a bomb builder," chuckled White, a soft-spoken former college professor with prematurely white beard and hair; he has a low-key demeanor that contrasts markedly with the attitudes of some of his preternaturally self-confident colleagues. He laughs frequently and easily acknowledges the contradictions in his business.

During his twenty-some years at Los Alamos, White has served as group leader of X-2, division leader of applied theoretical physics, and program manager for advanced nuclear weapons design. He was also the deputy director of the Center for National Security Studies (CNSS) at the laboratory, an organization of scientists, political scientists, economists, and historians that focused on the interaction between technology and national defense, a subject that had deeply interested White since his days of teaching physics at St. Edward's University in Austin, Texas. "I was teaching about it before I really knew any of the secrets," he said, "and I was after more and more. So I decided to come here and do it for real." Several of White's designs are still in the stockpile, he said, although he is especially proud of a weapon that ended up being dismantled. The Pershing II—created by his design team—was deployed in West Germany in January 1984, an alarmingly mere ten minutes from Moscow, and quickly brought the Soviet Union to the negotiating table for an unprecedented arms control agreement. The Intermediate-Range Nuclear Forces Treaty, signed on December 8, 1987, and ratified by Congress on May 27, 1988, was a significant turning point in arms control because, for the first time, instead of just setting limits, both superpowers agreed to the dismantling of warheads. It was the beginning of disarmament.

White and I first met over breakfast at Ashley's Restaurant, across Trinity Drive from Ashley Pond, a shallow pool that had once been the geographic center of the old wartime laboratory and was now the centerpiece of a small downtown Los Alamos park, its grassy sward full of sculptures, ducks, and playing children. In the restaurant the tables and booths were crowded by the army of middle-aged men that seems to constantly travel the government and science circuit. The sotto voce rumble of their discreet conversation was punctuated by quick blips of laughter and the clink of flatware against dishes. I began to notice an oddly out-of-place young man who arrived soon after I did and settled at the table next to ours. He had a broken nose, a deep tan, and a particular alertness; his presence reasserted that uncomfortable feeling I'd had of being watched, although I told myself he was probably just a skier fascinated with the talk of bombs and secrets. He remained at his table for most of the hour and a half that White and I spent at the restaurant.

White had just returned from a meeting in Washington, D.C., of the group of government and science leaders who coordinate U.S. assistance to Russia in its warhead dismantlement efforts. It was part of a 1992 agreement between U.S. president George Bush and Russian president Boris Yeltsin to share technologies and training to make the dismantlement of both nuclear arsenals as safe and secure as possible. The committee White serves on is also concerned with a closely related problem—the threat of nuclear materials theft and smuggling. Because of the dismantlement process, warhead components and nuclear materials are being shifted about in unaccustomed ways, leaving them far more vulnerable to thieves, White said. Furthermore, the economic chaos in Russia has left nuclear installations poorly guarded. This problem has been the focus of intense concern because of the possibility that weapons-grade materials could find their way into the hands of proliferant countries or terrorist organizations. Experts estimate that there is enough weapons-grade material in the former Soviet Union to build some hundred thousand nuclear weapons.

And as predicted, materials began to show up in odd places—on planes out of Moscow, on the backseat of a Czechoslovakian car, in a German garage, and in the breast pocket of a hapless smuggler who eventually died from radiation poisoning. By 1994 German authorities had made over seven hundred arrests related to the smuggling of radioactive materials.[2] German intelligence seized 12.8 ounces of plutonium from operatives that had arrived at the Munich airport on a plane from Moscow in August 1994; authorities later arrested a Colombian and two Spaniards. German police found a fifth of an ounce of plutonium in a Stuttgart garage, and Czech police intercepted a shipment of some six pounds of highly enriched uranium that was not quite weapons-grade, but a level of enrichment that linked it to a military storage site or a fuel manufacturing center. The smugglers were all former nuclear workers from the Czech Republic, Belarus, and Ukraine.

Some experts point to the possibility that organized crime, working in concert with disgruntled KGB, is taking the trafficking of radioactive contraband to a level of expertise and greed that is far more sinister and more difficult to stop than the desperate efforts of out-of-work technicians. After a series of high-profile arrests, Russia signed an agreement with Germany pledging to crack down on nuclear traffic, while the FBI opened an office in Moscow, presumably to keep tabs on organized crime and the burgeoning black market trade in nuclear materials, said Bob Kelley. U.S. law enforcement officials have offered training for their counterparts in Eastern Europe and the former Soviet Union.

While a General Accounting Office report confirms that there have been four major thefts of weapons-grade material from research facilities in Russia and other former Soviet states, Paul White said that the amount of real weapons-grade material smuggled out is still quite small, and is mostly worrisome because, first, it shows that it can be done, and second, it raises the potential that more could have slipped out undetected. Of course, there is no good evidence that this is true, he mused, adding that so far most of the detected thefts had been the work of con artists who operated on the fringes of Russia's nuclear infrastructure and took things that were mainly useless to proliferants. Indeed, some of the contraband had been lifted from smoke detectors or consisted of stable substances that had simply been contaminated with radioactivity in order to look like something they were not. "If they can get something that makes a Geiger counter tick," White said, "then they can try to sell it for a big profit to some middleman who doesn't know anything about the underlying technology and is easily fooled." However, the potential for disaster was sufficient to warrant the level of assistance offered by the U.S. Department of Defense.

Whereas the Soviet Union had once relied upon armed guards, worker loyalty, and the threat of harsh consequences in order to discourage theft of plutonium, uranium, and other radioactive materials, its former republics have recently turned to technical solutions from the United States. High-tech detection systems, computers, software, and training were offered to Russia, Kazakhstan, Ukraine, and Belarus to help them account for and secure their nuclear weapons materials. In September 1994, scientists and technicians from the Russian Ministry of Atomic Energy and Russia's two top weapons laboratories visited Los Alamos to learn how to use state-of-the-art technology designed to assess the damage resulting from a nuclear weapons accident and to stabilize the devices for safe transport and storage. Included in the equipment package were X-ray systems, portable radiation detectors, a special silicone liquid that can be poured over damaged high explosives to stabilize them, fiberscope systems that use high-intensity light and video cameras to view and record the condition of an inaccessible damaged weapon, and also protective clothing.

White said he feels relatively confident that these efforts have made a positive difference, but noted that we will never know for certain that the Russians have actually implemented the advice and protective systems that they have been given. "We're never going to have access to that information," he declared, calling it a frustrating situation for those who resent the very idea of sending U.S. aid to the archenemy. "They think we don't owe a penny to anyone in Russia," he said, "and to a certain extent that's true. The situation over there is of their own doing. On the other hand, the U.S. has a very compelling interest in helping to stabilize their materials, institutions, and people." Nevertheless, skeptics would like to see a scorecard showing the number of missiles destroyed and kilograms of material under control, White said. "But they will have to be satisfied with the knowledge that the Russians are at least thinking now about better ways to protect their materials."

A distinct irony in all of this, Bob Kelley suggested, is that until the end of the Cold War most of the weapons materials in the world had been pretty effectively isolated. "The safest place we've ever found to store plutonium is in the core of nuclear weapons, surrounded by high explosives. Now we're in a situation where all the old rules are gone, we're tearing bombs apart, and we don't have places to store the materials." Currently the United States has 75 percent of its plutonium stores still housed in the active weapons stockpile. With the quick dismantling of Russian and U.S. warheads it is essential that the whereabouts of weapons-grade material be closely tracked. However, a significant limitation on the security and accountability efforts in the former Soviet Union is the absence of a baseline quantification of their weapons material, said Bob Kelley. He compared it to running a bank without any records to account for the amount of cash in the vault or tied up in investments. In the case of nuclear materials, this situation puts the weight of control on intelligence and border security to prevent materials from leaving the country, Kelley said. It should be noted that during the height of Cold War weapons production, the United States wasn't always careful about its own record keeping. The Department of Energy recently revealed that it cannot account for some three metric tons of plutonium.

Critics of the program to share nuclear safety and accountability expertise and equipment with the Russians have worried that the plan could backfire and the technology somehow used against the United States should the relationship between the two former enemies grow cold again. White dismissed this. "Monitors that detect when nuclear materials go in or out of the gate cannot be used as offensive weapons, nor can any of the technology involved in them be used to bolster offensive capability."

I met with White again at his CISA office the day before he was to leave on yet another trip to the former Soviet Union. He would spend ten days there, representing the Los Alamos laboratory at the fortieth-anniversary celebration of the founding of Chelyabinsk-70, one of the former Soviet Union's two main weapons laboratories. "The worker's paradise," he noted ruefully about a facility that was, in fact, much less than paradise, especially now. Morning light slanted through a large window in White's office, past a transparent plastic seed cup attached to the outside of the glass. Tiny birds fluttered against the window, while beyond was a pine-filled canyon. The office building was so quiet that the air seemed to whisper. Down the hall was a library where Russian scientists visiting the laboratory could take quiet breaks from whatever task had brought them to the mesa. That week there had been several visitors from the National Nuclear Center at Kazakhstan.

White wanted to show me a present the visitors had brought him. It was a shiny slice of agate—a vivid swirl of deep mineral color—that had been picked from the grounds of Semipalatinsk, one of the former Soviet Union's two weapons test sites. Although White, who has a long resumé of U.S. test site experience, was involved in negotiating the protocols for the 1974 Threshold Test Ban Treaty, he was not able to go to Semipalatinsk during joint verification experiments in 1988. He was very pleased with the agate. "I didn't go to Semipalatinsk, but Semipalatinsk has come to me," he said, smiling. He had made friends in Russia, and despite the difficulties of travel, the discomforts of accommodations that were marginal by Western standards, and increasing worries about crime on Moscow streets, White enjoyed going there because he liked many of the Russian people he had met.

Bob Kelley, who describes himself plainly as a Cold Warrior, still does not completely trust the Russians and worries about a resurgence of "the big bad bear," as he described the old Soviet Union. "I've been part of this thing for a long time. You want my gut feeling? I worry that we are building down very quickly and destroying our capability, while it is not clear that the Russians are doing the same thing. I happen to believe that there are still some really bad dudes over there," he concluded.

Steve Younger took a different tack: "Russia is a great nation," he said. "Their weapons program was of urgent importance because they didn't trust us, and with some reason. They had lost over twenty million people fighting the Germans during the Second World War, although as many as ten million died at the hands of their own secret police," he added as an aside. "Nevertheless, they felt they needed a weapon that would defend their homeland against the kind of invasion that they had suffered in what they called the Great Patriotic War." While there were those in U.S. government who would be happy to see Russian institutions collapse and their people starve, Younger and his colleagues considered this an imprudent attitude. "Their problems aren't going to last forever. If we work with them now, we're going to have a partner in the future, rather than an adversary," Younger said.

To that end, Los Alamos scientists proposed early on that they engage the cream of the Russian nuclear weapons program in meaningful collaborative experiments that would prevent them from taking their expertise to proliferant countries. That possibility—what the Russians referred to as *diffusion*—is another important factor in the current global nuclear danger. "A competent designer could save a proliferant many billions of dollars and produce a weapon that is a thousand times the size of any weapon they could produce by themselves," Mercer-Smith told me. "That's a very dangerous capability and, as a result, you really want designers to have a very strong sense of responsibility." However, the scientists at Russia's top weapons laboratories have been hard-pressed by economic conditions. They have gone for months without getting paid, and even though they had once enjoyed "red border priority" on everything they needed, those deliveries no longer arrive with such efficiency. Scientists began tending their own small gardens for food and were unable to get milk for their families because, under the new Russian economics, nearby farmers found it more profitable to sell their goods in Moscow.

Furthermore, the loss of status suffered by the Russian weapons program has contributed to a problem that is equally familiar to its U.S. counterpart. The average age of Russian nuclear weapons scientists is advancing; young people are no longer interested in the work.

Younger, White, and their colleagues at Los Alamos saw in all of this a danger that was at least as worrisome as the black market trade in nuclear materials. So, using the communications network that had always connected the world community of science, Los Alamos National Laboratory began to discuss collaborative scientific experiments with their former enemies. Researchers from both the United States and the Soviet Union—even weapons designers—had managed to meet one another at international conferences and had read one another's papers on nondefense research. Younger, for example, has published over sixty papers in atomic and plasma physics and is a Fellow of the American Physical Society. He and his counterparts in the Soviet Union were never allowed by their governments to visit one another's labs, Younger said, and the Russians even carried fake IDs and concealed their addresses. Nevertheless, even before the dissolution of the Soviet Union, both superpowers' scientists were considering joint research projects.

The first collaboration was in 1988 when Joint Verification Experiments were conducted at the test sites of both nations. When the Cold War finally ended, Los Alamos scientists were in 1990 the first to visit the Soviet Union's premier nuclear weapons laboratory at Arzamas-16, which Los Alamos now refers to as its sister city, and the All-Russian Institute of Experimental Physics as its sister laboratory.

Sometimes called Los Arzamas by its residents because of perceived similarities with its American counterpart, the secret town of Arzamas is located about two hundred miles east of Moscow and has a population of some hundred thousand people. Formerly a provincial center called Sarov, it was removed from official maps in 1946. This secret city was first opened to the outside world in 1990, when it was visited by a small group of treaty verification specialists, including two scientists from Los Alamos. They were invited to share an autumn picnic. Now the town is again called Sarov and in 1994 appeared again on Russian maps.

Unlike Los Alamos National Laboratory, the All-Russian Institute, which was first housed behind the walls of an old monastery, is still closed to the world by barbed-wire fences and armed guards; but like its American sister city, Arzamas was the birthplace of its nation's nuclear weapons program. It was patterned after Los Alamos, just as their first bomb had been a copy of Fat Man. And like Los Alamos, which is located in forested northern New Mexico, Arzamas-16 is flanked by deep, thick woods and is infused with history. It has fine old churches and is graced by a winding river. Steve Younger said the city had been cleverly constructed to resemble a holiday camp. "Very nice architecture, but small apartments, because people spent most of their time working. For forty years some of them lived in dormitories because they just didn't want to be bothered, even with taking care of an apartment. All they did was work; it was their whole life." The Arzamas laboratory's founder—Yulii Khariton—had created an institution with a strong scientific orientation, similar to Oppenheimer's plan for Los Alamos, Younger said, noting that the similarity between the two men also was uncanny. Younger had recently attended Khariton's ninetieth birthday party.

The joint experiments between the Russian and U.S. scientists began with a high-profile directors' exchange at Arzamas-16 in February 1992, "with formal handshakes and vodka toasts to world peace and stuff like that," Younger noted wryly. "That, by the way, is the easy stuff. Everybody comes back and says, 'Oh we had a wonderful time! We toasted to peace!' Now write a contract. Now do some work. By the time we met in June of '92, the bloom was off the rose."

Both the Russian and the American scientists quickly learned that if they were going to bring off this unprecedented collaboration, they would have to overcome not only their own governments' deeply entrenched mutual distrust, but also the inertia that affected both bureaucracies. "We occasionally debate whose bureaucracy is the worst," Younger said, flushing slightly with irritation. "Ours is, by the way. At least they are able to get a decision from their government."

The cooperative programs being worked out between U.S. and Russian weapons specialists came to be known in both countries as Step-by-Step. "Because we realized that if we tried to take too big a step at one time, we'd fall down," Younger said. "So we took a series of small steps." They began by asking their governments for permission to simply exchange reprints of their research papers. "I mean, it's already published!" Younger said, exasperated. Then they asked to speak with each other about research details not included in their papers. "We adopted a policy of telling the U.S. government everything we were going to do. I've got a list of sixteen offices that we briefed, because nobody in United States government talks to one another," Younger sighed. "And people would say, 'I'm not comfortable with that.' And we would say, 'I just told you what we're doing. I gave you a handout so that it's in writing. If you don't like that, you've got to write a letter to my boss Sig Hecker, telling him to stop us from doing it. Otherwise we're going to go ahead and do this, because we're not breaking any laws.' When we talked about putting a contract together they said, 'Well, why the hell should we give money to the Russians to improve their technology? They might turn out to be bad guys again!'"

But it was not a matter of simply giving technology to the Russians, Younger said. The proposed series of experiments would be based on work that had actually been pioneered by Russian scientists, under the leadership of weapons designer Andrei Sakharov, the physicist credited with developing the Soviet Union's hydrogen bomb. Sakharov was later exiled by his country for opposing the arms race, a stance that won him the Nobel Peace Prize in 1975; he was eventually welcomed back to his homeland shortly before he died. Russian work in magnetic fusion, built upon Sakharov's discoveries, surpassed U.S. achievements in the technology, Younger said, adding that the American scientists went into this partnership expecting to learn something. And there were other advantages to working with the Russians, benefits that went beyond the obvious nonproliferation issues. The collaboration would advance each group's knowledge of the physics involved, and, he said pointedly, if the U.S.-Russian relationship did, indeed, go sour, then the United States certainly would have a much better understanding of its enemy. And, even though millions of dollars were going to the former Soviet Union to shore up its materials storage facilities and to engage its scientists in peaceful research, all these programs would be cheaper in the long run than conducting another arms race. During the Cold War the U.S. government had spent $8 billion collecting intelligence against the Soviet Union. "Whereas we can waltz right in and say, 'what's that?' and get an answer. Seems like a pretty good value to me," he said, with high sarcasm. Furthermore, the rapport that had developed between them would enable each cadre of weaponeers to better advise their own governments concerning threat assessment. It would dispel the myths, Younger noted wryly. "I mean, the Russians are not ten feet tall, they don't all dress in black, and they can die, too. So, we have been able to put a little rationality into things, finally, and that may be the real payoff in the end."

Through a series of four meetings, both at Arzamas-16 and Los Alamos, the Russian and U.S. scientists managed to come to agreement on the details of the collaboration. At one point, the director of Arzamas became frustrated with the slow wheels of American bureaucracy. "He was not a particularly happy camper," Younger said. "I still remember this. He said, 'Americans talk, talk, talk, but never do anything.'" The remark lit a fire under the group of chagrined U.S. scientists, including its leader Steve Younger, who were visiting the Russian lab; they vowed to have a working agreement within the week. "We had some knock-down drag-out discussions about what we were going to do, and by the end of the week, a collaboration existed." The Americans had taken a very hard-nosed approach, Younger said coolly. "The fact of the matter is, we *did* win the Cold War and they *did* lose the Cold

War. Our economy is flourishing, comparatively speaking, and theirs is a catastrophe. So we're not going in as complete equals here." But the Americans took great pains to convince the Russians that they viewed them as equals in science and that they were not there just to buy and take away Russian hardware. They wanted to work side by side with them. Nevertheless, the Russians were reluctant to share information, and a meeting would break down sometimes for that reason. "One time I pounded the table and said, 'Stop! We're not going to do this anymore. If you guys want to work together, we'll work together. If you want to keep secrets, this isn't a collaboration. Just go home!'" Younger sighed then and said that while the Russians were tough negotiators and should get points for being pushy, they finally backed off and gave the Americans the data that they had requested.

By November 1992, the two groups were able to sign a contract at Los Alamos agreeing to conduct joint experiments in high magnetic fields and electric currents. The Russian technology—magnetized target fusion—had been little understood by Western scientists until recently, although it had similarities to the two kinds of fusion technology developed in the West—*magnetic confinement fusion*, in which a plasma is confined by a magnetic field and heated to the point that its atoms are stripped of electrons and fusion takes place, and *inertial confinement fusion*, which uses lasers to compress a fuel pellet to pressures sufficient to force fusion. In the Russian technique, employing both implosion heating and magnetic field confinement, high explosives are used to generate an intense electrical pulse that compresses and heats a magnetized gas or plasma until it achieves pressures and temperatures near those found inside stars. "Super-intense electrical impulses. When the current is flowing, it equals the generating capacity of the planet. We're talking serious electrical energy here," Younger said. Sakharov had hoped at first to develop a nuclear weapon based on magnetic confinement fusion, a scheme that wouldn't have worked, Younger said. But the research would yield valuable insights into the atomic structure of solids, high-pressure chemistry, and high-energy particle accelerators.[3]

"And to be quite honest, we're interested in this technology because we are in the nuclear weapons program, and since we aren't testing them anymore and probably never will, this helps us to understand some of the things that go on in weapons," Younger said, making sure to add that U.S. weapons scientists were not conducting weapons re-search, as such, with the Russians. Interestingly, shortly after the col-lapse of the Soviet Union, Russian scientists sold to the United States a huge amount of information about the history of the Soviet weapons testing program. Under a $250,000 contract with the U.S. Defense Special Weapons Agency, two hundred scientists from the former So-viet Union compiled a two-thousand-page tome about the 715 Cold War nuclear tests. Not only did the project occupy scientists that might otherwise have transferred their skills to some rogue nuclear state, but it also provided the United States with invaluable details about the Soviets' nuclear program. It also contributed to a better understanding of how proliferators might develop and test nuclear weapons in the future.[4]

✦

The political and economic chaos that swept the former Soviet Union after its collapse made the collaboration between U.S. and Russian sci-entists even more difficult. In Russia during September 1993, to take part in the first experiment at Arzamas-16, Younger, who has made many trips to the former Soviet Union, got caught in the middle of the coup waged by Communist party hard-liners protesting Russian presi-dent Boris Yeltsin's reforms. Younger watched from his hotel room window as Russian army forces stormed the parliament building.

Meanwhile, the state of Russian communications technology also caused problems. "Nothing worked—phones or faxes," Younger said. "Sometimes it would take two weeks to get a fax over." U.S. scientists were equally surprised by the primitive quality of Russian technology, in general. While it may be true that the Soviets had recruited their best minds for weapons research, Younger said, they had not had the best of technology. "Things that we take for granted—like wire! They bought copper in bulk and made their own wire!" Younger said, in-credulous. "They had to make vacuum tubes." In fact, in the beginning of their program the Soviet scientists had built equipment for their first nuclear tests with the parts available from a Canadian radio station that had been built there during World War II. "Now, this sounds incredi-ble, but it was actually true," Younger said, adding that this had been done, in part, to protect the secrecy of the weapons program. The Soviet scientists had gone to such drastic lengths because they didn't want the outside world to know what they were doing. "Nevertheless, these people achieved remarkable things and still do, basically working away in the forest." During their first joint experiment, Younger recalled, they had needed to erect a shield around some of the equipment. "In America we'd just go buy some four-by-fours and put it up, and it would look great," Younger said. "They went out and chopped down trees! We have pictures of these tree trunks providing shielding for our experiment. And that's how they do things." Nevertheless, with a lot less money to spend, the Soviet program had produced weapons science that was at least as good as the U.S. program, Younger admitted. "Sometimes they ding us by saying, 'You've become too dependent on technology,'" he mimicked the rebuke. "Which is true. 'And you haven't had the challenges we have had,' they'll say. 'You spend too much time running your computers and not enough time thinking.' Which is also true. On the other hand, we've done some things that they could never have done because they simply didn't have the machining accuracy." The United States can do high-precision experiments, examining them from every angle and extracting immense amounts of data, Younger said, while the Russians, because of their poor quality control, have to do five times as many experiments to get the same amount of data.

Because of such basic differences between their technologies, Younger added, it was impossible for U.S. scientists to duplicate the results of that first joint experiment. While the science involved was the best in the world, the quality of the work put into the device was embarrassing, he said. "Boy Scouts could do better. But, as Lenin said, 'Better is the enemy of good enough.' And that has been their philosophy—to not excel where it was not necessary." They had produced, without high technology, a nuclear weapons stockpile that was just as good as ours, Younger noted ironically. "And it kept us running for forty years."

The future will be different, however, he warned. Now, if you drive from the airport into Moscow, there is a sea of Sanyo, Daewoo, Sony, and other high-tech companies. Before the former Soviet Union opened its doors to Western technology, its people had believed what they were told, that they had the best of everything in the world, while the United States supposedly was oppressing its starving people. Now Russians watch American television, Younger said, and realize that we had it better all along. They're getting minicomputers and precision machining for legitimate industrial purposes. "And they're making astounding progress economically, even though, right now, they're having one hell of a time. If we go back to a Cold War with them, it ain't gonna be the cakewalk the last one was."

The first joint experiment between these old adversaries was an exhilarating success, in which the science worked and the participants labored shoulder to shoulder, handing tools back and forth. "You couldn't tell the work of the Americans from the work of the Russians," Younger said. There was yellow sticky tape on the device in both Russian and English, telling what the parts were, where you plugged in cables. Afterward, both Russian and American physicists and engineers gathered for a banquet to celebrate. The room was filled with light, music, and some of the brightest minds in Russian and U.S. nuclear weapons research, Younger said. They gathered together as friends in the most secret city of the former Soviet Union, and instead of clustering together in their own groups, the Russians and the Americans started dancing with each other. Vodka and cognac flowed freely. There were many bear hugs, toasts, and jokes. "It was amazing," Younger said, his face softening a bit as he stared into the middle distance. "We had done it! Both sides had been absolutely determined to conduct this experiment or get fired trying; and it almost came to that," he noted. But they had pushed relentlessly on the system and finally had their way.

At the end of the banquet Younger gave a toast: "Think about what you've done. We are the Cold Warriors that gave our two countries time to solve their problems. Now, we don't need all those weapons anymore. We have done this experiment and proved that we can work together. We have both won the Cold War."

3

The Plague

While the harrowing Cold War years of threatened mutual self-destruction seem to be over, and there are determined international efforts at work to prevent the spread of nuclear weapons technology to other nations, there remains yet another, darker possibility: nuclear terrorism. With the ambiguous security of Russian nuclear materials and weapons components, the possibility exists that nuclear terrorists will someday use a crude nuclear weapon or nuclear contamination to further their goals. This fear is fueled by the existence of nations like Iran that are known to support terrorism and are themselves thought to be working on nuclear weapons programs.

We should be very worried about this, explained Jas Mercer-Smith, because anyone wishing to make a big statement in the world would try to hit the biggest target. "The one everybody wants to hit—the United States," he warned. "And it may not be as difficult as you think. Why not just sail a boat into San Francisco harbor?" he mused. In an era when nuclear weapons are relatively small and compact, you don't need ICBMs to deliver them, Steve Younger said. "You could deliver a bomb on a bicycle or in an old Corvair." And why not use one of the drug cartels to smuggle a nuke into the country, suggested Mercer-Smith. "They transport stuff across U.S. borders as a profession and in much larger volumes," he said. This would not be an unprecedented association. In Europe and the Middle East there is said to be a cozy relationship between arms smuggling and drug trafficking, with profits from narcotics sales being used to buy technology and materials and with both commodities using the same secret trade routes. Nuclear materials have been used as assassination tools in the former Soviet Union, and, indeed, there was a June 1996 arrest in the United States of two suspects who threatened to use radioactive materials to kill U.S. political and public figures. DOE officials assisted Suffolk County, New York, police in recovering the materials.

Until recently, the idea of terrorist nuclear threats against U.S. cities seemed altogether far-fetched. But after the bombings of the federal building in Oklahoma City and the World Trade Center in New York, the idea has become more plausible. Mercer-Smith insisted that it was just a lucky break that the World Trade Center bombers were so incompetent. They could have rigged the explosion to poison everyone in the building, he said. Or they could have obliterated a large chunk of Manhattan. "You can make a real mess if you know what you're doing," he said.

And as it turns out, there have already been serious nuclear threats against major U.S. cities, prompting local and federal officials to consider massive evacuations. A credible bomb design was presented to officials in a Florida city in 1970 to back up a threat of certain destruction unless the city came through with a million dollars. The blackmailer turned out to be a fourteen-year-old boy, who, instead of being sent to jail, was remanded to the guidance of two scientists in the area so as not to waste the youngster's talents.[1] A threat against Boston in 1974 was realistic enough for President Gerald Ford and local officials to consider evacuating that city's residents. The threat proved to be a hoax, but a similar incident in New York City the following year was frighteningly believable to federal officials. The ransom note included a drawing that showed that the perpetrator may have had the technical know-how to make a nuclear bomb. The extortionist failed to show up to collect the ransom, however, and thereby avoided an FBI trap.[2]

More recently, in September 1995, New York City was the target of another threat, this time from an unnamed Middle Eastern group that claimed to have a Russian nuclear weapon poised to go off in that city. A thorough FBI investigation concluded that this threat was also a hoax. Meanwhile, New Yorkers carried on as usual, unaware of the drama unfolding in their midst.[3]

In order to cope with such threats, the U.S. government formed the Nuclear Emergency Search Team (NEST), a clandestine multi-agency investigative force managed by the FBI and involving the Department of Energy, the Department of Defense, and the Federal Emergency Management Agency. NEST's mission is to search for, identify, assess, and disable any nuclear weapon directed against the United States for purposes of terrorism, coercion, or extortion. Los Alamos National Laboratory serves as the large, silent partner in the team, providing technical expertise as well as the search and disablement equipment needed to find a bomb in a large urban area, a terrorist's most likely target. During a crisis, scientists and technicians from Los Alamos and other national laboratories and research institutions volunteer to be drawn from their normal lives and sent into a strange and potentially dangerous new world. It can be high adventure, said Kelley, whose responsibilities as program manager for counterproliferation and emergency response include the laboratory's involvement with NEST. People seem to like being on a NEST team, he said, chuckling. "They know something interesting is bound to happen."

Their job, in the case of a bomb threat, is to find the device, figure out what it is, and take it out, Kelley said. "There was a case a few weeks ago where the teams were actually stood up and the message went out: make sure you know where your people are because there is something unusual going on," Kelley said. In this case, a box had been found with markings that suggested nuclear materials. It ended up being pretty routine, Kelley said, but strange. Some variation on this pattern is repeated several times a year, in which one or two NEST investigators are dispatched to a site. More often than not, though, Kelley explained, a large deployment will go in to search, "and they never find anything," he said. "Which doesn't surprise us, because our chances of finding anything aren't very good, anyway." While investigators slip quietly into a city carrying their highly sensitive detection equipment in the normal-looking luggage of ordinary citizens and drive around on city streets in unmarked vans packed with detection devices, they will be hard-pressed to find a nuclear weapon, Kelley said, because nuclear weapons do not emit large amounts of radiation.

The best hope for stopping a terrorist nuclear disaster is good intelligence work that keeps track of suspected bombers and stops them before they can arm a bomb, Kelley said. That responsibility falls mainly to the FBI. "We really don't want to have to go out and cut the wire. That's pretty late in the game. Nobody understands this better than the British. In all their troubles with the IRA their focus has been on finding the bomb before it's there, by tracking the people who would make it and finding out where they get their materials."

So far, NEST has not had to disarm a real nuclear device, Kelley said. When that time comes, the specialists will try to reduce the yield as much as possible. "Hopefully to zero," he said. "But we can't guarantee it." If they find the bomb, and have a little time with it, though, he feels pretty sure that they will be able to disable it or at least reduce its potential yield.

"People sort of think that a generic terrorist bomb is going to be something like ten kilotons—a Hiroshima-sized thing," he said. And given the amount of damage that such a weapon can do, NEST will be pleased to reduce that yield to a kiloton. That would be a victory, Kelley said, although maybe not for the people living nearby. He holds out hope that NEST's experts would be able to reduce the yield of a terrorist bomb to a few tons of high explosives. Even then, it could be formidably damaging to any community unfortunate enough to experience it.

NEST also stands ready to deal with conventional explosives and offers its assistance to local authorities who are unable or unwilling to deal with a device because of its size or peculiar features, Kelley said. "In that case, NEST will be called in by the feds." The United States also offers assistance to foreign governments who ask for it. While a few governments have similar teams in place, NEST gets many queries from those countries that do not.

In 1989 NEST was called in on a case in which a reactor-powered Russian satellite fell out of orbit and crashed in the Canadian wilderness. "It happened to fall on the northern part of Canada in January, up around the Great Slave Lake," Kelley explained. "The U.S. knew this was going to happen and immediately contacted the Canadians and offered the resources of NEST." The Canadian adventure not only proved to be one of the team's biggest deployments, it also tested people and equipment under unusually harsh conditions. "At that time of year there's only an hour or so of daylight with temperatures of fifty below zero. It was really, really rugged," Kelley said. While the searchers had some idea where the wreckage was headed, their task was complicated by the fact that the reactor had broken up high in the atmosphere upon reentry, the wind scattering the small, burned pieces of debris all over the tundra. It was only a lucky break that led the searchers to the crash site. "A group of young men had decided to put the world behind them and trek across Canada in the middle of the winter. They had their dogsled and they were just going along—totally isolated from the world—when, in the middle of the night, they heard a tremendous bang. When they got up in the morning, there was this hole in the ice and a piece of junk lying right next to them. They radioed in and said, 'We were out here in the middle of nowhere and this thing just landed next to us.'" The irony of the situation amused Kelley. "Here they were, they wanted to get away from the world and the next thing you know there were helicopters landing and guys in white coveralls and masks checking them for radiation. Proving, after all, that there really is no place where you can hide." As it turned out, the piece that landed near them was nonradioactive and the young men were quite safe. Finding it helped the investigators to map out where the satellite had gone, based on the trajectory of that one piece.

Ironically, in most instances, the gravest dangers to NEST investigators are the natives of the environment. In Canada it was grumpy polar bears, Kelley said, while in urban areas the biggest threat is the human predator. In a 1994 team exercise in New Orleans called "Mirage Gold," in which over a thousand people participated, NEST volunteers went into some pretty rough neighborhoods, Kelley said, and were in more danger from getting mugged than anything else. Every few years NEST conducts such an exercise in which a fake nuclear device that gives off a telltale signature is hidden within an urban area. In New Orleans, the team, working from an abandoned warehouse and using intelligence clues provided by the FBI, managed to defuse the "bomb" just thirty minutes before it was set to go off. In a real crisis, the people right next to the device would be at extreme risk for a very short time, Kelley noted. "But if something does happen, they'll never know it, anyway." Everyone else will be kept at a safe distance, based upon the estimated nuclear yield of the bomb.

It seemed odd that Kelley would be so emphatic about the odds against NEST's finding a terrorist nuclear device, and that he could not be very reassuring about the prospects of NEST experts' disarming one. "We just don't like to tell people what we're doing," he said pointedly. "And the reason is, we're kind of a bomb squad and we're only going to be as effective as we can be if the bad guy doesn't know what we're trying to do. That way, if somebody goes out there and plants the bomb, he doesn't see us, doesn't see what we're doing, and doesn't see how we come into it. So, you tell me if you want the bad guy to get me before I get him."

But there is a growing public fascination with the subject, Kelley noted, and this attention was a threat to the team's effectiveness. He shook his head as he described the Internet chat groups that mull over NEST's activities, surprised at what they know. "It's probably just a bunch of curious hackers. But we know that they're out there," he said, worrying that the team members' identities will become known, making it easier for any terrorist organization to carry out its plans. Because he has made public his own connection to NEST, Kelley does not go along on the investigations.

In the final analysis, Kelley is not convinced that a terrorist nuclear attack against a U.S. city will ever happen. Given the fact that designing and building a nuclear weapon is a difficult, time-consuming, and expensive project, he reasoned, the more likely form of nuclear terrorism would probably be a contamination event, achieved with conventional explosives that just scatter some plutonium around in order to scare people. Terrorists or organized crime groups could thereby use the threat of nuclear contamination to blackmail governments or corporations. The United States contemplated using a contamination weapon against Germany during World War II. "I am more of the opinion today that if you give a bunch of smart guys some material and tell them to go build a bomb, they're going to be a long time doing it. Years, maybe, to build a yield-producing bomb. Unless you give them the freedom to get away with finished components or a whole bomb, you're looking at quite a big buck return. That makes you think that terrorists probably aren't going to be real successful in a few months in someone's garage. They might cobble together something that makes a mess, but to build a bomb that gives a lot of nuclear yield and kills a lot of people? Not too likely."

Then Kelley chuckled and noted that the Manhattan Project had been sort of a terrorist operation, hadn't it? He echoed the words of theoretical physicist and former Los Alamos weapons designer,

Theodore B. Taylor, who stressed that the first atomic weapon had been built in an old ice house from scavanged materials. The glove boxes had been made out of wood, while some other pieces of equipment had been fashioned by engineers working at home on the weekends. "The early bomb work was something like what might happen in a garage now."[4]

Nevertheless, Kelley views building a plutonium bomb as a formidable technical challenge that would necessitate melting down and molding a perfect sphere of the substance, which must then be surrounded by a shell of conventional explosives that, upon detonation, will precisely and evenly compress the plutonium ball or pit and thus achieve critical mass and nuclear fission. While a terrorist organization would be better off starting out with an already fashioned plutonium pit, they would still need sophisticated engineering expertise to develop the rest of the bomb, Kelley believes. There are easier ways to terrorize.

What we really should be worried about instead, he explained, is the possibility of chemical or biological warfare, which would be cheaper and much easier to do. "If their goal is to just kill a few people and make a big splash," Kelley said. "It would take only a few guys, a little bit of chemical knowledge, and some equipment. And maybe, if they're lucky, they won't kill themselves in the process." The recipes for making chemical weapons are widely available and doable by any good chemistry student, and the ingredients are increasingly available, as well. Kelley cited the sarin attack by a radical religious group—called Aum Shinrikyo or Supreme Truth—that killed eleven people and injured over five thousand on a crowded Tokyo subway system in 1995. The poison the Japanese group used was a degraded version of the deadly nerve gas that was invented by the Germans during World War I. "It was the smart way to go—from their twisted, warped point of view," Kelley said, making sure that I understood that with that remark he was not condoning their actions. I had heard him predict in a talk the previous year that a terrorist chemical attack like the one in Japan was bound to happen any day. "And it turned out pretty much the way we thought it would," Kelley nodded. "Not that big a deal in terms of numbers of deaths, because chemical weapons are not very effective at killing lots of people in that kind of environment." While raids on the group's facilities reportedly found evidence that the cult was studying uranium enrichment, officials from the International Atomic Energy Agency dismissed the idea that the zealots were planning to build a nuclear bomb. However, raids on Aum Shinrikyo's safe houses had turned up evidence that they were also working on biological warfare, Kelley said, grimly noting that this would be far worse than a chemical attack or even plutonium contamination.

Biological weapons such as anthrax are cheaper and easier to make, needing only a small, simple manufacturing facility, easily obtained laboratory equipment, formulae available at any big college library, and pathogens that can be easily bought. A small amount of bacteria can be multiplied quickly into a fiendish killing machine in a matter of days. A warhead containing anthrax spores could kill more people in a large city than a Hiroshima-yield nuclear weapon. Furthermore, any soil harboring the spores would make the area uninhabitable for a very long time. However, there are much cheaper ways to deliver biological weapons like anthrax. A plane or a cab could spray a mist of it over or throughout an area and kill hundreds of thousands of people without the perpetrators even being detected.[5] And while there are attempts at international control of nuclear and chemical weapons of mass destruction, there is little or no international cooperation aimed at preventing biological warfare or terrorism.

Increasing worries about biological, chemical, and nuclear warfare and terrorism are reflected in research and development at Los Alamos. Among the high-tech detection systems the lab is working on is a laser-based detector that can zero in on clouds of biological warfare agents from a distance of up to twenty miles. Carried on a helicopter, the device scans the area with laser pulses that are reflected by particles in the air. A telescope captures the reflections and funnels them into detectors for analysis. The device, which has been successfully tested on a benign bacterium, is capable of scanning a million acres per hour.

Los Alamos researchers are also working on a portable detector that can be used on the ground in battle or after terrorist attacks to detect biological agents. A flow cytometer, based on technology pioneered by the laboratory, uses laser or other light sources to detect molecular tags that attach to biological material. The result of a collaboration between LANL and a commercial laboratory, this detection system will have commercial uses in pharmaceutics and clinical microbiology, as well.

Another tool, the acoustic resonance spectroscopy system, uses sound waves to identify the chemical signature of substances in closed containers. This tool will be helpful to international chemical weapons inspectors enforcing the Chemical Weapons Convention, an international effort to control the proliferation of chemical weapons of mass destruction.

What terrorists would achieve with any method of mass destruction, beyond coercion, extortion, and fear, Kelley explained, would be the diminishment of civil liberties. The fallout from a plutonium incident, for example, given the public's fear of this and other radionuclides, would be more political than radioactive. "If somebody took a bunch of plutonium and blew it up in New York, you'd see prompt deaths of a few tens of people, a few other people would get sick from it and the rest would be outside of statistical limits." Experts would be hard-pressed to measure the effects on large numbers of people, he said, "But I'll bet you that for the next fifty years every New Yorker who got cancer would blame it on that incident, whether or not it was the cause."

Our political reaction to such terror, Kelley said, would be similar to the response to airline hijackings. "Remember just how quickly we adopted airport metal detectors and submitted to random searches?" he asked. Our reaction to a terrorist attack that employed radioactive materials would be especially severe. "I would like to make sure that Americans don't have to give up any more freedom of movement than they already have," Kelley said.

Throughout our talk I was struck by the quality of weary sorrow in Kelley's sketches of the world as he saw it. It was true, he said; he is a realist about human nature, and sometimes that's a little sad. "I'd like to be a flower child and believe that everybody's good and everybody's happy and everybody wishes me the best. But my experience is that it just isn't true."

✦

Every year in New Mexico, there are a few cases of bubonic plague—a deadly antique of a disease that infests the plentiful rodent population scurrying in the canyons and arroyos and spreads by way of flea bites to family pets and finally to people. Jas Mercer-Smith is fascinated by this black death that managed to wipe out half the population of fourteenth-century Europe. "Certainly what I do is closely related," he said.

We had arranged to meet at White Rock Overlook, an observation platform cantilevered over the breathtaking eight-hundred-foot-deep White Rock Canyon and the serpentine path of the Rio Grande. Poised on the pointing finger of a mesa several hundred feet below Los Alamos, the overlook, just outside the community of White Rock, offers a broad view of hazy blue mountains, deep canyons, and desert.

Mercer-Smith tore into the parking lot in a rusty yellow 1970s vintage LTD, a boatlike bomber of a car. I had suggested we meet somewhere natural and quiet, like a park, away from the white and gray interiors of the laboratory and the hovering presence of security and public affairs. I was surprised when he suggested this beautiful place.

"So the guards bothered you?" Mercer-Smith asked as we walked along the rocky path to a bench on the overlook platform. A raven was sitting in a nearby tree, cocking its head and staring at us with one eye. Suddenly it lifted its wings and pushed out into the air over the deep canyon, its croaking call echoing off the walls of the mesa. It was near noon on a breezy, cool day; the bench radiated rivulets of heat under the full sun. Mercer-Smith, who is asthmatic, began to cough. He hunched over, pressing his hands between his knees and said, "You get used to the guards after a while. They are there to protect us. If you were living in a major city, it would be like having a policeman on every corner to help you." Not surprisingly, Los Alamos remains one of the most crimefree places in New Mexico, its residents feeling free to walk alone at night without fear. Carefully trained police, laboratory security forces, and a world-class fire department work hard to keep the isolated community safe.

The firefighters are specially trained to handle fires involving high explosives and radioactive materials. "We have a fire department that is trained to handle class-one industrial fires involving plutonium," Mercer-Smith said. "To them, a house fire is just a toy. These people would be the best at any fire department in the United States, but they're here." And for good reason. The tinderbox dryness on this heavily forested high plateau makes Los Alamos especially vulnerable to fire. In the summer of 1977, a catastrophic fire—the worst on the plateau during this century—destroyed more than twenty-three thousand acres before it was stopped. You can still see evidence in the blackened skeletons of trees along the highway that skirts the southwest edge of laboratory property. It took a week for firefighters from the lab, the park service, and the forest service and other agencies to extinguish La Mesa Fire, as it became known. Cinders and ashes rained down upon White Rock and parts of Los Alamos, while the roofs of some laboratory buildings were sprayed with water to keep them from catching fire.[6] "They stopped it just before it reached bunkers full of high explosives," Mercer-Smith said, laughing. "That could have caused some *real* problems."

Most recently, in April 1996, another massive forest fire, the worst since 1977, came within a mile of laboratory buildings containing explosives and small amounts of tritium. Safety procedures tested in La Mesa fire saved the laboratory and the town from the Dome Fire, as it was named for an area road. Skipping wildly through canyons and whipped by high winds, the fire burned some twenty-five thousand acres of the Santa Fe National Forest and Bandelier National Monument. In one of the driest summers in years, the conflagration was started by careless campers.

A bigger security concern on the mesa, however, would seem to be the threat of a concerted terrorist attack aimed at stealing nuclear materials from the laboratory. TA-55, the lab's plutonium facility, a brilliantly lit compound surrounded by a minefield, electrified razor wire fences, and guard towers fitted with bulletproof glass, holds the largest cache of plutonium in the United States. Recently the laboratory was designated the manufacturing site for all of the plutonium pits that will be needed for the much-reduced American nuclear weapons arsenal.

Terrorism against the lab had been especially high on the community's mind just lately because of a bomb threat during the previous week. The device—planted outside the Oppenheimer Study Center at the administrative heart of the laboratory—turned out to be a crudely fashioned concoction of explosive powder and bullets. A few days later, worried lab employees reported two other suspicious objects that turned out to be just a sandbag and a caulk tube. "Fake bombs," Mercer-Smith said with disdain and then laughed, adding that if the previous week's bomber was a disgruntled lab employee, he really should be fired for incompetence because of the crudeness of his attempt. "It is a worry, though," he added grimly. "If it's not a teenager's prank, then you wonder if it's someone who really intends to do something danger-ous." Ironically, bomb threats are a favorite prank at Los Alamos High School.

Joe Martz can't believe terrorists would even consider trying to steal plutonium from what may be the most heavily guarded facility in the country. "The last thing a terrorist is going to do is come break down the gate at TA-55. They're going to buy plutonium on the streets of Moscow or Baghdad or Teheran." Bob Kelley agreed that the nu-clear materials at Los Alamos, like those at other DOE sites, are quite secure. "I'm a trusted employee of the laboratory, and it's a really big deal for *me* to get into TA-55," he said. And the chances of someone on the inside trying to smuggle plutonium out are slim, at best, he insisted, given the security measures in place. "But if it happened, I don't think the FBI would have any trouble finding a person like that," Kelley said with certainty.

This is not to say that the laboratory has not experienced problems inside the facility. In September 1995 a behavior problem, as lab spokesmen described it, led to a stand-down at the facility while inves-tigators tried to figure out who had been repeatedly shutting down monitors that detect radiation in the air. The four hundred workers were warned that such tampering could result in dismissal and criminal prosecution.

Security has always been tight at Los Alamos, but within recent years the protection of nuclear materials has become much more strin-gent, to the dismay of some veteran lab employees. During the Man-hattan Project, the plutonium components that were used in the test at Trinity Site were driven there in the trunks of two sedans through pop-ulated areas like Santa Fe. As recently as twenty years ago researchers felt free to carry as much as a gram of plutonium in their cars from one technical area to another. Now, as LANL physicist Jim Smith put it, "if you want to haul a few grams of plutonium down a road, you have to close the road and bring out the machine guns. All these changes came about because somebody was worried. Nothing ever happened the old way. I never diverted any plutonium. But people in Washington de-cided it had to be done 'right.' "[7]

Doing it right means that several times a week, public roads in Los Alamos County are closed so that plutonium samples can be transported from one technical area to another. This is done not just to protect the plutonium from being diverted, but also to comply with Department of Transportation (DOT) regulations governing the movement of hazardous materials on public access routes. In addition to having to plan for terrorism, the laboratory has had to consider public and environmental safety in a way that it was never required to do in the past. Sometimes the regulations don't make sense, said my public affairs escort, who complained that roads wouldn't need to be closed if the lab were willing to use special DOT containers for transporting plutonium. But the containers are no different from the DOE containers already in use except for their labeling and their prohibitive cost, something the lab has decided not to pay, he said. Meanwhile, road closures are announced in the local newspaper, and motorists calmly put up with them. If they can't avoid being stopped by a closure, they wait patiently in their cars, some using the opportunity to catch up on their reading. Nevertheless, all of this extra security for nuclear materials is expensive, Smith said, adding $600,000 to $700,000 to the cost of each plutonium worker at Los Alamos.

Much of the security force that encloses Los Alamos is nearly invisible to the casual eye, but its muscular reality is made manifest by TA-55. "Which looks exactly like a prison," said lab employee and Los Alamos native Tom Ribe, who had just gone inside the facility for the first time, under escort by someone with the necessary security clearances to pass through its gates. Ribe, who manages the lab's Community Reading Room, looks more like a Santa Fe antinuclear activist than a government bureaucrat. He has the craggy, weather-worn appearance of a western outdoorsman, clad in denim with sun-bleached hair pulled back in a ponytail. His visit to TA-55 and the nuclear materials storage facility next door to it had been a shock to his system. "It weirded me out in a major way to go and see this stuff today. I felt very strange, and still do."

In his role at the Community Reading Room, established in 1989 to give the public access to documents related to the laboratory's attempt to identify and clean up environmental contamination on lab and town properties, Ribe often has to answer questions concerning laboratory matters. The new $17 million nuclear materials storage facility—where the raw materials for uranium and plutonium research would be kept—had been designed wrong and needed to be redone, Ribe said disdainfully. "They got the robotics, the basement, and even the paint wrong, and they put the doors in the wrong places," he said. Fixing it would cost another $35 million. The laboratory rightly expected there to be public questions about the mistake and Ribe was able to tour the building so that he could answer any that came his way. But first he had to wade through the security that surrounds TA-55 like a moat. Ribe walked through a metal detection system, like the ones used in airports. "And then I had to talk to a guy who was behind bulletproof glass and had a machine gun slung over his back. He checked my badge and my papers, which all had to be cleared in advance." After touring the materials storage facility, Ribe and his escort took a shortcut through the corridor to another building. There he saw people wearing military uniforms and anticontamination clothing, Ribe explained; they also wore dosimeter badges to monitor their radiation exposure. "And they all looked like androids," Ribe intoned. "It was really bizarre." These were basically working-class people who were moving stuff around or repackaging it, Ribe said, and as the escort had explained to him, these workers had to take extended breaks from their jobs as soon as their radiation load reached a certain level. "But rather than the lab providing these people with other work, they have these game rooms—with Foosball, Ping-Pong, and basketball—where they spend weeks until they get into a new four-week period where they're able to get their dose level up again. I walked by a room and here were these guys playing games and cards, talking and eating, and that's what they did eight hours a day. They punch the clock and then sit around like prisoners."

Paula Dransfield, a second-generation lab employee and the daughter of Manhattan Project physicist Raemer Schreiber, agreed with some of what Ribe had to say: "I think it's a creepy place. But unfortunately, I guess that's what's called for in order to do that kind of work." Dransfield is a group leader with Reliability Programs at the laboratory. Her team is responsible for ensuring the reliability of plutonium and uranium workers through random drug tests. She qualified Ribe's description of the working conditions in TA-55 by saying that managers there are sensibly very careful not to put workers in positions where they will get heavy exposures to radioactive materials. As a result, there's a lot of standing around in hallways as part of doing the job safely. Workers executing tasks at a glove box have to do it piecemeal, she explained, completing one part of a task, stepping out into the hall, waiting, and then returning to the glove box for the next step. In that way, they are not unnecessarily exposed to radiation. The nature of the work, in addition to the strict security measures at TA-55 and other facilities, make for an odd and stressful working environment, Dransfield acknowledged, explaining that laboratory management realized this and were trying to think of ways to improve these working conditions.

"It is an interesting place," said environmental chemist Matthew Monagle, who described TA-55 as moonlike and impressively immaculate. "But the things you go through just to walk around," he remarked. "You have to jump through a lot of security hoops. But my short and dirty rule of thumb is to take nothing in there with you and keep your hands in your pockets," he said, smiling. If you put something down, it has to be swiped and counted for radiation before you can get it back. "It's real straightforward and not scary at all if you pay attention and do what your escort tells you to do." The security forces are concentrated at the front of the facility, he said, while inside, the biggest concern is actually radiation control. As a result, the heavily conditioned and filtered air inside the facility is much cleaner than it is outside. However, not everyone who works inside the facility has total confidence in the safety of the environment. One day I was shopping for bottled water in a Los Alamos grocery store and overheard a comment by a woman who said she worked in TA-55. She was buying bottled water, she told her companion, because she wouldn't dream of trusting the safety of the drinking water in TA-55.

On another occasion Ribe had a chance to visit an office building that was "way behind the fence," as he put it, "out in this remote area with guarded fences, completely surrounded by wild country." When he entered this building he noticed that people immediately started posting signs on the wall warning that there was an uncleared person in the area. Down the hallway he noticed that there were bars across the office doors, with guards posted outside. "And you look inside through the jail bars and there are people just carrying out a normal day in the office. Behind bars!" Ribe claimed, amazed. "You have to wonder what it's like for a person's psychology to work in that atmosphere year after year after year, going through gates and barbed-wire fences, past guards, minefields, and bright lights."

Along with these physical security measures, designed to protect dangerous materials and sensitive information, as well as the people who work with them, there is a strictly observed security clearance system in place that is, in reality, a substantial invasion of privacy, said Joe Martz, who holds a Q-clearance, the higher of the two granted by the DOE; it allows him to do his research with plutonium and other nuclear materials. Under a program called Personal Security Assurance, Martz submits to random drug tests, and his credit reports and IRS history are carefully scrutinized. He is required to have medical and psychological evaluations every year. "And if I were to go to a psychologist in town, it would be reported," he said. "Despite assurances otherwise, I would lose my ability to work. This is a personal sacrifice and a lot of people around here make it." Nevertheless, Martz considered himself fortunate to live in what he considers a paradise, making a good salary. "Although, I'm not in it for the money," he insisted, adding that he could double or triple his current salary in the outside world. "We make these personal sacrifices trying to do good, trying to solve problems. I don't think people appreciate that. When activist groups accuse us of being warmongers and evil scientists, it's painful."

Jas Mercer-Smith pooh-poohed the thought that a Q-clearance means much of a sacrifice. "It's not a big deal if you live a normal, legal life," he said. "The thing that really looks suspicious on a security clearance, though, is financial irresponsibility or a problem with drugs or alcohol." The laboratory provides an alcohol treatment program for its employees, but you risk your job by taking part in it if you work in certain areas, said Karen Brandt, whose husband works at TA-55. Brandt, a reporter for the *Los Alamos Monitor*, also described increasing discord in the community over the annual recertification process required of people who have Q-clearances. The controversy concerns the validity of the questions being asked, "and whether the investigators are digging into matters that are none of their damned business," she said, in describing the attitude she had observed. The van that travels from lab site to lab site collecting urine samples to test for drugs is informally known as "the golden retriever," Brandt laughed.

Contrary to popular opinion, though, drug use at the laboratory is minimal, claimed Paula Dransfield. "Oh, we catch people every once in a while," she said. "Although, I had a manager tell me the other day that his people are so well educated that if they were using drugs they would know how to get around a drug test," she said. "That's probably possible. We're just there for deterrence." The drugs of choice seem to be marijuana and cocaine, "as with most of the rest of the country," Dransfield added.

Anyone working with plutonium or uranium is subject to a more serious background investigation. Part of Reliability Programs' job is to report to the DOE on anything that might be a security concern, Dransfield said, while supervisors and managers keep a careful watch on those individuals.

People in town do feel that there is a lot of security surveillance going on, said Tom Ribe, who confessed to never feeling watched himself. "I'm pretty naive," he added. "but I think you're fine just running around town or talking on the phone. A lot of people worry about it, though. They think they're being watched." There are posters about espionage and security displayed around the laboratory, and Ribe speculated that these may also contribute to the atmosphere of surveillance. "Plus they're always handing out pencils and bumper stickers that say 'Security Is My Responsibility.' And this place is crawling with people in uniforms, carrying machine guns—our security force. We all know they're just a bunch of people with a job. They're trained, but they're not exactly the Israeli army," he said, laughing uncomfortably.

There is a time-honored attitudinal conflict between scientists and security at the laboratory that dates back to the Manhattan Project, when security was extremely tight. Physicist Richard Feynman, for example, took boyish pleasure in getting around military restrictions and censorship by crawling out of holes in the fences, along with the children of other scientists, and inventing codes to get his letters past censors. Oppenheimer was convinced that security at Los Alamos had been overdone, a sentiment still echoed today by researchers who don't always like being reminded of the need for guards. The laboratory often seems more like a campus than a government facility, and the fact that it is managed by the University of California only contributes to that aura of academe. The UC connection is very important to Los Alamos scientists even though it is undeniably true that the laboratory's budget and overall mission are based on defense work, while otherwise unrelated research benefits from those weapons budgets. This situation contributes to the sense of frustration in researchers who wish to draw a line between their work and the weapons research taking place around them. They tell stories about their run-ins with security that are laced with this worry, and peppered with dark humor and titillating rumors that frighten newcomers with the prospect of being shot by guards for wandering into the wrong place at the wrong time.

Dick Tatro, a retired lab engineer who had worked in weapons testing since 1957, has lived with the presence of security forces for many years and accepts it with equanimity. The guards do their jobs quietly and unobtrusively until their ability to respond to an alarm is tested, he said. Then a test or a false alarm can bring armed guards rushing into a quiet laboratory area, ruffling the feathers of scientists and sometimes causing resentment. Los Alamos researchers face this trade-off between security and the ability to do their work without incident. "One of the problems is whether to tell enough people that it really is an exercise so that it won't get out of hand, or not telling people it's an exercise in order to see how they do," Tatro shrugged. "These security people carry real weapons—AK-47s and worse—and when you're carrying those things, there's always a possibility of something happening and somebody getting hurt." The most likely source of injury during such an exercise, he thought, was a traffic accident caused by too many people tearing around on mountain roads.

Tatro and his wife have lived in their tidy wood-paneled duplex in Los Alamos since it was built by the federal government in the 1950s. Their home is decorated with photos of their children and grandchildren. The garden wall in back of the house is made of tuff that was carved out of the mesa and sliced into blocks with a chain saw, the same material that had been used to construct the old icehouse near Ashley Pond, where the Trinity test weapon was assembled. Hanging from the branches of the pines that surround Tatro's house are many feeders for the legions of birds there, including the gray jays that shriek at one another as they dart in and out, strafing the army of squirrels that compete for dominance of the backyard. I noticed a vivid blue shape darting past the dining room window. That was a stellar jay, Tatro explained. He had taught it to eat from his hand.

Earlier that morning Tatro had trapped a skunk in a live trap out back, a necessity because the skunks and raccoons were always digging up the lawn, he said. He liked to take his captives out to the forest and let them go, and his favorite spot was in a canyon near S-site in TA-16, where the laboratory machines and tests explosives, "experimental sorts of things—small amounts of new explosives or combinations of stuff just to collect data." Tatro, wearing a brown plaid shirt, jeans, and work boots, looked every bit the kindly grandfather—calm and quiet with a soft western drawl.

"Well, I was in the process of letting this skunk out of the trap when a security guard who patrols the roads stopped and asked me how I was doing," Tatro said. "But I knew he was trying to find out *what* I was doing. Because maybe I was interested in stealing something from the laboratory or trying to do something bad, but he never really said that." The guard had probably written down the license number of the truck so that if something came up missing, they would know whom to look for, Tatro said. "I know that's part of his job, but I was outside the fence and he didn't even begin to tell me that I wasn't supposed to be there. He was just keeping an eye on things."

I asked Tatro what he thought about the young man who had sat at the next table in Ashley's Restaurant while I talked to Paul White. "Oh, I can't think that he was there to watch Paul," Tatro replied, with avuncular goodwill. "Paul's a good man. He knows exactly what he can say or not say. Maybe that fella was just watching you?" he teased, eyes twinkling.

The pervading sense of being watched in Los Alamos has long roots in cautionary tales of espionage from the community's past—the most notorious being the story of Klaus Fuchs. The young physicist was a German-born naturalized British citizen who came to Los Alamos with the contingent of British scientists assigned by their government to the Manhattan Project. However, Fuchs was a spy for the Soviet Union, giving Stalin's scientists everything he knew about the atom bomb project, including how much fissionable material was needed, how to calculate the yield of the bomb, and how to put it together.[8] The extent to which his efforts accelerated the Soviets' program to build their own bomb has been controversial. Recent estimates suggest that Fuchs saved the Soviets, who detonated their first atomic bomb on August 29, 1949, some two years in reaching their goal.[9] In October 1996, the British government released secret documents that confirmed the extent to which Soviet spies had penetrated the Manhattan Project; agents arrived soon after the effort began, as early as October 1941. The documents showed that another British physicist—Theodore Hall, who also was at Los Alamos during the war—passed information to the Soviets.[10] Hall, a university professor who retired in Cambridge, England, was never arrested for his deeds.

With the end of the Cold War and the opening up of secret documents from the KGB and the Soviet foreign ministry, there has been a rehashing of these wartime atomic espionage stories. And, in the best Western tradition, old Soviet spies also have been writing books. A 1993 autobiography by a former member of the Soviet secret police reopened still-tender old wounds by accusing J. Robert Oppenheimer of leaking information to the Stalinist government. Other respected Manhattan Project scientists, including Enrico Fermi, Niels Bohr, and Leo Szilard, were also implicated. *Special Tasks: The Memoirs of an Unwanted Witness—A Soviet Spymaster* by Pavel Sudoplatov, coauthored with his son Anatoli and former *Time* Moscow bureau chief Jerrold Schecter and his wife Leona Schecter, suggested that the scientists worked together to plant moles in the laboratories at Los Alamos, Oak Ridge, and Chicago and that they left important papers on their desks for these moles to find and copy, an unlikely scenario, given that army security officials swept the offices every night and would surely have noticed such a gaffe and set things right.[11]

Sudoplatov also accused highly respected Danish physicist Niels Bohr (1885–1962)—a veritable father figure for the Manhattan Project—of leaking top secret information about the development of the bomb to a young Soviet scientist named Iakov Terletskii during two interviews in November 1945. Bohr, along with American physicist John Wheeler, had authored the theory by which scientists were able to predict an element's ability to capture neutrons and undergo fission, identifying uranium 235 as the only such substance at the time, and had lent his considerable expertise to the Manhattan Project.

The clandestine interview had been set up by Lavrentii P. Beria, Stalin's brutally efficient and much-feared security officer, with the hope that Bohr would spill some new bit of information that would help the Soviets with their own efforts to construct a bomb. Bohr had just returned from the United States to resume his work at the Institute of Theoretical Physics in Copenhagen, Denmark; he met with Terletskii at the urging of a Communist member of the Danish Parliament, but only after informing Western authorities that he had been asked to do so. Bohr revealed nothing new to Terletskii, a claim verified by the Soviet researcher's own memoirs, published after his death in 1993, and by another witness to the conversation—Bohr's son Aage, who had also worked at Los Alamos during the war. Bohr's other son, Ernst, had stood guard in the next room, armed with a pistol and the distinct concern, also shared by Western authorities, that Bohr was about to be kidnapped. Instead, young Terletskii—not up to the task of understanding Bohr's discourse and reliant upon translation by a nonscientist—spent most of the interview discussing former colleagues of Bohr living inside the Soviet Union. During a short second meeting, Bohr gave Terletskii a copy of the Smyth report, a document about the Manhattan Project that had been published by the U.S. government shortly after the bombs were dropped on Japan. Contrary to Beria's boastful memo to Stalin, there was nothing in the transcript of the conversation, according to Bethe, Kurt Gottfried, and Roald Z. Sagdeev, that incriminated Niels Bohr.[12]

The one detail that the Soviets claimed was crucial to their bomb program and would not have appeared in print was a description of the number of neutrons that were emitted from each split nucleus in the fissionable material in the bomb. But when asked, Bohr answered only that there were more than two. The Smyth report had simply stated that the number was somewhere between two and three neutrons. Bohr explained to his questioner that the exact number was not important as long as it was more than two in order to sustain a chain reaction, an assertion that Bethe and his coauthors say is certainly untrue and was meant by Bohr to be vague.[13]

Information gleaned from Soviet intelligence files by U.S. researchers working with the Woodrow Wilson Institute's Cold War International History Project found that there was no factual support for the accusations of espionage against Niels Bohr. Nor did the FBI find any support in its review of classified files for Sudoplatov's allegations against Bohr, Oppenheimer, Fermi, and Szilard. According to Les Aspin, who was the chairman of President Clinton's Foreign Intelligence Advisory Board at the time, the FBI had corroborating evidence to support its conclusion.[14]

Accusations of betrayal are deeply disturbing to the old friends and colleagues of these Manhattan Project icons. "It clearly hurt the people who knew and worked with Oppenheimer," Mercer-Smith told me, "people like Hans Bethe and Carson Mark." Mark, who headed the Theoretical Division at Los Alamos from 1947 until his retirement, and who lived in Los Alamos until his death in 1997, found the accusations "absolutely out of character" for Oppenheimer, and Louis Rosen, another physicist with the Manhattan Project who, like Mark, stayed with the laboratory after the war, said that Sudoplatov's charges were unfounded and insisted that he would need "considerably more evidence than I've seen so far even to entertain the notion that there could be any truth to this."[15] The old spy stories didn't matter so much to younger scientists like Mercer-Smith, who reminded me that he was only nine years old when Oppenheimer died in 1967. Nevertheless, Los Alamos still cares very deeply about its history, he said. "And I can tell you that it would hurt me desperately if one of my friends did this."

There have been more recent breaches of security at Los Alamos, most of them rather dull compared to the high drama of the wartime stories. In 1979 a librarian and a security guard were fired when a Department of Energy investigation found that there were more than a hundred thousand sensitive but unclassified technical reports concerning nuclear weapons shelved on the lower level of the library, an area that is open to the public.

Then, during the early 1980s, a former CIA agent who was later charged with selling U.S. intelligence secrets to the Soviet Union was reported to have close contact with LANL employees. Edward Lee Howard, a New Mexico native, had returned to the state after being fired by the CIA, and took a job with the New Mexico Legislative Finance Committee. He managed to escape capture by federal agents and defected to Moscow.

A congressional study in 1988 charged the Los Alamos and Livermore laboratories with lax controls over foreign visitors, failing to do adequate security checks. Visitors included agents from Soviet bloc countries, China, and other nations, including India, Pakistan, Israel, Brazil, Iran, Iraq, and Argentina—all of them believed at some time to have been working on their own nuclear weapons programs. Of the

6,700 foreign nationals who visited the weapons laboratories between January 1986 and September 1987, congressional investigators reported, there were 222 from Communist countries and 675 from other nations for which there were proliferation concerns.[16]

Ironically, an alarming number of America's so-called nuclear secrets are already a matter of public record. Engineer Charles Hanson has compiled a vast collection of documents that are available for the asking from government agencies and the national laboratories themselves, he says. In 1988 he published "U.S. Nuclear Weapons, the Secret History," and recently produced a four-thousand-page manuscript called "The Swords of Armageddon," to be published in CD-ROM format. Experts claim that Hanson's material is frighteningly accurate and could be useful to the right people.

However, nuclear secrets aren't much good without the enriched uranium, plutonium, and other materials that make them work. Someone from the laboratory's public affairs office confidently told me that "having a bunch of experts isn't going to do you much good if you don't have the right materials."

Jas Mercer-Smith seemed amused by the glibness of this claim; he pointedly disagreed. "I can get around that," he almost whispered the words. "I can get around things in ways that you never thought of." It is true that over the history of nuclear weapons development, designers have learned to get greater and greater explosive power from smaller and smaller amounts of fissionable materials. Furthermore, weapons scientists may someday find ways to use the fusion of naturally occurring isotopes of light elements such as deuterium and lithium to build nuclear weapons, according to theoretical physicist Theodore B. Taylor, who worked at the Los Alamos lab and is credited with miniaturizing the atomic bomb and with designing the largest-yield fission weapon that has ever been detonated. He spoke on this issue in a May 1, 1996, address at the University of California at Santa Barbara.[17] It is important to keep thinking and experimenting, as Mercer-Smith opaquely phrased it, in order to maintain the element of technological surprise that had served so well in the past. "Hiroshima is a fine example of the kind of rabbit you might be able to pull out of the hat. There may be advantages to having technological surprise on our side someday. Things that you would be able to do, interesting things that would keep you from getting killed—without having to incinerate a billion people."

I didn't doubt that there were still plenty of secrets to guard at Los Alamos. "Every time I talk to that guy, I can't sleep at night," muttered my public affairs escort after one such meeting with Jas Mercer-Smith.

4

The Perils
of Plutonium

People will argue that the world could have chosen not to invent the atomic bomb, denying this powerful potential at the heart of the atom. But to suggest that all scientists everywhere could have turned their backs on an emerging truth is to not understand what makes scientists tick. Researchers at Los Alamos use the word *inevitable* to describe the development of wildly destructive bombs based on nuclear fission. "Nature is there to be measured and discovered," said Joe Martz, in words reminiscent of those spoken years before by J. Robert Oppenheimer: "It is a profound and necessary truth that the deep things in science are not found because they are useful; they are found because it was possible to find them." Likewise, nuclear weapons were there to be found, Martz said. "If nature has some effect—as with nuclear reactions—I don't think we can just sit back and ignore it and not investigate it, even though it represents harm. Could they have done that in the thirties or forties?" he asked, referring to the very real fear that Hitler would develop and use an atomic weapon first. Indeed, as soon as the ground-laying research was announced, physicists everywhere realized what it meant. By June 1940 researchers in the Soviet Union were reporting spontaneous fission in uranium. And Japanese military engineers, like everyone else in the world scientific community, had been reading reports in international journals and saw the promise for such research. By 1940 they, too, were working on the problem.[1] There were a hundred of Japan's best young scientists laboring in Tokyo under the direction of Yoshio Nishina, a physicist who had studied in Denmark with Niels Bohr.

They were charged with the task of developing an atom bomb.[2] Scientists in Germany were actively investigating the energy potential of uranium, but only later did the Allies realize how far they were from actually developing a bomb.

Martz and I were sitting beside Ashley Pond, its placid face a vivid reflection of the uncommonly blue New Mexico sky. Martz pointed out the spot nearby where an old icehouse had stood, the assembly site for the world's first nuclear weapon. The small stone structure, as well as the first laboratory buildings that had stood around the pond, is gone now, and in the way of Los Alamos, is not remembered with descriptive historical markers. However, the park had most recently been the site of a sculpture show in celebration of the fiftieth anniversary of the founding of the laboratory. And it was lovely, Martz allowed, "but even we don't escape from the realities of twentiety-century life. Somebody vandalized one of the sculptures by spray-painting it," he grimaced. It was difficult to imagine Joe Martz ever being the kind of kid who would scrawl graffiti across public property. He is the straightest of straight arrows.

"It's not our job to put our heads in the sand," he continued, referring both to the exigencies of the times and the realities of nuclear weaponry. "Our job is to learn to control these forces." But putting the knowledge of nuclear weaponry back in the bottle may lie beyond the skills of the world's best scientists and politicians, he intoned; the most sensible strategy for slowing the proliferation of doomsday weapons and preventing their ultimate use may be to reduce as much as possible the amount of weapons-ready materials in the world and tightly control what remains—especially plutonium, a substance that offers more efficient explosive power per gram than other fissionable materials and whose most stable isotope has a half-life of 24,200 years. "This stuff isn't going away naturally on any kind of human time scale," Martz said.

Plutonium was first discovered during the winter of 1940–1941 by radiochemist Glenn Seaborg and three other researchers, who named it for the planet Pluto, discovered a decade earlier. It had seemed like a logical choice for the new addition to the periodic table, following as it did after Neptunium, the element named for Neptune, Pluto's neighbor. It also brushed the substance with an unscientific tinge of poetry, in that Pluto, in Roman mythology, is the god of the dead and the ruler of the underworld. Seaborg has been quoted as saying that plutium would have been a more correct name for the element, but he and the others had liked how the word *plutonium* rolled off the tongue.[3] None of this really mattered at first because during the war years the given name of element 94 was classified top secret and was blandly referred to with the code words *material* or *product* instead.

Plutonium is often described as a man-made element, another usage that irks Joe Martz, who thought it the height of human arrogance. "Like we've got so much control over nature that we can make an element," he sniffed. Plutonium likely existed in greater abundance in the earth's crust ages ago, Martz added, noting evidence that the element had been produced in natural reactors that had formed spontaneously within a uranium deposit in west Africa some 2 billion years ago.[4] The phenomenon was first suspected by French mining engineers who had noticed a depletion of U-235 and the presence of its fission products in uranium ore. Water flowing through the uranium must have acted as a moderator and slowed down escaping neutrons, allowing them to fission enough additional uranium atoms to achieve criticality. As many as one hundred such natural reactors may have existed, alternately producing power when water was available and shutting down during droughts over a period of many thousands of years.[5] In addition, Los Alamos scientists have discovered natural traces of Pu-244 in nature, while the fission products of that isotope have been found in meteorites.[6]

Now, however, nearly all of the plutonium that exists on earth is human-made, produced in nuclear reactors by bombarding a solid uranium compound with neutrons and precipitating out everything except element 94. The most trivial shielding—aluminum foil or even paper—is sufficient to block plutonium's alpha emissions, and depending upon its isotopic composition, it will feel warm to the touch, like a living thing.

"Plutonium 238 is considerably warmer than that, though," said Martz, who described what once had been a popular exhibit at the laboratory: a box containing a sphere of Pu-238 that glowed red when the cover was removed. Lab physicists considered it a nifty illustration of thermal emissions, a characteristic that makes it useful as an energy source in spacecraft. But the exhibit scared other people, fulfilling as it did their worst misconceptions about nuclear material. "So we got smart and stopped doing this," Martz chuckled.

Indeed, the fear of plutonium runs so deep in our culture that, for many people, the element has become synonymous with evil, a bogeyman for the modern age. Martz is quick to refute this practice of personifying plutonium or any other technical fact or discovery as either good or evil. "It simply exists," he stated flatly. Nevertheless, even he had been profoundly affected when he made his first visit to the plutonium facility at Los Alamos as a summer student in 1985. "I had received all the proper training and had a tremendous amount of technical knowledge, and on an intellectual level, I understood the hazards. But when I walked into that plutonium-processing area for the first time, I was scared; it was an emotional, visceral reaction that I will never forget," he said, explaining that society had done such an effective job of making us afraid of things like radiation and nuclear materials that even he had had a reaction. "So I can fully understand why people who don't have a technical background would be scared," Martz acknowledged.

The roots of this cultural fear of plutonium reach back at least as far as the Manhattan Project, when weapons research and industrial-level production of the substance were under way well before its toxicity was understood. Fearing the worst, however, project leaders sought to protect workers by instituting at least some safety standards that were extrapolated from what was known about radium—a radioactive material discovered by Marie Curie at the turn of the century and that ultimately killed her by 1934. Before its dangers were known, however, radium had been a much-touted magic ingredient in any number of commonly used products: toothpaste, face cream, contraceptive jellies, and chocolate bars, for example. And, of course, it was used in crude medical therapies.[7] But the tragic experience of the radium dial painters brought to light the inherent dangers of radium. The dial painters, most of them women and girls, used a luminescent concoction of radium 226 and zinc sulfide to highlight watch dials, instrument panels for airplanes, and a wide assortment of novelty items. As they worked, they licked the tips of their brushes to achieve a fine point and, within a few years, began to die horribly from jaw and sinus cancers. Investigators traced the illnesses to the alpha radiation emitted by the radium the women had ingested. Specialists began to realize that any benefits to be derived from radioactive materials would not be simple and, indeed, might exact a heavy price.

So, in order to avoid a similar tragedy Manhattan Project leaders tried to establish exposure standards for the large numbers of people working furiously to produce enough plutonium for the secret bomb project. At the time, plutonium was thought to be fifty times less toxic than radium; an internal dose limit of five micrograms was established. This standard was fairly meaningless, however, because there was not yet any way of measuring the plutonium load in a human body.[8] But just to be safe, remote control devices, filtered exhaust systems, and dust dispersal methods were installed in some work areas.[9] But money for such refinements was scarce during World War II, and it was difficult to convince workers of the risks involved, anyway. According to Jas Mercer-Smith, that was when plutonium's reputation as one of the world's most toxic substances really began, with frightening warnings aimed at influencing worker safety. It didn't stop Manhattan Project scientists and technicians from taking terrible risks with plutonium, however, Mercer-Smith added. "There were people here during the war who got god-awful plutonium loads," he said. "Some of those guys accidentally tipped over solutions and were in it ankle-deep. Machinists worked without hoods." Furthermore, during those days, every speck of plutonium had to be saved because it was so incredibly rare and precious. One machinist who returned to Los Alamos for the Manhattan District Fiftieth Anniversary Reunion in 1993 told of having to pick up and save in a cup any of the tiny shavings that fell to the floor. Other men were part of a cleanup detail assigned the task of chemically extracting all of the plutonium left in waste liquids and on beakers, countertops, and floor tiles.[10] "Yet they lived to tell the story," Mercer-Smith said, "and they are the healthiest bunch of people you've ever seen in your life." A study begun in 1951 has followed twenty-six of the Manhattan Project veterans who were exposed to Pu-239 at Los Alamos, nineteen of whom are still alive and in their seventies, still carrying plutonium particles around in their bodies. Epidemiologist George Voelz, who was head of the laboratory's Health Division for a time during the 1950s and took over the plutonium workers study in the early 1970s, can confirm that these nineteen surviving Manhattan Project plutonium workers are still in pretty good health for seventy-year-olds. Their death rate was close to 50 percent of what would be expected for a similar group of U.S. males, Voelz said.[11] "The heavy smokers are all among the seven who died, while the others are doing quite well for men their age." Of the seven who died, three had cancer, three had heart disease, and one died in an auto accident. "Being chased by a jealous husband," Mercer-Smith contributed with an ornery grin. "But if you write anything I've said," Voelz quietly insisted, "write how dangerous it is to smoke." One could make a case, he added, that six of the deaths had more to do with smoking than with plutonium exposures. The death that had the closest relationship to plutonium exposure, Voelz said, was a rare bone tumor; finding one among a group of that size exceeded expectations. However, according to a 1994 study of all the people at Los Alamos who had received plutonium exposures, there were no other such bone tumors, putting that one case well within the expected number for a typical population, Voelz added. Nevertheless, Voelz reserves final judgment on the relationship between the plutonium exposure—about a quarter or a third of the traditional lifetime permissible body burden—and the development of a bone cancer. "I think we need to continue looking at it. If they were, in fact, related, then we may have underestimated the risk a bit," Voelz has said.[12]

The men in the study were informally referred to as the UPPU Club—meaning "you urinate Pu (plutonium)," since the presence of plutonium in their systems was ultimately detected in their urine. They had been chosen for the follow-up study because they had inhaled plutonium, the exposure that presents the greatest danger if the particle is fine, like the dust that forms on an ingot as it oxidizes when exposed to air. A small amount—one ten-thousandth of a gram—can cause lung cancer. Given access to the bloodstream or the lymph system, plutonium concentrates in the liver and on the surfaces of the bones. It turns off the mechanism in the bone marrow that produces white blood cells, making possible the development of cancers. And once a plutonium particle finds a niche in the body, it stays there forever, emitting radiation into the immediately surrounding tissues.

But inhaling a plutonium particle doesn't necessarily spell doom, explained lab physicist Jim Smith, because it has to be just the right size—neither too small nor too large—to cause lung cancer. Experiments carried out on beagles had shown that a large particle will be isolated by scar tissue, effectively blocking its damaging rays, while a very small particle will simply be exhaled again or carried away by mucus to the digestive tract and expelled from the body. A very large particle simply can't be inhaled. Human exposures have tended to be from large particles and have tended not to cause cancer, Smith said, citing an example from the Manhattan Project. The chemist who had cast the plutonium spheres for the Trinity test shot and the plutonium bomb used on Nagasaki inhaled three micrograms of Pu-239 in the course of his work. "And in those days the glove boxes were made of plywood," Smith noted, "and they were vented on the roof." The man never developed cancer, as shown by the autopsy that was done after his death at the laboratory from a heart attack in 1981. The plutonium he had inhaled years before had been effectively isolated by scar tissue in his lungs. "And he was incredibly proud of this exposure, by the way," Smith said. "He would tell me, 'When I'm dead, they're going to take my body.' He wanted that." For this man, who had not been able to fight in World War II because of a neurological problem that caused seizures, the plutonium exposure was equivalent to a chest full of combat ribbons, Smith explained, adding that people who work with plutonium, explosives, and other dangerous materials tend to be very proud of having done so.

Smith will even go so far as to say that no death anywhere can be clearly attributed to plutonium exposure, that scientific research has yet to establish such a link. A study of seven thousand workers employed at Rocky Flats between 1952 and 1979 found them to be healthier overall than the general population, with no reported bone cancers and fewer lung cancers. Those workers who had ingested or absorbed plutonium particles had a death rate similar to that of their colleagues who had not.[13] Tissue samples from hundreds of American nuclear workers have been analyzed at Los Alamos National Laboratory as part of the U.S. Transuranium and Uranium Registries, a database of U.S. nuclear workers. The lab also solicited donations of whole bodies from persons who had had significant documented exposures to radioactive materials. So far, eleven bodies have been analyzed at Los Alamos. However, federal budget cuts have undermined the ability of health physicists to keep track of the nation's plutonium workers. In 1994 the tissue analysis program was moved from Los Alamos to Washington State University.

One of the tricky things about plutonium, of course, is that laying blame with certainty for any cancer death is complicated by the distance of years and the existence of other carcinogenic environmental factors and genetic influences. Experts on the damaging health effects of low-level radiation contend, however, that the plutonium spewed into the earth's atmosphere by aboveground nuclear tests will be responsible for hundreds of thousands of lung cancer deaths as well as genetic abnormalities that, in turn, will produce more and more problems as the years go by. The nuclear energy industry tells us that nearly everyone born before 1962 has particles of plutonium permanently fixed in his or her body because of fallout from atmospheric tests, while several tons of plutonium reside elsewhere in the biosphere.[14]

Of course, death by plutonium was most vividly illustrated to the world in the bombing of Nagasaki during World War II. These were criticality deaths, however, and quite different from the slow damage performed by small particles. Blast, fireball, and gamma radiation were responsible for the seventy thousand deaths attributed by the end of 1945 to the plutonium implosion weapon Fat Man; the number of dead doubled after five years.[15] More people died from Little Boy, the uranium bomb that fell on Hiroshima, in part because of differences in the geology of both bomb sites. After five years the Hiroshima death toll was reckoned at two hundred thousand people.[16] Other differences between the Hiroshima and Nagasaki death tolls have been attributed to little-understood effects of the uranium weapon, a device that has been subject to far less research in general than the plutonium device. Disagreement among scientists over what kinds of radioactive particles showered Hiroshima continue. A number of tests have been done over the years to better understand just what made the uranium bomb so deadly. At Los Alamos, physicists and engineers built a twin of Little Boy out of warehoused period materials, tweaking its core close to criticality to find out what sorts of radiations it emitted. They concluded that gamma rays had done the killing at Hiroshima; but more recently, researchers at Livermore uncovered evidence of neutrons in the concrete and natural rock of Hiroshima. The solution to this mystery is important, because radiation standards worldwide have been based upon the health effects studies of high- and medium-dose radiation exposures to thousands of Japanese A-bomb survivors.

While it was immediately obvious after the bombings just how deadly the new weapons were, these extensive follow-up studies have characterized the more subtle long-term effects. The Radiation Effects Research Foundation (RERF), a joint effort by the Japanese and U.S. governments, estimated in 1996 that among approximately 50,000 survivors who received significant radiation exposures, 426 died subsequently of cancers clearly attributable to the A-bomb. Activists say that many more have suffered from their exposures, and that the dying continues unabated. The RERF research found that in utero exposures, especially those occurring between the eighth and fifteenth weeks of gestation, resulted in reduced IQ or mental retardation among the most severely exposed babies, as well as stunted growth and development. Data suggest that cancer death rates will increase among the most severely exposed of this group as they continue to age. No genetic effects have been found among children of A-bomb survivors, although blood samples are being saved by RERF scientists for the day when more powerful tools are available to further analyze DNA at the molecular level.[17]

Surprisingly, given the sometimes questionable safety practices in the U.S. nuclear complex, there have been few criticality deaths among researchers and technicians involved in nuclear weapons research. Indeed, at Los Alamos, there have been more deaths due to accidents with conventional explosives. The first two criticality deaths occurred within months of the bombings of Hiroshima and Nagasaki, during critical assembly experiments with metallic plutonium. The first was on the evening of August 21, 1945, when a young scientist, Harry K. Daghlian, began an experiment in which a subcritical sphere of nickel-plated plutonium was surrounded with a tamper of tungsten carbide bricks that would reflect neutrons back into the sphere in order to sustain criticality. As Daghlian was stacking the tamper bricks, he recognized a rapid increase in neutron flux and tried to push the last brick off the stack to prevent an uncontrolled chain reaction. Instead, he accidentally dropped it into the center of the assembly. A security guard sitting some twelve feet away with his back turned to the experiment saw the flash of light reflected by his newspaper. Daghlian tried to push the other bricks out of the way, but in the ten minutes he spent near the reactor he received a fatal radiation exposure and died on September 14, 1945. The guard received small doses of neutrons and gamma rays and died thirty-three years later of leukemia, an illness that may have been caused by his radiation exposure.[18]

On May 21, 1946, group leader Louis Slotin, about to leave for the Bikini Atoll test site, decided to give an impromptu demonstration of a criticality experiment to his successor and five other people. A sphere of plutonium was placed inside a tamper consisting of two hemispherical shells of beryllium. Slotin was holding the shells apart with a screwdriver, when his hand slipped and the shells abruptly closed into contact. There was a blue flash, and Slotin threw the shell to the floor, but not before he had absorbed a fatal dose of radiation that killed him within nine days.

Of the other men present at the experiment, two died nineteen or more years later of leukemia, most likely related to their exposures. Two others eventually succumbed to illnesses that could be related, while, of the remaining two, one died in combat in the Korean War and another refused to participate in follow-up studies.[19] Physicist Alvin Graves was one of the men in the room "when Slotin saw the blue flash," as a longtime Los Alamos resident put it to me in the myth/ history shorthand of Los Alamos memory. Another Los Alamos longtimer, Jean Dabney, was a WAC assigned to help Dr. Graves and electronics group leader Dr. Darol Froman. She remembered the effects Graves suffered after the accident. "It was frightening and yet very interesting to monitor the changing body effects occurring almost daily to his person. The positive, cheerful spirit and thoughtfulness he expressed is something I shall never forget," Dabney said.[20] Mercer-Smith fondly referred to Manhattan Project pioneers as wackos who performed such critical assembly experiments using things like pencils to hold tampers apart. They devised daring criticality tests, like the one physicist Richard Feynman dubbed "Tickling the Dragon's Tail." This involved assembling enough uranium 235 to make an explosion, but leaving out the core of the material so that neutrons could escape and the material would remain just short of critical until the core was dropped through the hole from above. As it raced through the material, there would be a momentary flash of criticality that the researchers could then study.[21]

Such imaginative yet risky experiments made it possible for Manhattan Project scientists to create the atomic bomb in record time. And while their derring-do is considered foolhardy by today's scientists, it is also viewed by some as heroic. This was wartime, one older engineer pointed out to me, and these civilian and military researchers and technicians were risking themselves as millions of other men and women had done during World War II. Only later did the lab establish a comprehensive health and safety program, because, as an official history of the Manhattan Project put it, "in peacetime the Laboratory could not afford to take any chances with human life".[22]

The one criticality accident to occur at the laboratory since the Manhattan Project deaths of Daghlian and Slotin led to a long-term research project—the Occupationally Exposed Worker Study—aimed at refining and improving radiation safety standards. The accident occurred on January 7, 1957, when plutonium worker Cecil Kelley received a fatal dose while cleaning a tank in the plutonium recovery plant at the lab. It happened during a materials inventory process when operations had been interrupted. Solutions containing plutonium-rich solids were inadvertently washed from two tanks into a single solvent-treating tank; when Kelley flipped a switch that turned on a stirrer, a mass of plutonium came together and achieved criticality.[23] Kelley, who had been standing on a ladder against the tank, was taken to the Los Alamos Medical Center emergency room semiconscious, incoherent, retching, vomiting, and hyperventilating. His skin had turned a deep red-violet and his lips blue. Over the thirty-five remaining hours of his life he suffered from severe cardiovascular shock, abdominal pain, increasingly manic behavior, then coma and death. Authorized by Kelley's wife, the laboratory collected autopsy samples, which were subjected to radiochemical analysis in order to determine the plutonium content in his body and compare it to urinalysis and whole body counting data obtained from Kelley while he was alive.

By 1957 more was known about the effects of such criticality exposures and about radiation, in general. As horrible as it was, Kelley's suffering, like Daghlian's and Slotin's before him, added valuable information to that growing body of knowledge. "We really didn't know very much about radiation at first," said a lab veteran. That the Manhattan Project was well under way before anyone knew the effects of plutonium on the human body seems crazy today. And, not surprisingly, at the time scientists involved with or aware of the secret work were getting increasingly nervous about it. "It has occurred to me that the physiological hazards of . . . say one miligram or less may be very harmful," wrote Glenn Seaborg, advocating that a research program begin at once to trace the path of plutonium through the human body. Then something happened in August 1944 to force the issue. The entire Los Alamos supply of plutonium, a total of ten milligrams, blew up in the face of chemist Don Mastick. Mounting pressure from a chemical reaction inside the sealed tube of plutonium solution caused an explosion that ruptured the vessel, splattering the contents against the wall and into Mastick's mouth. The young chemist ran to health director Louis Hempelmann's office to get his stomach pumped, whereupon he immediately set about recovering from the extracted contents as much as he could of the approximately ten micrograms of plutonium he had swallowed. As it turned out, by 1995 Mastick had suffered no ill effects from his exposure because, as investigators later came to understand, swallowing plutonium is less serious than other forms of exposure, the particles tending to pass unabsorbed through the intestinal system. Nevertheless, at the time, it was a frightening event that galvanized Hempelmann's concerns about the safety of those working with this new material when so little was known about its action in the body.

When they first began working with plutonium at Los Alamos, said George Voelz, there was no portable device for measuring alpha emissions. "If you wanted to see whether a benchtop was contaminated, you would have to take a filter paper, make a smear, go back in the laboratory, and count it. There was no easy way of surveying surfaces." Both Hempelmann and colleague Wright Langham had had a particular concern for these workers, Voelz has said. He later worked with Hempelmann during the 1970s and recalled that every time he saw Hempelmann, the physician inquired about "the boys," as he called the Manhattan Project plutonium workers. Were they still okay?[24]

What Hempelmann and Langham most needed at the time was an accurate way to ascertain the body burden acquired by exposure victims like Mastick, since plutonium could be traced only through its alpha emissions and, after ingestion, would be silenced to outside detection by the intervening tissues of the body. Animal studies had shown that plutonium's radiations were detectable in excreta, but little experimental work had been done to establish a reliable method of assaying the body burden that those radiations represented. Hempelmann sent a memo to J. Robert Oppenheimer outlining his own concerns and those of Mastick and his colleagues, urgently calling for further study. While "a full time chemist here and another at Chicago have been working on the problem," Hempelmann wrote, there was still no reliable method of quantifying exposure levels.[25] On August 16, 1944, Oppenheimer added his voice to those calling for research that would fill the gap, but also urged that the experiments not be carried out at Los Alamos. The Manhattan Engineering District soon authorized a cooperative research project with institutions in Chicago, Berkeley, and Rochester, New York. The first injection was administered at Oak Ridge, Tennessee, in April 1945. A group of eighteen people was injected with tracer amounts of plutonium in order to determine the fixation and excretion rate of plutonium in humans. Only the analysis of tissue samples and excretions would be done at Los Alamos.

"The world and the country needed data," said Jim Smith, adding that only later would the widespread program of human experimentation that began at that time be considered somehow evil. Experiments continued throughout the Cold War years, a time when a nuclear exchange seemed highly probable and more knowledge about radiation and nuclear blast effects was deemed essential. Furthermore, radioactive isotopes held great promise as tools for medical diagnostics and therapies; after the war, the Atomic Energy Commission (AEC), the DOE's predecessor, encouraged a wide-ranging slate of research projects with that in mind. Los Alamos scientists are quick to point out the lifesaving medical tools and the advances in cell biology that have resulted from such research.

However, there were some serious ethical breaches in the conduct of some of the human radiation experiments that would come back to haunt Los Alamos, the other institutions in the Department of Energy complex, and the medical facilities that participated in the studies. It appears now that some of the research subjects did not give their informed consent for the things that were done to them. This was again brought to public attention by a Pulitzer Prize–winning series of reports that appeared in the *Albuquerque Tribune* during November 1993. Reporter Eileen Welsome identified five of the eighteen people who had been chosen for the 1940s plutonium injections by researchers at the participating medical institutions. The patients, including one child, were selected because they were thought to be terminally ill and therefore would not survive long enough to suffer the mainly long-term effects of the plutonium. As it turned out, a number of these people lived for decades, some of them tortured with anxiety over what might have been done to them and what it meant. A few were tracked medically for years by the doctor who had injected them; they were treated to all-expense-paid trips to research centers where they were examined for long-term effects of the plutonium, but they were told very little.

George Voelz, who came to the lab in 1951, remembered that Wright Langham, the biochemist who performed the urinalyses and tissue analyses for the plutonium injection studies, "had a reluctance to discuss the project because he had an uneasiness about it," Voelz said. "In terms of the use of patients for these studies, I think Langham was just contributing what he knew about his procedure for urinalysis and the chemical management of the plutonium samples and solutions. As for the rest of it, he was just going along with what was proposed by others. I think he had a real uneasiness. I know he had a real uneasiness about the project, [but] not his end of it."[26] Langham's wife, Julie Langman Grilly, explained that her husband did not propose the plutonium injections and didn't want any involvement in the study beyond analyzing the samples, and that "it bothered him that these people hadn't been told."[27]

The *Albuquerque Tribune's* treatment of the plutonium injection studies was riveting and significant because it put human faces and personal stories to what had previously been anonymous case histories in scientific journals. In fact, Los Alamos scientists reminded me repeatedly that most of the information had been openly published in the scientific literature years before, and had made its way into the popular press, too. For some reason, there was very little public reaction to earlier stories about the experiments—published in 1976 in *Science Trends*, in 1981 in *Mother Jones* magazine, and later in several major newspapers when in 1986 Massachusetts Democratic representative Edward Markey released a congressional report titled "American Guinea Pigs: Three Decades of Radiation Experiments on U.S. Citizens."[28] The congressional report brought out details about the research that had been kept secret for years. Some information, as documents now show, was suppressed to spare the AEC both embarrassment and litigation.[29]

The revelations about the plutonium injection studies and the flood of press reports about other experiments were shocking to Energy Secretary Hazel O'Leary, who referred to it as the dark side of the nuclear genie. And finally, the information struck a deep nerve in the American public. One report told of retarded children in Massachusetts being fed oatmeal laced with trace amounts of radioactive material. In Ohio, a Department of Defense–sponsored program exposed cancer patients to total body radiation, while in Washington and Oregon, prison inmates were subjected to the irradiation of their testicles.[30] In a collaboration between the laboratory and the Argonne Cancer Hospital, under the management of the University of Chicago, tracer amounts of tritium and carbon 14 were used to study protein and cholesterol metabolism in the human fetus. The study results were published in medical journals of the time.

An early 1960s Los Alamos experiment was deemed to be particularly sinister because the researchers conducting it fed radioactive iodine to their own children. In the April 1964 issue of *Science* the study's authors explained that radioactive iodine—a substance that is released in nuclear explosions—can make its way through the food chain and deposit itself in the human thyroid gland. Data on the retention of this substance in children were scarce because of the reluctance of researchers to use traditional tracer techniques on the more radiosensitive young thyroid gland.[31] And the smallness of a child's thyroid presented detection problems, as well. The Los Alamos study, using a new highly sensitive whole-body counter, made it possible to trace in the body the retention and biological half-life of extremely small doses of radioisotopes, in this case about 0.01 microcurie of radioiodine. It was found that the rate of retention was similar in both children and adults, about 20 percent of the dose after one day, while the biological half-life of the substance was about ninety days. Eight adults, two teenagers, and eight children participated in the study. Sessions with the children, ages four through nine, were scheduled during afternoon cartoon time, with a television positioned in such a way that the children would remain still and in the proper pose for the fifteen-minute test.[32]

News stories that revisited the radioiodine metabolism study served to reinforce a common public skepticism about government scientists; some people, including a few in Los Alamos, misunderstood the reports, thinking that Los Alamos scientists had fed plutonium to their children. "'Los Alamos fed radiation to children,' was the headline in one of our local newspapers," said physicist Gary Sanders, who, like other Los Alamos scientists, was mystified by all the fuss and didn't understand why the lab was being accused of sinister secret tests when, in fact, the data had been published in the same year of the study with updates published as more results were found. "People went off to conferences to give prestigious talks about this stuff," Sanders said, stressing that the dose administered to the children had been a hundred times less than a diagnostic dose of today. "These researchers knew that this represented a very small risk, and were even willing to give it to their own children for their country and the greater good of society." Cell biologist Don Petersen, a lab veteran who had worked there since 1956, serving before his retirement as the program manager for the Chemical and Biological Program, had participated in the study and so had two of his children. "The six-year-old and the eight-year-old decided they wanted to participate. The four-year-old looked around and she decided she didn't want any part of it, so she went home," said Petersen, who has been laughingly characterized by Gary Sanders as someone who has tried to nosh his way through the periodic table. The radiation to which the children were exposed, Petersen said, was only a fraction of what they would experience from natural sources on any given day. For example, living in Los Alamos at an elevation of seventy-five hundred feet exposes residents to solar radiation far exceeding the dose in the radioiodine metabolism study. "We would never put our kids in harm's way," Petersen said.[33]

The press had made these researchers sound like a bunch of ghouls, Sanders said, as if they were so enamored of radiation that they were willing to immerse themselves in it and feed it to their children. "They were not above using themselves as human subjects," Sanders sighed with frustration. "In fact, their first thought was to use themselves." And in those days, said George Voelz, lab employees considered such volunteerism to be important work and a source of pride, an attitude that is not appreciated today, nor portrayed accurately by the press. No one had to twist anyone's arm to get people to participate in studies, he said. It was a common impulse among researchers and their families to volunteer themselves for research during the 1950s and '60s.[34] For example, during the development of the whole-body counter, Wright Langham, then the leader of the lab's Biological and Medical Research Group, had tested a prototype's efficiency by wedging himself inside its central chamber and holding a 0.2-microcurie radio source against his stomach, information that was published in *Nature* in 1953.[35] Los Alamos researchers swallowed tritium-laced water, one person dipped his arm elbow-deep into it, and others inhaled oxygen saturated with tritium water vapor.[36] Another group of lab volunteers, including Don Petersen, was reinjected with samples of their own blood that had been tagged with chromium 51 for a study of the life span of circulating blood cells.[37]

Another major public health concern at the time, of course, involved the possible effects from atmospheric testing of nuclear weapons. By 1958 studies were finding that atmospheric tests by the United States, the Soviet Union, and Great Britain, equal to 174 million tons of TNT, had generated a noticeable increase in the amount of global radioactive contamination. To determine the extent of contamination by such long-lived radioactive isotopes as strontium 90 and cesium 137, "Project Sunshine" had been established. The project leader—Willard Libby of the University of Chicago—had chosen the name because he believed that fallout would be as ubiquitous around the globe as sunshine. This research sought to collect samples of soil, water, crops, animal tissues, and human bones from around the world and analyze them with the whole-body counter that had been developed at Los Alamos. The New Mexico laboratory tested for plutonium in human tissue specimens from 1,520 persons from twenty-seven states, finding that the deposition of that substance was not as serious as first suspected.

The dark side of Project Sunshine, however, was that it was carried out under a pall of secrecy, with plausible cover stories devised to hide the real purpose of the effort. For example, tons of human infant skeletons from at least a dozen countries were acquired supposedly to measure concentrations of naturally occurring radium. Plant and animal samples were collected under the guise of nutritional research. All of this was accomplished through contacts with other government agencies, physicians, and private organizations, without ever telling the public what was really going on.

The details of this and many other studies were revealed when Secretary O'Leary decided that, with the end of the Cold War, it was time for the federal government to come clean on the past and disclose as much as it could about the past fifty years' government radiation research, including classified information about the experiments carried out on humans. At the same time, a congressional investigation revealed that government agencies—including Los Alamos National Laboratory—had made thirteen unannounced releases of radiation into the environment without notifying the affected populations.[38] A December 15, 1993, General Accounting Office report described three 1950 tests in which radioactive lanthanum was released during hydrodynamic tests conducted in Bayo Canyon near Los Alamos. The experiments employed conventional high explosives to test weapons designs, with the lanthanum used as a source of diagnostic X rays that made it possible for the researchers to see movement and compression of materials during explosions. Small quantities of strontium 90 were also released into the environment in the process. In a test that was conducted outside the nearby town of Abiquiu, radioactive lanthanum was used as a source of X rays that were directed into the sky, where a B-17 used them to calibrate instruments. That exercise did not entail explosions or releases of radioactive materials, however.[39]

Secretary O'Leary decided to make public as much of the information about human radiation studies, U.S. plutonium stockpiles, unannounced underground nuclear tests, radiation releases, and the disposition of spent nuclear fuel as was feasible without compromising national security. She called for the collection, declassification, and release of documents nationwide, finally opening the books on the Cold War.

As Martz and I talked, the weather on the mesa, often eloquent and unpredictable, had turned suddenly cold and cloudy, with gusts of wind and sharp rain blowing down from the Jemez Mountains. Martz, ready to talk all morning like the practiced lecturer that he is, suggested that we go somewhere warm and out of the wind—the nearby Los Alamos Community Reading Room. He described this lab-owned and -operated facility, located in the same oddly shaped dark brown and red structure that houses the laboratory's Bradbury Science Museum, as a promising sign of openness for an organization that is perennially portrayed as being closed and unresponsive to the public. He gestured toward the back of the room where a shelf-lined alcove was packed with fat binders full of previously classified documents. More were added to the library every week.

Secretary O'Leary's announcement of the Department of Energy's new openness policy came on December 7, 1993, catching Los Alamos National Laboratory completely by surprise. "And believe me, when Mrs. O'Leary said, 'Let's show the world what's gone on in the last fifty years,' and didn't let any of us know what she was going to do—this was a crisis," said Scott Duncan, director of public affairs at the laboratory. It couldn't have happened at a worse time for Los Alamos. Faced with a suddenly unclear mission after the fall of its old enemy, the former Soviet Union, Los Alamos was coping with decreasing budgets and deep staff reductions, not to mention a major internal reorganization. Moreover, lab managers and researchers had been charged by the new Clinton administration with finding ways to transfer their technological know-how into cooperative research and development agreements with U.S. industry, a quite different ball game from the operating style of a lavishly budgeted national laboratory. Morale was not good. Then, to have the quality and ethics of its research questioned was a painful blow, indeed.

Furthermore, the announcement occurred at the beginning of the Christmas holidays when the lab routinely shuts down, and any business that gets done is conducted at holiday parties, Duncan explained. It was at one such party that LANL director Sig Hecker suggested to Duncan and other key players that the laboratory respond to O'Leary's bombshell and the congressional report by putting together a committee to work on the problem. "We needed to get out ahead of this process," said Duncan, who had spent twenty-six years with the air force, most recently as director of public affairs for the air forces in Europe. The laboratory needed to show that it could lead the way and not be dragged kicking and screaming into this new era, he said, explaining also that he and his colleagues suspected the DOE had already pegged the lab as being uncooperative and secretive. "So we said, 'Hey! First of all, it's the right thing to do,'" Duncan noted with unctuous enthusiasm. Second of all, they would beat the DOE at its own game.

So, they quickly put together a Human Studies Project Team composed of people from every part of the laboratory—bench scientists, explosives experts, geneticists, and retirees—to set about the business of collecting reports, lab notebooks, letters, memos, and other documents to trace the history of the laboratory's involvement in human radiation testing. Gary Sanders was on the team, having recently been pulled off the doomed superconducting supercollider project and, as a result, was already weary of the press and the public's attitude toward basic research. George Voelz was one of the retirees in the group, as was Don Petersen, who was particularly resentful of the public outrage over what he knew to be good science. Sanders, who eventually served as the team leader, said the retirees were the most knowledgeable and helpful in finding documents and explaining why things were done the way they were, but they did not have much interest in openness. He had learned that much of the searching had to be done independently of the retirees, because they had a natural tendency to hold back on things that might raise questions. "They may understand something better because they were there and they may be qualified to say it's irrelevant," Sanders said. "But I have to question it." The retirees were justifiably proud of their work, he added, because they did good science and, in most cases, maintained reasonably high ethical standards. Now it was being put under a not very friendly microscope and this was a source of tension on the team. They met twice a week for two-hour sessions that were like twelve angry men on a jury, Sanders quipped, in a heated tug-of-war between traditional lab culture and this disturbing new policy of openness. "And it wasn't just the retirees," Sanders acknowledged. "The entire laboratory had worked for a long time in this era of secrecy with a high sense of national mission. Now that mission had seemed to disappear, with nothing really to take its place. And one of the first things to come along on these winds of change is this openness policy," Sanders said. Even current employees were struggling to learn how to be open, how to submit themselves to being questioned by the public. Look it at from their perspective, Sanders urged. "You work hard and go to graduate school and publish fifty peer-reviewed articles, give a lot of talks at international conferences, then along come the reporters to criticize your work. How dare they?" Sanders asked. The openness policy was butting up against a wall of arrogance and secrecy around a sheltered community that had realized it wasn't getting the kind of respect it had once known. The Human Studies Project Team and the rest of the laboratory were coping not just with boxes of papers but with all these other things, too.

The team collected and released to the public more than fifteen hundred documents consisting of over twenty-one thousand pages of information. A daunting amount of material was housed in the laboratory's records center, while more was still in the possession of the researchers themselves. They discovered that some things had been thrown away. That apparently happened with some of Wright Langham's records, Sanders said. Langham had devised an equation for excretion of plutonium based on his work with occupationally exposed workers and on the plutonium injection studies. He was the lead author on the report. "When he died in an airplane crash in 1972 his records were put into a file cabinet in the basement of the health research lab," Sanders said. "Eventually they just weren't there anymore, because someone decided to clean up. There probably was some interesting stuff there." Some records existed only because someone had made copies of their work when they retired and stored them out in the garage. "And maybe you'd have to go talk to their widow," Sanders said, acknowledging that there had been a certain amount of informality about records in those days. Of course, when the press and the public hear something like this, he shrugged, they assume it's a cover-up.

But, on balance, the team believes they have found what was important. "I can't say that someone way back didn't do something really awful and then destroy all the records," Sanders mused. "You always wonder why some people have oodles of records when they retire and other people only have one box." But they found no evidence in the records they searched that the lab had any involvement in the plutonium injection studies beyond analyzing excreta and, in the case of one of the injections, providing the plutonium solution. And the record shows that the lab played no role in selecting who would receive the plutonium injections. In the eleven human or environmental experiments in which the lab played a part, no one's health was shown to have suffered any ill effects. Furthermore, the lab was confident that participants had given their informed consent, although it was not always formally documented.[40]

By the end of the search phase of the Human Studies Project, the team had learned more about the laboratory than they thought humanly possible, said Scott Duncan. And, as painful as it was, this self-examination had helped the laboratory and the public to begin to come to terms with the meaning of the past fifty years. "We had to do things that I don't think anyone is comfortable with," Sanders said, "And now we're going to have to come to grips with what we did. All the getting under the desks during the air raid drills of the fifties, all those things—those images are all inside of us." Now we have the ability to look back over what was, in reality, a long, long war that stretched out over fifty years. Science had played a part in it all, coming through with useful tools during a time of great military need. You could look at the people who have worked in the nuclear weapons industry, the people at Los Alamos, as a kind of police force, Sanders said. "You always want them when you need them, but the rest of the time you're convinced that they're out there committing corrupt, brutal acts. Now, people are looking back and somehow, as a part of this reflective period, they will decide on a place for us, and that will be the basis for whatever we do in the future."

5

Death before Decaf

Surely one of the most pressing new roles for Los Alamos National Laboratory involves dealing with the overwhelming surplus of plutonium that remains after the Cold War. The scope of the problem is evident when you realize that the world stockpile of plutonium is more than twelve hundred tons, with an additional seventy-five tons produced every year in civilian reactors, a source whose output will soon be greater than that of defense installations. The U.S. government has identified some fifty tons of plutonium as surplus and in need of disposal. Given the expertise Los Alamos has with such materials, it would seem that the laboratory is uniquely suited to solving these problems and also devising the most efficient ways to clean up the environmental mess that was created by our own fifty-year nuclear arms buildup. However, one of the greatest residual effects of the human radiation studies revelations was their impact on an already crumbling public trust of government scientists and institutions. And, as the public has become more aware of the depth of pollution in the Cold War nuclear weapons complex, the distrust has grown. How could the people that created the problem be trusted to fix it? "And the only answer I can give to placate public fear is 'Trust me!' Well, what a terrible answer!" said Joe Martz, throwing up his hands in resignation. "What kind of trust did we develop in the past? It's just a joke!" Unfortunately, he shrugged, it is still true that the public needs to trust him and other government scientists to safely and sensibly resolve problems associated with plutonium and other Cold War artifacts.

The growing plutonium stockpile represents not only a potential for many thousands of ten-kiloton yield warheads and the proliferation of nuclear weaponry, but also an imposing long-term storage problem, given the element's tendency to migrate and gather together where it doesn't belong. "And it will interact with a container in various ways until that container fails, " Martz said. "This is not a static material. It doesn't just sit there and stare at you over time." Ironically, the most successful storage method for plutonium so far has been the one that has benefited from the most research—the spherical sealed container of fuel that fits inside a thermonuclear weapon. "If you were to sit down and design from scratch a storage container for plutonium with the sole goal of maximizing safety," Martz said, "you'd end up with something pretty close to a pit inside a nuclear weapon. A pit's geometry is critically safe, too, which means you can stack together an infinite number of them and still not get a critical mass. Furthermore, it is very well sealed."

But how long and how well plutonium can be stored this way is still unknown because there are no fifty-year-old nuclear weapons around to illustrate it. Someday a pit assuredly will fail, Martz said, and weapons scientists do not have the experience or understanding to precisely predict when it will happen. Furthermore, all these weapons-ready pits offer an enticing convenience for nuclear proliferators. It would seem prudent to make the plutonium less readily usable.

One thing plutonium scientists do know about pits is that, as they age, they become increasingly toxic to the workers who have to remove them from decommissioned nuclear weapons; plutonium changes into plutonium americium 241, a strong gamma-ray emitter that renders the surface of a twenty-five-year-old pit five times more radioactive than it was when it was made. This represents a serious safety concern in an already challenging technical problem: the dismantling of a nuclear weapon. That process entails removing all of the subsystems of the warhead: the high explosives in the primary stage, the fission device that triggers the explosion of the secondary stage or fusion component of the weapon, and the chemical explosives that cradle the secondary. This work is done at Pantex, a DOE facility near Amarillo, Texas, where most of the approximately fifty thousand U.S. nuclear weapons have also been assembled. The duty of the crews at Pantex is to insert the physics package into the weapon, do electrical installations, and perform reliability tests on the components of weapons randomly se-

lected from the active stockpile. In the process of disassembling warheads, crews crush the components in order to disguise their precise
purpose, while any useful materials—such as gold, silver, aluminum,
copper, nickel, and palladium—are extracted and recycled. Over eight
hundred nuclear weapons were dismantled in fiscal year 1995 and over
a thousand were earmarked for dismantlement in 1996. The missiles
themselves are sometimes recycled into other sorts of weapons, as in
the case of the air force's nuclear missiles that were converted into conventional weapons to be used against Saddam Hussein in 1996.[1]

Prior to 1989, pits from decommissioned weapons were sent to the
DOE's plant at Rocky Flats, Colorado, near Denver, where the plutonium was removed with acids, a process that also created huge amounts
of plutonium-contaminated liquid wastes. Ultimately, Rocky Flats was
closed because of environmental and safety violations. A new facility
for the recovery of plutonium is planned but has not been built. For the
time being, pits are stored in canisters in shielded bunkers at Pantex
until a long-term storage site can be established. While there is plenty
of room at Pantex to store all the pits in the stockpile, Martz said, residents of Amarillo have opposed long-term storage of plutonium triggers in their area for fear of accidents or contamination of the Ogalala
Aquifer that flows beneath them, events that he thinks are highly unlikely. There are over seven thousand pits and an unidentified number
of complete weapons stored in igloos at Pantex.

To make the task of removing and storing aging pits both safer for
workers and cleaner for the environment, government scientists have
devised the Advanced Recovery and Integrated Extraction System
(ARIES), which is essentially a robotic shuttle that trundles the plutonium pit into a glove box, slices it open with a lathe, and reduces it to
powder by exposing it to nitrogen gas. The americium is stripped away,
and the plutonium is melted into an ingot that is sealed into a can.
Martz was the principal designer of the system that was developed by a
group of researchers from Los Alamos, Lawrence Livermore, and Sandia laboratories. They have envisioned portable ARIES systems travel-
ing from site to site, including the former Soviet Union, to convert excess plutonium pits into canned ingots that will be easier to store and
less immediately useful to proliferators than complete pits.

"Of course, during the fifty years of the arms race and the Cold
War, nobody ever envisioned having *excess* plutonium," Martz said.

"My God, we were faced with plutonium shortages during those years. And so, from a technical standpoint, nobody ever asked the question 'How do you store this stuff safely outside of a nuclear weapon?' We had to store it for the short term, and the things we did were satisfactory for a couple of years." But even short-term solutions have been plagued by difficulties.

An incident at Los Alamos in November 1993 brought to light some of the weaknesses of short-term plutonium storage strategies. A can of plutonium inside a concrete bunker at Los Alamos swelled and burst open. The pewter-colored plutonium metal had been ground to red dust by oxidation, similar to the way iron rusts. The cascade of events that led to this breach was complex, unexpected, and unwittingly made possible by a handling technique called a *bag-out operation*. The procedure—designed so that workers could safely move a can of plutonium from glove box to storage—involved placing a plastic bag over a small portal at the bottom of the glove box, putting the welded-shut can of plutonium into the bag, closing it with a wire twist, and then putting that package into another container that was taped shut, with the whole multilayered shoebox-size parcel stored away in a vault.

But what they hadn't planned for, Martz said, was the surprising chain of events that was triggered by weather systems moving through the area. When a high-pressure system swept over the mesa, the barometric change squeezed the plastic bags inside the package and forced tiny invasions of air into the cans through breaks in the seal. When a low-pressure system moved through, the bag inflated a bit and the air came back out of the can, bringing with it traces of the fine oxide dust that forms on the plutonium as it oxidizes and depositing it on the plastic bag. This entire process would repeat itself until there was enough plutonium in contact with the bag to cause the alpha radiation to degrade the plastic and produce hydrogen gas. The hydrogen gas went into the can by the same mechanism and reacted with the plutonium, forming a compound called plutonium hydride. Eventually the bag became brittle and broke, allowing air into the container, where it further oxidized the plutonium, causing it to expand. Finally the can would burst open, just as a container of water will break as the liquid freezes and expands.

Martz could cite six instances in the past ten years in which plutonium had ruptured its containers and migrated into storage vaults. "A very frightening circumstance. No one has been contaminated or had a permanent exposure to plutonium, and it was contained within the facilities, but it represents a breakdown of your boundaries. Anytime you lose that much control, it's a concern," Martz said, adding that there would surely be more breaches in the future, owing to the fact that other containers, when x-rayed, were shown to have started the same process. "We're only beginning to recognize things that can change plutonium storage containers and lead to these sorts of failures," Martz said, adding quickly, "At the same time, I feel confident that we now know enough about plutonium to say with statistical certainty that it can be safely stored at least for the interim fifty to one hundred years until we decide as a country and as a world what to do with this stuff."

The state of plutonium storage throughout the DOE complex has not inspired confidence in those who naturally fear the worst from this strange element. A 1994 DOE internal review found significant hazards from leaking packaging and decaying buildings, piping, and machinery at thirty-five government sites in over a dozen states. (The study did not include the plutonium that was being stored inside warheads and pits.) Rocky Flats was found to still house 14.2 metric tons of plutonium, and the bill for cleaning it up at just this site would amount to at least $200 million.

Los Alamos was characterized as one of the least contaminated sites in the DOE complex and, as a working plutonium research site, had relatively few safety problems. After a 1994 internal assessment by laboratory employees, a DOE team spent two and a half weeks at Los Alamos inspecting technical areas and talking to hundreds of people in order to identify weaknesses in the laboratory's plutonium handling strategies. The internal assessment identified forty-nine vulnerabilities, most of them attributed to workers, while the DOE team identified only five major vulnerabilities, none of them considered high-risk situations that needed an immediate fix. The review committee cited the lab's practice of using non-DOT pressure-cooker-type containers to transport plutonium short distances on lab property, noting that a shipping accident involving fire could lead to a complete release of the material into the environment. The other four key vulnerabilities had to do with weak packaging of plutonium and the potential for accidents in plutonium handling that would jeopardize worker safety. Other vulnerabilities included locations in TA-55 where the geometries of the work space might allow liquids to get into glove boxes, a situation that could lead to criticalities. DOE team leader Fred Witmer acknowledged at a public meeting in Los Alamos that sometimes environmental laws intended to monitor stored materials and protect the public are in conflict with optimal safety practices for workers. For example, he explained, state laws required the laboratory to send someone into vaults every day to check stored wastes. "But every time you go into a vault, it costs you something and you take a risk taking on radiation," Witmer said, adding that Los Alamos had been trying to get relief from such legal technicalities that in the long run endangered workers.

The delicate balance between public and worker safety is only one of many problems associated with the storage of excess plutonium. The necessity for both the safest and the least expensive solutions is obvious. Everything has been suggested as a final resting place for the element—from launching it into space, to burying it in deep holes in the ground. One scheme suggested putting plutonium at a place where the earth's plates are moving under one another, so that the material would be carried deep into the belly of the planet, Martz said, shaking his head. The most likely scenario, however, is mixing plutonium and high-level radioactive waste together with glass—a process called *vitrification*—and burying it deep underground in the form of steel-encased glass logs. Vitrification of radioactive waste is already under way in the United States, Russia, Great Britain, France, and Belgium. Incorporating plutonium into these glass logs would tie it up sufficiently that proliferators would have a difficult time getting access to the weapons-grade material.[2] The first U.S. glassification plant opened in March 1996 at the Savannah nuclear weapons facility near Aiken, South Carolina; the $2.4 billion plant, the world's largest, will convert 34 million gallons of radioactive liquid waste into some six thousand ten-foot-tall, two-ton steel and glass canisters that will be stored in concrete bunkers until a permanent storage place is established. The cost has been estimated at some $4 billion.[3]

Because plutonium and other radioactive materials will outlast any human-made container, though, most organizations—such as the National Academy of Sciences, the United States Office of Technology Assessment, and the International Atomic Energy Agency—have agreed that deep geological disposal of high-level nuclear waste in salt caverns or other geologically stable earthen chambers is the safest option for long-term storage.[4] Other countries with nuclear energy programs, such as France, Sweden, Germany, and Japan, have decided upon deep geological isolation for their nuclear waste. It is thought that thermally fissile material, stored thus in subcritical amounts, would quietly and slowly decay over thousands of years.

However, research by two Los Alamos scientists challenged this assumption, concluding that long-term underground storage of plutonium could lead to serious problems, something activists and other citizens have worried about all along. Findings by Charles D. Bowman and Francesco Venneri suggested that plutonium, after thousands of years, could manage to achieve autocatalytic, or self-enhancing, criticality. In plain English, that means it could someday start blowing up spontaneously. To the displeasure of lab management, a draft of the Bowman-Venneri paper, whose theory opposes the official DOE position, was released prematurely to the *New York Times*. This caused heated controversy, but, as Bowman cheerfully put it, "If you can't take the heat, get out of the kitchen." Despite pointed criticism from his colleagues, he stood by his story that small subcritical amounts of fissile material, while placed in the ground in safe configurations, will eventually breach its containers and migrate into the underground matrix of water and rock, substances that would serve as moderators for escaping neutrons and produce a feedback effect that could lead to criticality. Even steel-encased glass logs would not withstand this process, having eventually crumbled under the influence of time and the elements. Bowman recommended burying the plutonium in smaller amounts placed further apart than originally planned, a much costlier solution to an already wildly expensive proposition.

The exploding waste story made for embarrassing headlines nationwide, and while some Los Alamos researchers ridiculed the notion, three other government scientists from the DOE's Savannah River weapons facility backed up the alarming study. Nevertheless, a LANL technical review of the Bowman-Venneri papers on the subject found "that the discussion in the papers does not describe a credible sequence of geologic events leading to super criticality and explosive energy release."[5] The review panel cited fundamental errors in concept and execution, declared that the authors had no grasp of the elementary concepts involved, and recommended that if this line of inquiry were to continue and the authors be associated with it, their activity should be overseen by a team of scientists who would check their calculations. "We find no technical merit in these papers," the reviewers concluded.[6]

The lab public affairs escort who accompanied me to Bowman's office put this spin on the situation as we walked along: perhaps the scientist had grown impatient that laboratory study of accelerator transmutation of waste, an effort for which Bowman served as project leader, was not getting sufficient consideration in the national discussion of what to do with surplus plutonium and other nuclear wastes. It was a theory that had been widely discussed around the laboratory, such that the director finally addressed the subject in an internal news publication: "Many people at the laboratory have questioned the connection between the Bowman-Venneri paper and the Laboratory's effort on accelerator transmutation of waste," stated Sig Hecker. Lab management did not consider the accelerator technology to be in conflict with the goals of the underground deposit site at Yucca Mountain, Hecker explained. "It may, indeed, complement the repository work quite well."[7] Yucca Mountain, in Nevada, has been proposed as the storage site mainly for high-level waste from commercial reactors, while a site in southern New Mexico near Carlsbad has been built as the repository for defense nuclear waste. The Waste Isolation Pilot Project (WIPP) near Carlsbad in southern New Mexico would store midlevel nuclear waste from Los Alamos and other research and production facilities in chambers carved into ancient salt deposits some two thousand feet underground. Natural salt deposits would seep into the chambers and encase the containers, sealing them safely away for thousands of years. The proposal, while it has created hundreds of jobs and millions of dollars in income for New Mexico, has met with determined resistance by many residents who do not want their state to serve as a depository for waste and do not want the materials being transported over state roads, which they contend are not up to safely accommodating such traffic.

The laboratory has optimistically predicted that transmutation technology, derived from its work on the Strategic Defense Initiative, or Star Wars research, would reduce the storage time required for long-lived materials, thereby reducing by a thousand times the mass of radioactive waste that must be stored, and reducing the half-life of such substances from thousands of years to hundreds. Study of transmutation of surplus plutonium and other radionuclides from both dismantled weapons and commercial reactors has been going on for over thirty years. The technology combines both accelerator and fission reactor technologies, using a high-energy proton beam from an accelerator to strike a target that is blanketed by an assembly containing the materials to be destroyed and a moderator such as heavy water or graphite to slow the escaping neutrons, thus promoting fission of the radioactive materials. The device would be fueled by thorium, which is abundantly available in reactors in the form of thorium 232. While thorium is not readily fissionable, it is transmuted by the system into a substance that is—uranium 233. This accelerator-based conversion scheme would operate at a subcritical level that shuts down when the proton beam is turned off, thus avoiding the possibility of a runaway criticality accident. And it would produce far fewer high-level radioactive by-products than a conventional reactor.[8] Moreover, the system could be used to generate energy for the nation's power grid at the same time that it is eliminating nuclear waste, an important feature, Bowman said, because a system whose only role was destroying waste would be an impractical expense. Transmutation, on the other hand, could pay for itself by converting waste heat from the system into electrical power. "When you fission stuff you're going to get all that energy out, anyway, and you're going to have to do something with it—blow it into the atmosphere or heat up the river or something. So we have designed all of our systems so that they are highly efficient in converting that heat into electricity," Bowman said. He envisions that the sale of electric power derived from transmutation systems will pay for the cost of destroying waste so that society will not have to carry that burden. He pointed to the aging reactors where waste is now piling up. They could be replaced with transmutation systems that would burn the waste on-site, and then efficiently continue producing energy and burning waste concurrently, Bowman explained.

Critics of Bowman's plan claim it would require fifteen years and $500 million to get up and running, and even then it and other similar technologies would require hundreds of thousands of years to consume the world's constantly growing stockpile of plutonium.[9] Deep underground burial of radioactive waste still remains the solution of choice, even for a number of prestigious antinuclear organizations, who oppose disposal schemes that involve burning excess plutonium as fuel, on the grounds that it represents a revitalization of the plutonium industry. The United States stopped burning plutonium fuel during the Carter administration, a move that other nations refused to follow. The Nuclear Control Institute, the Federation of American Scientists, the Institute for Energy and Environmental Research, the Natural Resources Defense Council, and the Union of Concerned Scientists have all lobbied the federal government in favor of mixing warhead and separated civilian plutonium with other high-level wastes, encasing it in glass logs, and burying it deep underground, an approach that sends a signal that plutonium has no useful purpose.[10]

A three-year DOE study finally concluded in December 1996 that the best plan would combine both deep geological storage of vitrified plutonium and the burning of some plutonium in electricity-producing commercial reactors. Simply storing the substance was deemed too dangerous.

However, none of us wants any kind of radioactive waste depository in our own backyards. Residents of Nevada, like those in New Mexico, have vehemently opposed the idea. The state of Nevada claims that the Yucca Mountain project was chosen for political rather than scientific reasons, that even though the proposed waste repository is situated over a volcano range and thirty-two known earthquake faults, billions of dollars have been poured into the characterization and development of the site and will continue by force of political and economic inertia. Furthermore, Nevada residents worry that waste canisters will crumble in as few as three hundred years, allowing radioactivity to leak into an underlying aquifer. They contend that the DOE can't be trusted to safely build and operate a nuclear waste storage site, anyway, given their track record so far of heavily contaminating most of the sites in the nuclear weapons complex. On the other hand, nuclear energy specialists claim that the natural reactor in West Africa offers evidence that geological deposits are capable of isolating waste, noting that there is no evidence that earthquakes and rains over millions of years led to dispersal of the by-products of that spontaneous chain reaction.

Recent research findings by Los Alamos scientists suggest that while rainwater can percolate through the complex geological structures overlying the storage facility site at Yucca Mountain, it seems to occur mainly by way of faults in the layer immediately underlying the topsoil. Called welded tuff, this layer of less porous volcanic rock is extensively fractured. But sandwiched between it and another lower layer of fractured rock that would house the repository and much of the tunnel, is a layer of highly porous volcanic rock that would slow the seepage of water such that it could take some ten thousand years for it to reach the third layer, a finding justified by the presence of ancient water (five to ten thousand years old) under Yucca Mountain. Using a chemical tracer and computer modeling, the Los Alamos researchers attempted to trace how rainwater has traveled down to that porous layer. The tracer is a combination of naturally occurring chlorine 36 and a man-made form—called "bomb-pulse" chlorine 36—so called because it was deposited in the atmosphere by aboveground nuclear tests. Of the 127 water samples taken from Yucca Mountain and sent to Purdue University for analysis, there were 21 with above-background levels of chlorine 36. It appears that faults in the porous middle layer facilitated more rapid migration of rainwater, since 85 percent of the elevated samples had been gathered within one hundred meters of a fault, but these were isolated occurrences and did not describe the hydraulics of the entire mountain, according to the researchers conducting the study.

Another source of anxiety for Nevada residents is the potential for accidents during the heavy trafficking to and from Yucca Mountain by trucks carrying high-level waste that might also leak radiation along the way. Critics contend that the presence of the storage facility will stigmatize the state as the nation's nuclear waste dumping ground, affecting convention and tourism revenue as well as new business growth, while also lowering property values along the truck routes. And if there was an accident, the physical cleanup would be extremely costly, according to the official Nevada position paper on Yucca Mountain waste storage. Nevertheless, even though some 80 percent of Nevadans have opposed the storage of nuclear waste in their state, Lincoln County, Nevada—in exchange for federal benefits—did offer to accept a transfer station where the waste could be loaded from railcars to trucks for final transport to Yucca Mountain.[11]

Surprisingly, the amount of spent fuel from commercial nuclear reactors and the surplus plutonium from defense represents a relatively small proportion of the entire radioactive waste stream, which overall is huge. One of the factors contributing to this situation is the problem of mixed waste. Daunting quantities of materials must be disposed of simply because they have been contaminated with radioactive elements. In the long run, disposing of weapons-grade plutonium may be an easier task than getting rid of mixed waste, Joe Martz said. "At least with weapons plutonium, you know exactly what you've got; it's well characterized," he noted. But when plutonium is part of a complex matrix, you don't know what all the constituents are, and as a result, all of it has to be treated like the most highly radioactive component of the mix and disposed of accordingly. Likewise, contaminated objects must be disposed of in their entirety because of the nature of their contaminants. A perfect example is the contaminated glove box. "It has to be gotten rid of through something called size reduction, which basically means compacting," Martz said. "Then you put it into barrels and throw it away." Ironically, disposal can cost more than twice as much as a new $100,000 state-of-the-art glove box. There are many other similar examples of this conundrum, including entire buildings at badly contaminated DOE sites like Rocky Flats—where everything in a structure, including pipes, light switches, floor tiles, and even the paint on the walls—is considered contaminated waste. By far the largest portion of the DOE's weapons-grade plutonium stocks, excluding what is held at Pantex, is located at Rocky Flats—as much as fourteen tons, with a surprising amount of it tangled up in the structures and ductwork of the facility. And so far the best way to get rid of the contaminated structures and contents has been to box it up and throw it away, a choice that is both cumbersome and shockingly expensive, Martz said. "Because throwing things away in a nuclear dump is not cheap, if you even *have* a dump to throw them into," he said pointedly, alluding to the nation's inability to provide such a storage facility.

However, Martz has patented a system that can recover plutonium and other radioactive materials from mixed waste. *Process plasma decontamination* combines a plasma—a gas of negatively charged electrons and heavier positively charged nuclei—with carbon tetrafluoride and oxygen to produce extremely reactive fluorine atoms. When exposed to a plutonium-contaminated object in a closed system, the fluorine atoms grab onto the plutonium and form plutonium hexafluoride, another gas. This gas can then be pumped out of the system and collected on a trap downstream, thereby entirely removing the plutonium from the object. Martz described his invention as an environmentally friendly way to decontaminate an object by remote control without using toxic chemicals or hazardous solvents. He envisions rolling an entire glove box into a plasma reactor, flipping a switch, and thirty minutes later rolling it back out, cleaned of plutonium and ready to be reused, recycled, or put into an ordinary landfill without worries about radioactive contamination. The plutonium is a waste product that will have to be disposed of properly, but it will take up much less space than a glove box, Martz said.

Manufacturers have shown a keen interest in plasma processing, a technology derived from nuclear weapons research that has applications in private industries unrelated to plutonium. However, industry has been squeamish about having their products associated with weapons technology. Recently, though, researchers from LANL and private industry have collaborated on developing a plasma system that can be used to clean silicon wafers for integrated circuitry. Because it eliminates the need for dangerous solvents, the system is billed as a cleaner, safer alternative both for the environment and for industry workers.

Indeed, Joe Martz and others at the laboratory contend that such solvents and other chemical pollutants are a greater danger to public health and the environment than are the radioactive by-products of the defense and energy industries. They will tell you that the proposed cleanup of the nuclear weapons complex is an overreaction that is grossly out of proportion to the risk the contamination represents and that it will be remembered as one of the most expensive environmental remediations in history. The bill for simply isolating the damaged environments at 130 sites in 30 states in order to protect nearby neighbors could total at least $170 billion, while a complete restoration could consume more than $500 billion, an estimate that Martz views as conservative. "Other analysts have suggested that it will cost a trillion dollars—money this country really can't afford," he said, suggesting that it is up to technologists like him and his colleagues at the laboratory to find the best and least expensive ways to do the cleanup.

The greatest Cold War remediation challenge is at Hanford, Washington, the main plutonium production factory for the nation's nuclear weapons complex. Hanford is shockingly polluted with radioactive materials and other chemicals that have accumulated for decades, some 1.3

billion cubic meters of it having been pumped right into the soil. Nearly every DOE laboratory, including Los Alamos, is involved in some way with supporting the Hanford cleanup, which will require an estimated $50 billion or more, as well as many years of work by technicians and scientists. There are approximately a dozen tons of plutonium on-site, not all of it well isolated, over two thousand tons of irradiated fuel stored in basins that are vulnerable to earthquake, and several large profoundly contaminated buildings.[12] But perhaps the most difficult challenge is the high-level waste tank farm at Hanford. The 177 tanks—ranging in size from 55,400 to 1 million gallons in capacity each—currently contain 56 million gallons of radioactive and hazardous waste, a nightmarish stratification of gases, liquids, and solids, and as many as 69 of them are leaking into the surrounding soil. Public interest groups claim that some of the contamination has penetrated the groundwater that feeds into the Columbia River, and they report that a plume of cesium has blossomed under the tank farm. Flammable gases build up inside some of the tanks, threatening explosions that could lead to dispersion of radioactive materials. At one point, it was discovered that one of the tanks at Hanford was burping, an eerie, disturbing thought for a public that was just coming to grips with the reality of the wasteland that once had been the U.S. nuclear weapons complex. "The tank was burping because it wasn't being stirred," according to Los Alamos chemist John Watkin. "That allowed crusts to form on the surface, so that when gas evolved low down in the tank, the bubbles couldn't escape through the thick sludge." Watkin, a young Oxford-educated Welshman with rusty red hair, likened the mechanics in the burping tank to the innocent bubbles in a rising cake. "The sludge would swell until the crust suddenly gave way and all the gas would come out," he continued. Then the process would start all over again, operating on about a one-hundred-day cycle. An enormously expensive sixty-foot-high pump was installed in the tank to churn up the contents. "And I believe they have not had any more burps," Watkin smiled, explaining that this item could now be checked off on the long list of problems at the Hanford site.

Eventually, Westinghouse Hanford Company, the DOE's operations and engineering contractor, ended the potentially dangerous venting of flammable gases from the underground storage tanks. But fixing all the other problems with the Hanford tanks alone could easily consume as much as $50 billion, a cost that insiders say is due in large part to the strict regulatory environment in which they work, a notion with which two key U.S. senators on nuclear issues have agreed. Senate Energy Committee chairman Frank Murkowski, a Republican, and ranking committee Democrat Bennett Johnston concluded that the Hanford cleanup is mired down in contradictory laws and regulations. A Senate Energy Committee study suggested that while a total of $2 billion is spent every year at Hanford, the biggest public works project ever, the cleanup of the 560-square-mile plutonium production complex is an expensive failure. The workforce at Hanford has increased by 20 percent over the number of workers there during the heyday of Cold War plutonium production, with the federal government paying some $800 million annually in salaries.[13] The chief beneficiaries of this slow, expensive cleanup, critics contend, are the contractors involved in the work. Just the tab for monitoring the Hanford tanks each year is a whopping $80 million. The National Research Council concluded that one reason the cleanup appeared to be getting nowhere was that federal budget allocations decreased as the research they funded succeeded. There wasn't much incentive to finish the job.

The ultimate goal of the Hanford tank remediation is to characterize the waste present and then process it into vitrified glass logs for safer storage, but because the contents are so toxic and are still chemically active, sampling the waste mixture is tediously dangerous.[14] Watkin is one of the Los Alamos researchers who has gotten involved in the cleanup of Hanford's tank farm. In the hardy entrepreneurial spirit required now of a young government scientist wishing to keep working, Watkin had gone after research money available for Hanford cleanup projects. For the previous eighteen months he had been working on red oil, an organic material that is a by-product of uranium reprocessing. "Red oil was really a thorn in their sides up there [at Hanford] and they needed something done about it," Watkin said. "That was one area where I thought a chemist could get involved." Red oil is a big problem because unlike other organic substances, it has a tendency to sink to the bottom of an aqueous solution. The normal tactic for eliminating organics from a vat or tank is just to skim them from the surface, but that won't work with red oil. If the mixture was heated in order to boil off the water, any red oil lurking at the bottom of the tank could explode, a catastrophe that had actually happened the previous year at a Siberian nuclear facility at Tomsk, Watkin said. "What if some of this nasty material had been formed sometime during the Hanford processing operations and has been sitting in a waste tank waiting for somebody to come along and heat it up?" he asked. So Watkin went into his laboratory and simulated as best he could the chemical soup of a Hanford waste tank; then he made some red oil and laid it onto the surface of the waste. Surprisingly, the red oil, on contact with the typical complex Hanford mixture, simply died and decomposed. That's one more problem solved, Watkin noted, but there are plenty of other things needing attention. Every element of the periodic table is in the soils and waters of production sites around the country, he said. "You name it, it's got to be cleaned up and pulled out."

A committee report from the National Research Council urged the federal government not to rush to judgment on the best long-term strategy for cleaning up Hanford. By September 1996, after billions of dollars already spent, there was still not enough information available about the contents of the tanks, their potential for harm, and all of the possible technical solutions.

Indeed, experts as well as lawmakers are becoming increasingly skeptical that a complete cleanup of the nation's weapons production complex is even possible. "There isn't enough money in the world to clean it all up," said one young environmental specialist at Los Alamos. According to a congressional study, cleanup standards have been set unrealistically high, anyway. In fact, they may be much higher than the capability of current technology to achieve them. A study by the National Research Council cited the inefficiency of multiple approaches to the cleanup by various agencies. The report called for a unified and consistent ranking of waste sites as well as collaboration and consultation among agencies, making the process more objective, fair, and incidentally, more open to scrutiny.

John Watkin's office was located in the laboratory's TA-21, the predecessor to TA-55 and long one of the most heavily contaminated parts of the Los Alamos laboratory. It's where early research with plutonium, uranium, and other radioactive materials had been done. It is also the technical area where Cecil Kelley received his fatal criticality exposure in a plutonium recovery plant in 1955. Much of the contamination in TA-21 had never been cleaned up. Building 3 North, where the first gram of americium was isolated, is a 120-foot-long and 40-foot-wide structure that until recently had not been decontaminated since it went into operation in 1945. "Look at the walls," said chemist Jeff Bryan, whose office in Building 3 was badly stained by water that had seeped down from the roof. It's really frightening, Bryan said, because out on the roof, where the glove boxes were directly vented in the old days, there were still hot spots of plutonium and americium isotopes. The attic was contaminated, as well, and cramped with utility lines and asbestos. Above Bryan's desk, the wall was festooned with heavy rust stains, many of them deposited the previous year during unusually heavy rainstorms. "The leak was really bad—just streaming through there and splattering all over my desk." Not surprisingly, he had made a point of keeping his desk very clean, monitoring often for radiation. "Fortunately, I've never found any," Bryan said, adding that a burgeoning population of mice was also a constant worry. "Because they run all over out here, into the areas with contamination, possibly dragging it around with them," said the young chemist, who had often found mouse droppings behind his computer and worried that they might be radioactive. "I set a trap down under my desk and it hasn't caught anything in over a year, so I'm feeling better about it. It was actually a big worry, though," he said, laughing halfheartedly. The role of animals in spreading radioactive waste has been a cause for concern for some time and an object of several studies. A 1982 Los Alamos study examined the effects of pocket gophers burrowing in low-level waste trenches, and concluded that while the animals moved impressive amounts of soil, they did not seem to be dispersing radioactive elements in excess of global fallout levels. At Hanford, burrowing rabbits were found to have consumed radioactive salts in waste trenches and then deposited them on the surface in their droppings. Nevertheless, the bigger worry had to do with the possibility that burrowing animals might facilitate the channeling of water through the trenches of waste materials.[15]

In today's new world of openness and environmental regulation, Los Alamos scientists have found themselves having to acknowledge that mistakes were made in the headlong race to outdo their Soviet counterparts during the Cold War. "I think we have been careless," said

Paul White. "In some cases, we were in a hurry, and when you're in a hurry, you don't always think about where you left things. You just go on to the next step." When scientists first came to the mesa, most people believed that beating Hitler was a national emergency, he explained. Then during the arms race of the Cold War, there were other considerations. White offered a domestic comparison: you drop everything in the sink when you hear the baby fall in the next room. And you worry later about coming back and cleaning up. "Well, now it's time to come back," he said. At Los Alamos there have been many surveys done in an attempt to locate abandoned underground piping, for example, and map old spills in the canyons. "We haven't found it all yet," White said, "but most people think we have to keep looking." The extent of contamination throughout the nuclear weapons complex and at military installations isn't even completely clear because no one knows for sure where it all is. That is the case at Los Alamos, too. In the early days no one kept any records of how much waste was produced and thrown away.

Jim Smith is quick to point out that during those early years plutonium was too valuable to waste, anyway. As a result, very little was allowed to disperse into the environment. "The smartest people were here," Smith insisted. "We didn't do anything stupid with the environment. Now, that may have been because we didn't want to waste the plutonium, but we weren't fools." However, he went on to describe an incident during the late 1950s in which critical masses of plutonium were buried a few hundred feet down in the dirt for a test that was in defiance of the recently signed test ban treaty. The purpose of the exercise was to determine whether a nuclear explosion would occur if the explosives that surround and serve to detonate the warhead were subjected to some assault, such as a rifle shot, a so-called one-point failure. Later, nuclear weapons would be extensively tested to ensure their one-point safety. The plutonium is still buried off the road by the back gate, Smith said. "We didn't get around to digging it up. It's geologically stable because we put it in a good place."

Tom Ribe claimed that one dedicated independent investigator had been haunting the Los Alamos Community Reading Room for months trying to uncover in the environmental documents there some concrete evidence that the laboratory had also inappropriately buried irradiated fuel rods in the landfill. It's important to note that while reams of documents have been released to the public, they are not easily digested and understood by the average person. A dedicated researcher with a technical background may indeed find useful information in the many binders displayed in the Reading Room, but even academics have found it difficult to mine and use the vast stores of government documents available to them since 1990 about the activities of DOE facilities like Los Alamos National Laboratory. Accused of setting up roadblocks to delay access, the laboratory claimed that the real problem was lack of funding to process requests. Furthermore, much of the early data that might yield valuable insights on laboratory behavior exists in a raw state as handwritten notebooks of laboratory researchers. Interestingly, the sheer volume of material to be released has so stymied the DOE that documents that should remain secret are occasionally released by accident and withdrawn, merely reinforcing the public's suspicion that the government is still hiding the truth. For example, a DOE nuclear weapons internet site was closed down after a newspaper unearthed documents there that seemed to contradict the government's claim that no new nuclear weapons were being designed.

Because they do not believe laboratory assurances, people in New Mexico fear that plutonium and other elements will wash out of the canyons of the Pajarito Plateau and find their way into the Rio Grande and the water supplies of communities down the line. "It's true that we vented plutonium onto the roofs of buildings during the Manhattan Project and that rain washed it down into the dirt. We've made an effort to find it. And some of the runoff could get into the Rio Grande," Smith said. "But the doses are really small." Los Alamos geology is unusual in that the aquifer underlying the mesas and from which the town gets its water supply is a static pool of very old water that does not flow in the way that the Ogalala Aquifer flows from the upper Midwest to the Gulf of Mexico. Furthermore, the Jemez Mountains, because they are remnants of long-ago volcanic eruptions, are riddled with mineral-rich springs. One of those minerals—arsenic—is dangerously high in the Los Alamos water supply that is drawn from eight two-thousand-foot-deep wells, said Smith. He noted that he is unable to breed certain South American fish because the arsenic causes them to lay sterile eggs. "And it's not because of anything the laboratory is doing. Frankly, I think it's worse." But if any radiation did leach from the laboratory down to this aquifer, it would affect only Los Alamos since only that town uses the water, Smith added. "And, by the way, we'd notice it."

Los Alamos scientists have observed that a large chemical plume has formed deep inside the mesa. Its source is thought to be TA-54, where drums of solvents have disintegrated and disgorged their contents into the soil and rocks. The drums had been buried during the 1950s when the accepted practice was to dispose of them by stacking them in layers on pallets inside pits and then covering them over with soil, said Matthew Monagle, who works in the Organic Analysis Section of the Environmental Chemistry Group at Los Alamos. "The problem is, all those drums went crunch," he grimaced, and now the solvents have leached into the rock of the mesa and become a plume that expands and contracts with fluctuations of the barometric pressure. "In other words, the mesa is breathing in and out. So that the plume is slowly but surely moving up, down, and laterally," Monagle said. "It cycles at night as the mesa cools and then warms again, and it cycles when storm fronts pass through." The mesa also appears to respond to the tug of the moon, cycling approximately every twenty-eight days, drawing the plume along with it. Los Alamos specialists have punched holes into the mesa through which they draw samples of the plume and attempt to keep track of where it is going. But no one really knows what will happen to it, said Monagle. It's been estimated that the plume may take as many as four to six hundred years to reach the nearest groundwater nine hundred feet down. "Now, do we really have to do anything about it? I don't know," Monagle said. "We could use the holes to suck off the plume, but what you really need to do is remove the source. But how much money and personnel exposure are we willing to spend on that? And even then, when you try to clean things up, sometimes you end up with something worse than the original problem."

As frightening as such stories sound, the level of contamination at Los Alamos is still small compared to places like Hanford, Monagle said. That's because the Los Alamos laboratory is fundamentally a research institution with comparable levels of contamination, he added; it's the production facilities like Hanford that have real problems. "And everyone is just salivating to get involved with the Hanford cleanup."

The day we met, Monagle came striding down the dimly lit hall of his building wearing a button that read "Death before Decaf!"—a fitting declaration for the fast-talking young man whose brain seemed, indeed, to be running on high-octane fuel. The recent boom in environmental remediation had meant many fifty- and sixty-hour weeks for Monagle, a skilled analyst who reads patterns in the miles of paper spit out by the automated sampling systems in his laboratory. "Our bread and butter is generating paper," Monagle laughed. "You start with a sample of dirt and end up with a report." His laboratory is crammed with metal boxes that are basically high-tech separators; they examine samples of dirt and water and sort out the contaminants that are in them. Such auto samplers bubble nitrogen through a water sample so that the components are pulled into the nitrogen bubbles and passed through a charcoal trap. When the trap is heated and the flow is reversed, the trapped chemicals are loaded onto a gas chromatograph, wherein each chemical whirls through a column and emerges at a distinct time and with a characteristic pattern. "Think about the world—there are lots and lots of patterns," explained Monagle, whose automated systems are PC-based. "We keep teaching the computer these patterns, but, of course, you can never completely replace the experienced analyst." In fact, the more automated such a device is and the more reliant it is upon expert systems, the more inclined people are to doubt it, still not trusting the word of a computer. That may be because the stakes are so high. An analysis performed by such a facility can determine how difficult and costly a remediation plan will be or whether any is needed at all. "When there's a two-thousand-dollar bill sitting on top of each barrel that needs to be disposed of, people get nervous," Monagle said.

Monagle's lab did only *cold work*—that is, nonradioactive sampling, while alpha and gamma counting, including bioassay tests for internal exposures and analysis and final calculations on samples for the transuranium registry program, was done elsewhere in the division. Monagle was interested in doing more in the way of process monitoring in which effluents are eliminated before they hit the pipe. By placing automated monitoring systems at each facility, it is possible not only to track the source of a contaminant but also to stop it before the damage is done.

In addition to Monagle's Organic Analysis Section, the Environmental Chemistry Group has other facilities scattered around the laboratory, including one at TA-50, the radioactive wastewater treatment plant. Another facility was being readied for the expanding remediation program, but the $1.2 million remodeling job had been bogged down in engineering and regulatory problems for years. There's something strange going on there, said Monagle, a self-confessed type A personality who isn't afraid to say what he thinks. The environmental chemists at the laboratory had always been viewed as service personnel and were lucky just to get enough money to update their equipment now and then. This sudden change in status was exciting. "Everything has changed," said radiochemist George Brooks Jr., who appears to be having fun with this change in fortune. "Now we're on the high side with all the funding, and we can buy a lot of stuff." Brooks designs and builds mobile laboratories that are sent out into the canyons on lab property to sample soils and analyze them on-site for various kinds of contaminants. Another fast talker, Brooks is part of a laboratory family, with a father who is a radiographer in the weapons program, and several other family members who either work for the lab or for laboratory contractors. His small mobile laboratories had placed Los Alamos on the cutting edge of radiochemical analysis. "When the big environmental push came, the emphasis was on doing analytical work in the field, since it's very expensive to bring samples in and then contract them out," Brooks said. Like the PC-based auto samplers, however, the mobile labs had met with some resistance from people who didn't trust that the tidy little setups could do analysis equivalent to that of a larger laboratory. Brooks had created several of the mobiles, refining them with each iteration. At first they were used just to screen samples for radiation. But the vans were too expensive to be used just for that. So Brooks worked on establishing better procedures and instrumentation so that the mobiles alone could determine whether a site needed remediation or could be closed out. He worked to establish a standard platform in the mobile laboratory so that the instrumentation could be adapted to support organic, inorganic, or radiochemistry. In collaboration with Oak Ridge and Sandia national laboratories, Pacific Northwest Laboratory, Idaho National Engineering Laboratory, and the universities of Florida, Tennessee, and Texas, Los Alamos has been developing automated contaminant analysis systems that combine robotics with plug-and-play modules that can be customized to meet the needs of specific sites. Beginning first with contaminated DOE sites, the systems will eventually be used in the private sector. Meanwhile, procedures developed at Los Alamos have been incorporated into a methods compendium that is accessible to anyone else in the DOE system.

Interestingly, in the two and a half years they had been working the canyons, Brooks said he had seen only three hot samples coming out of these sites. "A lot of people believe that Los Alamos is contaminated beyond belief, but the truth is, we have very minimal problems." Furthermore, the technical process of cleaning up should be, in his words, a piece of cake. "It's the bureaucracy that goes along with it that kills you, though," he said. "If they just let the people go in and do their work, it would be great." Brooks attributes the high cost of remediation to the maze of environmental guidelines pertaining to air emissions, transportation, and radiological work plans. "The paperwork probably accounts for 60 percent of the cost of a lot of these projects. It's ridiculous, and it's getting worse," Brooks said, adding that public perception about radiation seems to be at the root of the problem. "They think we are contaminating everybody, and so therefore we need to be watched." There are even those among the laboratory ranks who are spooked by radiation, he noted. "You have highly educated people that don't have much radiological knowledge and, just like the general public, what they don't know, they fear. When we go to radiological sites, people are more interested in the radiation than in the organics and inorganics, which are just as nasty and can kill you just as quickly, maybe more so. But they don't worry about that. And it's fine. I'll take their money," he quipped, adding that when he goes out to take samples he is expected to screen them first for radiation, before other specialists will check for other constituents in the soil.

One of the benefits of working with the mobile labs, however, Brooks said, is that the canyons they visit are often quite beautiful, populated by deer, elk, and bears. "I'd live here," said Monagle, who doesn't live in Los Alamos because of the unavailability of affordable housing. Having lived in California for two years analyzing fish for a commercial facility, he would rather take his chances on Los Alamos. "California has more problems. This is by far the cleanest place I have ever worked." Indeed, most Los Alamos workers and residents seem to have made peace with the chemicals and the hot spots left over from less enlightened years of weapons research on their mesa, and don't worry overmuch about any slightly elevated risk. They cite the greater statistical probability of death from such other hazards as smoking or riding in a car on nearby state highways, and wonder why the public isn't more sensible about the nature of risk.

However, a brain tumor scare a few years ago had many Los Alamos residents uncharacteristically worried. In 1991 a Los Alamos sculptor—Tyler Mercier, the grandson of a lab nuclear safety engineer and by training an engineer himself—presented information to the laboratory indicating that there had been a cluster of brain tumors among Los Alamos citizens living in the Western Area, one of the early prestigious sections of the city. The artist had spent a year gathering a list of more than fifty names of residents and former residents of Los Alamos who had fallen victim to brain cancer. He had begun by investigating radiation levels in Los Alamos and comparing them to those reported by the laboratory, which were lower. At the time, he was living there in one of the old government-built homes from the early fifties with his wife, a computer specialist at the laboratory, and their young child. When the lab did not respond to his revelations in a way that seemed appropriate to him, Mercier took the information to a Department of Energy meeting.

As anxiety increased among residents over the implications of Mercier's revelations, the DOE funded an epidemiological study to investigate the incidence of cancer in Los Alamos. Phase I of the multiphase study found that Los Alamos did experience an elevation in brain and nervous system tumors during the mid- to late-1980s, although in small numbers. The incidence of such tumors in Los Alamos County for the period from 1980 to 1990 was 70 to 80 percent higher than that found in reference populations elsewhere in the state and the nation and followed a pattern of increasing incidence starting in 1970. The study concluded that the increased incidence of brain and nervous system cancers could not be attributed to chance alone. There was also a marked increase in thyroid cancers in Los Alamos County—four times higher than the New Mexico population—in the years from 1986 to

1990. Nevertheless, the study's findings were not conclusive enough to convince residents that their community was a dangerous place in which to live. And Mercier's research into radiation levels, which had started it all, was dismissed by Los Alamos scientists as inaccurate and unskilled.

Los Alamos Monitor writer Karen Brandt also dismissed the study, calling it a waste of funds. "An incredible amount of money was spent, and nothing came of it. Just absolutely nothing came of it. All a person like Tyler does is cost all of us a great deal of money. Whether or not that's a good thing depends upon your point of view."

But there was another cost, of course. Some parents in Los Alamos lost a little of that sense of security that life in a sheltered community had always given them. For decades some of the worst things about the outside world had been shut out. This was a threat from the inside. "My wife and I did think long and hard about this because we live three blocks from where these brain tumors are supposedly concentrated," said laboratory archivist Roger Meade. "I have children, and if I thought for a minute that there was any danger, we would be out of here like a shot. And I think there would be twelve thousand other people who would be right behind us. Nobody is going to put their family in jeopardy." Meade could not understand how the public could so deeply misunderstand the motives of Los Alamos scientists, who aren't robots, after all, he declared. "We're all human around here. We work hard, we have families, and we want to live long lives." Meade and his wife had followed the brain tumor study closely and, in the end, felt good about staying put. Paul White, who lives in White Rock, had also carefully studied the incidence of brain tumors and concluded that it was still a safe place to live and raise a family. Jeff Bryan was a relative newcomer to Los Alamos, having lived there with his wife and children for only four years. He too felt comfortable staying on the mesa. "Although I guess we'll find out for sure in twenty years," he said with a grim smile. "Maybe we're all going to die of cancer?" A level of anxiety had to exist in most rational people here, he mused, adding that he himself had been somewhat anxious about the health risks, although they were secondary to his misgivings about the focus of the laboratory. "I'm not a big fan of weapons research, and that to me has been more troubling than worrying about potential contamination." Unlike most of the people I talked to at the laboratory, Bryan was sympathetic to outsiders who were afraid to set foot in Los Alamos because of their fears about radiation. "Of course, it helps to have worked with radioactive elements and to understand dose rates and the probability of cell damage," he explained, admitting that there was indeed some very small additional radiation exposure risk in living in Los Alamos, and that it would take only one event, some kind of particle or radiation going through your body, to initiate a problem. However, chances are that you will get that from your average daily background dose as you're walking around on planet earth, he said. It's just a matter of probability. But the fact that Los Alamos adds an additional risk, no matter how infinitesimal, is unacceptable to some people. "And I can understand that argument. I think it's entirely reasonable," he said.

Meanwhile, Tyler Mercier moved to Santa Fe.

When I left TA-21, John Watkin escorted me to the gate, stopping first at a checkpoint to drop off the dosimeter badge I was required to wear—because of what TA-21 used to be, he explained—and to sign me out of the building. Like Bryan, Monagle, and so many other Los Alamos researchers, Watkin made a point of saying that he wasn't involved in any of the weapons research done at the laboratory. "Weapons have got nothing to do with my being here at all. And that's just fine with me." As we walked, he pointed across the parking lot to an area surrounded by high barbed-wire-topped fences. "In all those fenced-off areas there's plutonium and other things just buried a few feet down in the soil," Watkin said. "In the old days—the forties and fifties—when the attitude was 'let's make maximum bombs for maximum money,' they basically had runoff pipes going directly into rubble-filled pits. When a pit was full, they put soil over the top of it and went on, kind of knowing that it was bad for the environment, I think. But you have to remember that the Cold War was going on and they thought the Russians were getting more bombs than we were. I can kind of understand that. It wasn't the 1990s. At that time, anyone who came out here and accused them of messing with the environment would have been locked up as a traitor to protect the national interest." Unfortunately, though, Watkin added, now the nation has to spend millions of dollars to put things right. At this site, technologists were taking core samples, finding that the buried waste was trickling slowly down through the bedrock. "It's going to take a long, long time to clean it all up." Later, during the summer of 1996, the laboratory would begin tearing down Buildings 3 and 4 North in TA-21, recycling and decontaminating the metals and crushed concrete, at an estimated cost of $2.5 million.

For his part, Watkin didn't feel at all jeopardized by what the laboratory referred to as dangerous contamination in his building. "Not for a second," he said. "If you know anything about radiation, you realize it's not as nasty as everyone thinks." Then he cocked his head to the side and smiled. "It's interesting, though. Here you have this gorgeous blue sky, clear mountain air, and about twenty yards that way there's more radioactivity than you care to think about. That's just this funny old place," he said, as he gave a friendly wave and turned to walk away.

6

Habits of Secrecy

During the summer of 1994 work crews began to tear down a group of government-built duplexes on Trinity Drive in Los Alamos. The walls facing the street had been peeled away, revealing small kitchens with tattered linoleum and sagging cupboards; shreds of shingles, insulation, and the wood and plaster from thin walls were heaped in the yard, soggy with rain. It was more than just a shabby diorama of 1950s and '60s domestic life. This demolition site somehow seemed to symbolize all the changes that were occurring at the laboratory and in the community. Everything was being turned inside out, examined under new light, and redesigned or thrown away.

After the boom times of the Reagan arms buildup, the Bush administration's announcement in September 1991 of strategic reductions in nuclear weapons, and the unbelievable end of the long Cold War brought budget cuts, staff reductions, and a suddenly unclear mission. But with the pressures of the arms race diminishing, there was also time to examine more closely the cost of what Los Alamos scientist Lou Rasocha referred to as "this little exercise in man's lizard brain." We had spent somewhere between one and three trillion dollars and now this unfortunate part of history was over, he said; now it was time to deal with the legacy. The extent of the environmental damage at Hanford, Rocky Flats, and Savannah River had already leaked into the country's consciousness, such that increasing pressure from the public and Congress had induced then–Energy Secretary James Watkins to issue in 1989 a more stringent regime of environmental and safety regulations for the DOE system. Los Alamos managed to stay above the fray until the brain tumor scare, which attracted inquiry into past and

current health and safety practices at the nation's elite weapons research laboratory. Anticipating trouble, the lab did its own assessment
of its situation and came up with 770 violations of federal health, safety,
and environmental standards.[1] A subsequent visit in 1991 by a DOE
Tiger Team identified some 2,300 solid-waste disposal sites that
needed further study and excavation, estimating a $2 billion cleanup
that would extend into the year 2019. The team also found that the laboratory—the site of fifteen nuclear reactors, one of them the oldest operating facility in the country—was ill-prepared for emergencies, an assessment with which lab director Sig Hecker had to agree, saying the
lab had lost ground on emergency preparedness in recent years.[2] The
Tiger Team visit yielded a thousand-page report and a striking blow
that was "so overwhelming," wrote Hecker, "that I concluded massive
changes were required for us to stay in busness."[3] He set the laboratory
on a path of quality improvement that would lead to deep and sometimes disturbing changes for the thousands of people who worked
there, but that would yield only mixed results after five years of effort.
The quality improvement journeys of other organizations—primarily
Motorola—had been studied, the lab's organizational structure and
business practices had been radically engineered, and while it had
forced some progress, "I am sorry to report that we haven't gotten
there yet," wrote Hecker in 1996. "It is difficult to lock onto a guide
star when the constellations are constantly changing."[4]

From the beginning, the biggest stumbling block to change would
be the deeply ingrained culture of the laboratory, explained Basil Swanson—a materials scientist who served as the project leader for a strategic planning group assigned to come up with a functional alternative to
what was clearly a dysfunctional management structure, as he put it. He
had experienced this old way of doing business when he was a group
leader. "I remember having staff in my group say, 'Swanson, your job is
to bring in money for me and to leave me alone and not question me
about the things that I'm doing.' Managers were there to bring in
money and leave them alone to play in their sandboxes." This business
style harked back to the 1950s and '60s, the so-called golden age of research culture at Los Alamos, before the first hints of accountability
and funding pressure in 1970 had begun to steal some of its glitter.
That was when people first had to start writing about what they were

working on, thereby defining their programs, Don Petersen explained. Increasing legal requirements and funding restrictions that simply hadn't existed before that time had managed to kill this golden age, he said. "It's amazing that people find it so hard today to believe that nothing was written down. The whole time, [we] operated under a sort of handshake mentality that required documentation only in terms of what we published." It was part of an informal management style that extended into the 1970s, when then–lab director Harold Agnew held his monthly staff meetings at his home. "I provided the liquor, which I guess would be considered scandalous, but it certainly allowed people to forget their inhibitions. We didn't have that many division leaders or associate directors, so everybody could come and speak out."[5] The early bygone days of the laboratory were characterized by camaraderie, enthusiasm, and excitement, Petersen said. It was this and the fact that so much was accomplished so quickly, not the unlimited funding, that had made it such a special time. "The only way you could tell the difference between night and day was whether the lights were on," Petersen said. "The people worked around the clock, and they worked in an almost driven mode."[6] Not surprisingly, the influence of that time still resonates in the laboratory and influences the character of the institution today.

But, those who had worked since 1955 in that protective atmosphere were slow to recognize the crisis that was looming ahead. "And crisis didn't really start to occur in this business until the Department of Defense [DOD] budget started to fall," said Public Affairs Director Scott Duncan, who was working at the Pentagon during the 1980s, at the apex of lush DOD budgets. So much money was being pumped into the defense budget that "we kept advising the Reagan administration that it was too much money, we couldn't absorb it that fast," he recalled. "We were very concerned about the defense industrial base being able to handle the quantities of cash that just couldn't be absorbed effectively or efficiently. So we kept trying to slow it down. Then, of course, it started to head into the dumper," Duncan noted wryly, adding that the laboratory did not perceive the risk this represented for several years thereafter. The institution's budget, while it is administered by the Department of Energy, is most closely aligned with the defense budget. It took the implosion of the Soviet Union and the fall of the Berlin Wall to make the scope of the crisis really obvious, Duncan said. "'Like, jeez, maybe we have a problem here?' Hmmm. No lie," he said, his words suffused with sarcasm. Amazingly, though, many at the lab were still slow to get it. "In fact, there are still people who believe that the Brinks truck will always arrive," Duncan said.

For over forty years the lab had lived apart, operating on generous budgets with little oversight, while every year six percent of incoming funds was skimmed off the top to support laboratory-directed research and development. This was discretionary money that could be assigned to any interesting idea that lab management deemed promising. A December 1990 General Accounting Office audit criticized what it called the laboratory's excessive use of this discretionary funding, an accusation that Hecker labeled unfair. He explained that the lab had been encouraged by the AEC and the DOE to use these research dollars to continue to attract top scientists to the mesa. Nevertheless, the DOE increased the paperwork for the national laboratories in order to better track research funding and began writing more detailed contracts with the institutions that manage the labs. The contract between the lab and the University of California, which manages it, evolved from a gentleman's agreement into a several-hundred-page document.[7] "For a long time this was a kind of billion-dollar-a-year sheltered scientific workshop," Lou Rasocha said, "But not anymore. Economic change is here to stay. If the laboratory doesn't get used to that, it won't survive."

Getting used to it would require doing business at a reasonable cost, historically a somewhat alien idea at the laboratory. Younger scientists who came to the lab understood the meaning of budget constraints and the intense competition for funding in science, while veterans who had been at the lab for many years were deeply resentful of the changes that were taking place. "It's really much more difficult to do your job," said Ed Flynn, who had spent twenty-five years at the lab as a nuclear physicist and was a lab fellow, a designation that honors a researcher for having made fundamental discoveries and for being a recognized authority in his or her field, with a strong publishing history and outstanding contributions to important laboratory programs. Only 2 percent of the laboratory technical staff are recognized as fellows. He and other members in the lab's Biophysics Group had developed an improved method for measuring the weak magnetic waves that are emitted by the brain when neurons are activated. Magnoencephalography is a noninvasive technique, Flynn explained, that shows how the brain functions. It employs quantum mechanics principles and a device that operates at superconducting temperatures. It's expensive research and getting funding is a continuing problem. "To actually get funding you have to be part of some mafia," he said, bitterly. "It's hard to break in, and even though you may have a good idea, well, you're just not on the right list." AIDS research, for example, never seemed to have trouble getting funding and people, he noted. Flynn complained that he spent half of his time writing proposals for funding. Increased accountability documentation, while designed to enforce goals and keep projects on track, also added to the paperwork demanded of managers and group leaders. "Now you have to do quarterly reports to show that you meet the milestones. You can't just say, 'I have a great idea, fund me and I'll come out with some good publications.' That's not enough, anymore." Flynn said he tried to protect the technicians and postdocs in his group from this onerous chore of writing reviews and funding proposals. He said it was necessary to build into any budget he devised at least 20 percent just to cover the administration of the money, and he morosely predicted that it would only get worse.

One of the strengths that the national labs have over industrial labs or universities is their ability to form core competencies that cross over the boundaries separating disciplines. Scientists from very different fields can more easily be brought together to solve problems. Groups like Ed Flynn's perfectly illustrated this. "It's tremendously cross-disciplinary," said Flynn, "with people in physics, electrical engineering, computer science, and neural science all working together. It makes for incredible depth in this group. We can interact amongst the various divisions of this laboratory much better than in a university, for example, where departments are much more isolated. This is still something the national labs can do, at least for now, " he added, laughing ruefully.

Another advantage is the ability to do big science, the kinds of things no one else could afford to do, said physicist Jim Smith. "This is a place full of physicists, and these guys like to have the biggest, the most powerful stuff. It's all about energy, and they like energy. That's why they like nuclear weapons. They want to make the biggest laser, the biggest accelerator, they want to have the most concentrated energy, and if they're materials scientists, they want to have the biggest press." Smith pointed to a building whose sole occupant was a five-thousand-ton press that had been used to crimp steel bands around the big cables that were used at the Nevada test site. Now it was used by geologists and materials scientists. "The principal reason for having a national laboratory is that you have to have a place to put the biggest stuff, like the biggest laser. And we want that stuff here. This is large-scale science that is state-of-the-art." However, along with that comes the potential for making really big mistakes, he said, citing as an example, the Antares project, built to support Star Wars research. "We were pouring concrete for years trying to get that building ready, and we put all these lasers in there, and come to find out, we had the wrong energy lasers and it didn't work. We couldn't change it," Smith said, laughing. "And when I say it didn't work, I mean it *really* didn't work. Now, maybe we should have known this in the beginning. And maybe not." The building is being used for other things, and some of the technology from the project has been folded into other research. "But my point is, only the United States government can make mistakes on that scale, because somewhere you've got to have the really big, powerful stuff."

The ability to form core competencies and to do big science makes national laboratories the ideal research institutions to address grand scientific challenges, the big-ticket problems. Nuclear weapons design had been such a challenge, demanding the world's most powerful computers that would be relied upon more than ever now to assure the safety and reliability of the stockpile. The computing power at Los Alamos would continue to be applied to other grand challenges, like global modeling of the planet's atmosphere, oceans, and interior.

But the inertia of the culture and increasing regulation were keeping the laboratory from being as productive as such a research institution needed to be, said Hecker. "Finally, we realized that if we didn't do something, we were doomed, because the government seemed to be bent on ruin with the way it was controlling the environment in which we had to live."

Hecker asked consultants from Motorola—their productivity and efficiency training team known as Motorola University—to visit Los Alamos. "While we were fighting other battles, American businesses were threatened with being wiped out by international competition, and they found that they had to do their job in a totally different way in order to be more competitive," said Hecker. The laboratory had missed out on that quality revolution, and by the time they'd stuck their head out from behind the Cold War, it was almost too late. If Los Alamos didn't catch up with the quality movement soon, they would become obsolete. As it turned out, the Motorola team told them what they didn't want to hear. Their organizational structure was bloated and Byzantine, and the staff was cynical, their performance unrelated as it was to their pay. Furthermore, there was so much red tape and bureaucratic redundancy that it took forever to get anything done.[8] They also observed that the large number of proposals for funding churned out by LANL researchers consumed tremendous resources, while only 25 percent of them actually brought in any money. Motorola called that a disaster and suggested that individual scientists put more effort into working for the good of the entire laboratory and not just for their own pet projects.[9]

Scott Duncan had been shocked by the state of lab culture when he first arrived to take over the public affairs office. "I was very surprised when I got here. R & D establishments should be very flat, very free-wheeling," he said. What he found was a hierarchical silo, as he put it. Most organizations, including the military, he said, had abandoned that sort of vertical structure long ago, because it made quick decisions and nimble movement all but impossible. He illustrated his observation about the institutional gridlock such a structure created by telling a story about what happened when he tried to order refreshments for one of his first staff meetings. What should have been a simple task turned out to be impossible. He learned that while he could *order* refreshments, he couldn't get them *delivered*. Only the lab director could do that. "But since the lab director is seldom here, how does anybody get any refreshments?" Duncan wondered. "'Well, the director's secretary could sign for it!' they told me. How fascinating! We absolutely required multiple, multiple decisions and signatures for the most trivial things that had to be done. You had to wait for weeks for the most routine requests to make their way through the bureaucracy. It was mind-boggling. There were all these stovepipes and ways that you simply could not do business."

Part of the problem, Swanson said, was that the rules and responsibilities for different levels of managers were confusing, with too much overlap. "In fact, it was very unclear what the job function of some senior managers really was. It wasn't that they weren't good people. They were. They just had undoable jobs." As a result, lab management had a hard time making decisions and planning for the future, he said. The organizational structure was equally confusing, with more than one group doing such similar work that they even competed with each other. Furthermore, the accepted way of getting new business for the laboratory was poorly managed, unfocused, and chaotic, Swanson said. "I have worried about the future of this place. This lab and other national labs are absolutely unique in their ability to address critical national problems, and we need to make them work better in order to allow them to do that."

But big organizations just don't change willingly, said Duncan, and Los Alamos National Laboratory would be no different. "You want to believe that big organizations like that are brilliant and altruistic and all that other stuff," he said. "But they aren't. They're stupid. They only change when they're facing a crisis. Then they decide that if they want to live they will have to make massive changes. When they do, of course, they emerge tougher and stronger."

What it came down to, Swanson said, was that the entire culture of the laboratory was going to have to change, and it would mean overcoming a formidable institutional inertia. What was needed was a major shake-up. So, after a lot of painful self-analysis by task forces and committees, Hecker announced in October 1993 a new organizational and management structure, designed to make the most of the laboratory's strengths. Layers of management were removed, creating one single layer of twenty-eight directors who answered to the laboratory director. The laboratory was organized into divisions that sought to cluster capabilities and eliminate duplication throughout the institution. The divisions were closely aligned with the core competencies of the laboratory, and nine programs were created that would choose from among the different divisions or capability organizations to get what they needed to address a particular problem. The programs were mapped directly onto the laboratory's major customers. Swanson described an organizational structure of concentric rings, with the customer in the center, the programs occupying a ring around that center, while the divisions or capability organizations occupied the outer ring. "The program people get on the superhighway and travel around the divisions gathering what they need to serve the customer in the middle," Swanson said. Plus, practical streamlining measures were instituted, reducing, for example, the number of signatures needed for approvals. The entire reorganization quickly yielded an $11 million savings, according to lab sources.

Nevertheless, after all of this, progress was still slow, hampered by what Hecker characterized as a constantly shifting target—the slate of environmental, safety, and health requirements from the DOE. "The ink was barely dry on the Tiger Team report when we were faced with new and different requirements. These requirements continued to shift as the DOE sought an acceptable approach to performing its oversight role. Each of these directions represented major efforts not in sync with the previous direction. So much of the focus in the early activities was compliance-driven that it appears we lost our focus on those factors that control the real safety of the workplace." In the pressure cooker that the laboratory had become, accidents continued to happen.

The weapons community, which had functioned for years in an unreal world, was now subject to the same kind of scrutiny that the nuclear power industry experienced after Three Mile Island, said Bruce Matthews, director of nuclear materials technology, the division responsible for plutonium research and for overseeing TA-55. "We are where nuclear power was fourteen or fifteen years ago. It was just chaos in that industry because all of a sudden the public became aware of what was going on and what the potential dangers were. So, the regulatory environment changed enormously. That's exactly what's going on for us. We're in a fishbowl right now and everyone is looking at us."

The unblinking gaze of the public manifested itself at the laboratory in the form of ceaseless audits, nearly one every day, said Scott Duncan. Matthews would spend most of the day we met working with the Defense Nuclear Facilities Safety Board, who were there to perform an audit. "They'll be here for four days," he said. "And right now we also have an audit team from the DOE's Office of Nuclear Safety." They would stay at Los Alamos for weeks. Other types of security audits would be going on at the same time, in addition to the laboratory's own internal audits. "The Congress think they run things, so you get the General Accounting Office [GAO] audits all the time, too," said Mike Berger, a program manager in one of the environmental programs at the laboratory. "For every project there's a seventeen-page questionnaire from the GAO about future funding, interactions with universities, and interactions with industry," he said. "You could spend your whole career just filling out forms. I don't have time to fill them out. I don't even understand them. Nobody in this organization understands them." Berger had once recommended that a special department be created and labeled "non-value-added science." Lab managers and researchers could just send all their forms there to be filled out so that they would have time to do their real work.

The extra regulations and paperwork vastly increased bureaucracy and overhead at a time when the lab was trying to tool a leaner organization and was also being asked to produce more results with less money. One Tiger Team finding—a not altogether surprising requirement to extend a vent stack so that the radioactivity in gases would decay before being expelled into the air—had cost the laboratory budget $3.5 million to fix.[10] "It takes up a tremendous amount of resources just dealing with regulatory issues," said Bruce Matthews. The changes that were implemented in response to the Tiger Team findings had added to the annual budget some $70 million of overhead costs—"work that does not contribute to our technical product," Hecker said. At least as much had been lost in terms of technical productivity because of the time spent dealing with bureaucratic chores associated with the increased bureaucracy. Day-to-day operations were vastly more difficult. For example, regulation of chemicals used in the laboratory was so stringent, said materials scientist Don Sandstrom, "that we are not allowed to have in our laboratory things you have in your own home. It's made doing chemistry a lot harder." Joe Martz said there was a materials safety data sheet for every chemical he used in his lab. "We have one for water! And one for sodium chloride. That's table salt! It recommends that if you get this stuff on your hands, you wash them for twenty minutes and see a physician. Table salt!" he said, exasperated. Chemist Pat Rocoff offered a slightly tongue-in-cheek assessment, noting that increased safety regulations had given birth to a bad case of sign pollution at the laboratory. "There are signs on everything, telling you what to do and what not do," she said, "when all we really need is for people to take responsibility for learning how to do their job carefully and then just doing it."

What seemed to bother people most, however, was the lack of trust these changes represented. "Everything I do is second-guessed," said counterproliferation specialist Bob Kelley. "When I came into this business, I had a tremendous amount of authority, responsibility, and trust. I was twenty-one years old and a reactor supervisor out in the Nevada desert. I could do what I wanted to do, but there were rules and I followed them. They weren't very complicated, because I was paid to think. These days no one gives me that authority. They second-guess you on things as simple as purchases, on money, and on safety rules, to the point that people are becoming almost totally frozen in their ability to make decisions and do things. It's one of those classic bureaucratic cases in which making no decision is the safest thing to do," Kelley said, adding that the effect is deadening, as it produces lethargy, resentment, and resignation among staff members. "I don't mind being regulated," said Jill Trewhella, group leader of Biochemistry and Spectroscopy, who had come from Australia to the United States in 1980 and was later hired by Los Alamos to start their structural biology program. She is the only woman so far to be named a lab fellow. "I just want to be trusted. We're not two-headed monsters that disregard the environment or want to poison our neighbors. We're fairly ordinary people who take pride in what we do and we want to be positive contributors to society."

In the midst of reorganizing itself, the laboratory also realized it urgently needed to forge a new relationship with its overseer, the DOE. The relationship had changed radically over the years, said Martz, and not necessarily for the better, from the laboratory's perspective, that is. "At first they were our patron, and as you know, a patron is someone who gives you money without reservation, because he knows you're going to do good with it." Then the DOE assumed the role of a sponsor, "someone who will champion you because he likes the work you do and knows that you're capable of doing it, but, at the same time, wants to see how the money is going to be used," Martz said. Finally, though, the DOE became a customer. "And customers can be cranky, demanding service and efficiency. That's where we are today," Martz concluded.

Of course, Congress is also a customer, and that relationship has deteriorated in a similar fashion. Paul White chalked it up to the culture of secrecy that had dictated business as usual for years in the nation's weapons laboratories. The Reagan and Bush administrations had been arrogant, as had the laboratory, White said. "We knew what was right, and we stonewalled Congress. The thing is, you can have the right answer, but you still need to exercise a certain amount of skill in order to convince others. I don't think that was done. In the end, Congress wasn't buying any of it," White said. The Hatfield Amendment called for a complete nuclear test ban and that may have had as much to do with this arrogance on the part of the administration and the weapons community as it did with whether or not nuclear testing was the right thing to do, White said. "Some senators said this very explicitly."

We mustn't forget that Los Alamos and the other laboratories had played a part in creating this political quagmire, said Bob Kelley. For example, they had impeded the debate over nuclear testing with their own arcane discussions about the many ways that the Soviet Union might cheat on the test ban treaty or how difficult it would be to verify compliance. "We propagated all sorts of scenarios whereby the Russians could conduct a clandestine test that we wouldn't be able to observe and therefore they could beat us, couldn't they?" he said in disgust. "I think the policy community finally just had to tell the laboratories to shut up! 'We asked you what the possibilities for cheating were, we asked you what the consequences of cheating were, thank you very much! We are not going to sit here and listen to these endless technical arguments about how complicated we can make the verification regime in order to deal with a tenth of a percent possibility that somebody might try to cheat on us! If you have something useful to say that can contribute to the debate, speak up!'" But then, Kelley wearily added, Senator Jesse Helms would get on a soapbox and say he's got some guy at Los Alamos who tells him there's some possibility, some way they could cheat. "But so what if the Russians pulled off a test? If they went and did something that dumb it was probably for some safety problem they wanted to double-check." One of the most egregious examples of pork-barreling may have been the Star Wars project, as Steve Younger, who had worked on the technology at Livermore, described it: "You just knew it wasn't going to work. You just knew it! But Teller was pushing the story that the Russians were ten years ahead of us and so on," he rolled his eyes to the ceiling in exasperation. "Well, I think I have every clearance known to man, and I could say that it just ain't there. Honest to golly! So, I had a fairly serious difference of opinion with some of the Livermore people about what it meant to tell the truth." It was at that point that Younger decided to leave Livermore and come to Los Alamos.

None of this was lost on the American public, who had become increasingly distrustful of the defense arguments of scientists. And now the public had a voice. In the language of Hazel O'Leary's DOE, they were stakeholders. "It's just ironic," said the Reading Room's Tom Ribe. "Now the public is trying to interact with the laboratory at a time when the institution is totally unclear about what it's doing and where it's going. And obviously, the country is completely confused about what it's going to do with this laboratory." It would be more difficult now to get the public on our side, Swanson said, adding that it was a relationship problem whose tone had been set by the Atomic Energy Commission years before. "They were very bright people back in Washington and they did a very good job of running the labs, but they were extremely arrogant in terms of having a mandate. So they tended to just push things down people's throats. It was a very arrogant stance that lingers." Tom Ribe views the AEC as "almost a criminal agency in terms of what they were doing to the people in the 1950s and '60s," he said, citing the exposure of soldiers and citizens to radioactive products of nuclear explosions in the Nevada desert. The public had trusted that somebody in the AEC was really seeing to our best interests. "That somebody would draw the line," Ribe said. "But the military drive in the forties, fifties, and sixties to create nuclear weapons was so strong that it was 'The public be damned, we're going to do this.' It wasn't in the public's interest, anyway; go ahead and destroy a lot of things, including your own credibility as a government, but it's necessary because we're in this Cold War, this race. I think that a lot of things got swept aside, very definitely." And science was being blamed for all of it, decisions that were essentially political, added Jim Smith. "The public is horrified by what science has done in the past. But we did what we did because the people wanted it," he rationalized. "But we'll fix all the problems. Science isn't evil. It's just information and it all depends on what people do with it."

So, as much as researchers complained about the unfriendly attitude the country currently held toward basic research and the work of the national laboratories, they could blame themselves in part. "In fact,

I think pork-barreling has been devastating for science, in general," said Jill Trewhella. "To do things for political and economic reasons and not for the science that you are trying to produce is a sin and it has hurt us badly." She blamed it for the current difficulty researchers had getting funding and for the introduction of improper criteria for evaluating research. "We should not be funding mediocre or second-best science. I think researchers have to develop some integrity and not go to Congress and try to pull that anymore." The laboratory should only sell things on their benefit to society to solve problems society wants solved, she said. Furthermore, only the best fundamental research would yield competitive technologies. It should be that simple. Society wants good answers to its problems—how to clean up the environment, how to get nondestructive energy, how to have more competitive biotechnology, how to fight disease better. And an appropriate balance must be struck between a quick turnaround now and investment in a future we can all live with, said Trewhella. The public is hostile toward basic research, said Gary Sanders, who had worked on the superconducting supercollider before Congress had pulled the plug. Basic research is expensive, but it is absolutely necessary if our nation is to continue to be able to solve big societal problems and also be competitive in the marketplace. By failing to fund basic research, we are, in essence, eating our seed corn, Sanders said.

As the laboratory struggled internally with all of the questions confronting it, Sig Hecker tried to remind his staff that the problems they were facing were bigger than just their laboratory. "Don't you realize that this is not just us?" he said. "This is threatening the whole support of science in this country." The United States had used the defense argument to justify the support of science, but the end of the Cold War had changed everything. "The Cold War had given this country a covert, where we were able to do science without necessarily having to get full public consensus for what we were doing," said Hecker, who had been thinking a lot about this lately. "Now we have to turn our focus to civilian issues, but what we're finding is that we can't agree on the civilian issues. We can't even agree on the basic role of government for supporting civilian issues." There would have to be a new rationale for supporting science with public money.

Swanson wanted to believe that the public would be sensible enough to keep the national labs, to recognize what a value they were to the nation. They have an essential role to play and it would be a disaster to lose them. But there was a distinct possibility that some labs might close, a not entirely far-fetched idea, given what had already happened—the closing of the production complex and the closing and consolidation of military bases by the DOD. On the positive side, however, those DOE survivors might emerge as a more integrated whole. "In fact, all this angst that is flowing around the national labs is not entirely bad," said Swanson. "It's given us a real kick in the butt. In justifying our existence, we will get a much better idea of what we are and what we're good at."

One possibility for bolstering the shrinking budgets at national labs was collaboration with industry. As early as 1986, the year President Reagan and Soviet president Mikhail Gorbachev signed an agreement limiting strategic warheads, Sig Hecker started talking to Congress about the prospect of transferring some of the government-funded technology base of the national weapons laboratories to American industry. This wasn't a completely new idea; as early as 1980, with the Stevenson-Wydler Technology Innovation Act, Congress had tried to encourage the nation's government laboratories to cooperate with industry, with mixed success. LANL began to forge such collaborations in 1988, with the Superconductivity Pilot Center, and in the following year, the Oil Recovery Technology Partnership. The National Competitiveness and Technology Transfer Act of 1989 continued the theme, with the Cooperative Research and Development Agreement, or CRADA. In 1990 defense program funds became available for collaborative efforts with industry, under the Technology Transfer Initiative. CRADAs and many informal agreements with industrial partners were developed in which cost-shared partnerships made use of the brainpower and resources of the national laboratories while industry retained intellectual property rights to the research. At Los Alamos an Industrial Partnership Center was established.

Researchers at the national weapons laboratories were cautious about boarding this new train, however, being unclear as they were about the destination and the cost of the ticket. Weapons designers themselves, who were already feeling the pinch, did not see how their expertise applied. "We need this technology to build nuclear weapons, but it will not build a better toaster," said weapons designer Merri Wood, who believed that there were very real barriers to sharing weapons technology in a world where proliferation is an urgent concern.[11]

By August 1996, the laboratory had participated in two hundred technical partnerships with industry, bringing in over $50 million annually. However, the slow grind of bureaucratic wheels made it difficult for the industrial partners, who needed a quicker turnaround and stricter attention to the bottom line. This was particularly problematic for small companies that could not afford to wait for the DOE bureaucracy to hammer out a deal. Consequently, 82.5 percent of the funding for lab/industry cooperative agreements at Los Alamos and Sandia National Laboratories went to businesses with more than five hundred employees.[12] Large corporations like General Motors (GM) reaped the most benefit from cooperative research agreements. In a $14 million collaboration with GM and the University of Wisconsin, laboratory researchers are using technology from the Antares project to harden the surfaces of such objects as automobile parts, machine tools, and ball bearings to make them more resistant to wear and corrosion. The process, *plasma-source ion implantation*, forces ions that have been accelerated to high energies into the surface layers of objects, transforming the chemical and physical properties of near-surface layers of the material. The process is being billed as a cleaner process since it doesn't use the chemical solvents involved in conventional electroplating. When President Clinton came to Los Alamos, the first research facility he visited was the site where this experimental technology is being developed.

For small businesses, the bureaucratic delays involved in technology transfer were an unaffordable hardship. For example, Vista Control Systems, a small Los Alamos company established by former laboratory employees, got caught in the squeeze. Their small staff had left the lab, taking technology they had developed and shaping it into a marketable product. In the course of doing a collaboration, they found themselves stalled for eighteen months waiting to sign an agreement. They lost a critical year in the marketing of the technology. Virginia Martz, Joe's wife, works at Vista, designing drawing tools similar to MacPaint that are used in control software. "Basically it's a set of software tools that are used to control hardware," she said. However, they had lost sales due to the fact that the laboratory also had continued to develop the software and was giving it away free as part of a collaboration.

DOE bureaucracy was problematic in other ways. The agency had failed to devise and implement a way to quantify the outcomes of the cooperative research agreements, so as to prove that government dollars were being well spent. It fueled the complaints of a cost-cutting Congress that these collaborations were a form of corporate welfare. The budget for the Technology Transfer Initiative was cut to the bone, to the disillusionment of the researchers who had worked hard building industrial partnerships. This was a further drain on the staff's morale. However, a compromise was worked out in Congress whereby funding would remain for industrial partnerships on the condition that their research would support the laboratory's core mission of national defense. So, research developed jointly by the laboratory and industry would not only benefit the industry, the economy, and presumably the public, it would also be folded back into the laboratory's defense programs.

Meanwhile, the factors that had hampered the laboratory all along still remained—regulatory oversight and its attendant paperwork, and looming budget shortfalls. Recognizing a need to make the national laboratories more efficient, the DOE had announced in February 1994 the Task Force on Alternative Futures for the Department of Energy National Laboratories. Its objective was to examine ten labs in the DOE system and make recommendations for restructuring, redirecting, and streamlining those institutions. The task force would make suggestions for how the nation could best benefit from these national resources in which they had invested. The chairman of the task force was former Motorola CEO Robert Galvin.

The Galvin Task Force, as the group became known, made sweeping recommendations, including one that raised a sigh of relief at Los Alamos. The burden of regulation and bureaucratic paperwork should be lifted from the shoulders of the laboratories if they are to be expected to do valuable work, and the DOE should stop micromanaging these institutions. It was clear that regulation had neither increased productivity nor prevented accidents. At the same time, environmental cleanup, one of the important missions now for the laboratories, had been slow, inefficient, and expensive. The task force also determined that collaborations with industry were not the appropriate focus for the national defense laboratories unless the projects were closely aligned with the missions of the labs. Any economic benefit should be a derivative of those laboratories' performing their core missions. The DOE should sustain and strengthen the kind of long-term fundamental research that is best done at such large-scale facilities as those in the national laboratories.

Hazel O'Leary responded to the task force's recommendations and announced a plan—the Strategic Alignment Initiative—to streamline DOE bureaucracy, while in Los Alamos, Sig Hecker recognized that it was now time to pare away the excessive bureaucracy that the Tiger Team report had wrought in 1991. He announced a new team that would examine the situation and come up with a plan. With continuing budget shortfalls looming, this new plan, Hecker said, would no doubt mean hardship and sacrifice and would probably rival any of the challenges the laboratory had faced in recent years. Jobs would change and some would disappear. The Workforce Productivity Project was announced in June 1995 and recognized that of the 10,173 employees, over half were support positions. Managers had expected the lab's budget to be cut by 10 percent, and by the end of November, 915 of those positions were eliminated, for an estimated savings of $60 million. However, the budget had not been slashed, and the workforce reduction, instead of eliminating technical positions as a previous layoff had done, hit minorities and women especially hard and created an explosion of bitterness and recrimination. The lab was accused of targeting specific groups and performing a force reduction when it was not necessary. Hecker responded by saying that the force reduction was necessary, because the DOE had been all too clear about the need to reduce costs. At the same time, Hecker was worried about losing technical staff, those people who made the laboratory the scientific research institution that it was. Otherwise the lab was in peril of drifting toward mediocrity. "Unless we follow through with our productivity project, we will go out of business as a world-class scientific institution. All that may survive is a 'Jiffy Lube' for nuclear weapons, rather than a great scientific laboratory that can live up to the challenge of science-based stockpile stewardship and one that can serve the nation with distinction in other critical areas," Hecker wrote.

Nevertheless, citing a better financial picture because of savings reaped from the previous layoffs, the lab backed away from another round in 1996 that would have cut as many as five hundred more jobs. Another factor may have been the fact that the always supportive New Mexico congressional delegation had thrown its support to the laid-off workers, not the laboratory. Senators Peter Domenici and Jeff Binga- man and Congressman Bill Richardson prevailed upon the DOE to in- crease the separation packages for the workers who had voluntarily left their jobs. In December, the laboratory's public affairs office issued a press release describing the institution's economic impact on northern New Mexico. It accounted for almost 5 percent of the total economic activity in the state and almost one-third in Los Alamos, Rio Arriba, and Santa Fe counties, where most of the employees live. The report was funded by two major subcontractors of the lab and prepared by an- alysts from New Mexico State University, the Albuquerque office of the DOE, and the University of New Mexico.

Scott Duncan said he thought the laboratory would do fine, com- paring it to a stockbroker who makes money in an up market or a down market. In the lab's case, the up market had been the nuclear weapons buildup of the Cold War, while the down market was dismantlement and cleanup afterward, which would also keep the bright minds of Los Alamos scientists busy for many, many years. Lou Rasocha thinks that the confusion and cynicism of this time will pass and that new genera- tions will come to the lab "and do fantastic things again. I'm hopeful," he mused. "After all, I'm a child of the space age; the space program had just started when I was starting elementary school. Sputnik went up when I was seven years old. It's all I know."

And it is that kind of spirit, Duncan said, the kind of drive and en- thusiasm that characterized the Manhattan Project, that will solve this institution's problems. This current age of accountability and regula- tion had made that seem impossible, said Duncan. But he, too, had hope, citing an example during the Gulf War of the laboratory's ability to still pull off nimble and ingenious coups under extreme pressure. The Defense Department asked Los Alamos to invent technology that could be used to detect chemical and biological warheads. "And our guys said it was going to take a year to get it done, and the DOD said, 'I don't thing so! You've got sixty days.'" So, researchers representing a cross section of disciplines actually fielded LIDAR—for light de- tection and ranging—a laser-based detection system, in just seven- teen days. But it took breaking some rules to get the job done. "It was actually done over the holidays when we were closed," Duncan said. "There were no systems in place to support a project like this." So, as it turned out, warehouse people just threw their keys at the team and said, "Get what you need; we'll figure out the paperwork when we get back." Later, LANL scientists converted the technology for use in detecting air pollutants. The entire experience proved that the spirit that had made the Manhattan Project a success could still be summoned from what was now a much larger and slower organization. Los Alamos had simply grown fat on its own success, illustrating one of Peter Drucker's famous comments, Duncan noted. "Those whom the gods would destroy, they first give forty years of success." At Los Alamos there had been steadily increasing budget lines all the way from the lab's beginnings in 1943 up to about 1986. "And what happens is you get to thinking you're the best in the business, that you know it all. There's no reason to reorganize anything, because God knows, you know everything," Duncan said, grinning. Now, what the laboratory needed to do was recapture that youthful spirit of the Manhattan Project, that spirit of urgency. "But I don't know how you're going to do that without a war."

7

Mechanical
Ants

It's not unusual in successful organizations to find
that the kind of creative eccentricity that helped
to make them great is not easily tolerated by the more sanitized hierar-
chy of hugeness. This can't be said of Los Alamos National Laboratory
as long as there are people like Mark Tilden on staff. Tilden builds robots, and unlike most of the robotic creatures born in labs around the
world, these are made from junk for mere pennies; they move on their
own without the benefit of a computer brain or an umbilical to a main-
frame. Furthermore, Tilden believes that his creations are actually alive.

He was waiting for me in the hallway outside his office on my first
visit and he wasn't at all what I had expected. This man looked more
like a bouncer at a rowdy bar than a laboratory researcher. The six-
foot-two-inch, three-hundred-pound British-born Canadian computer
engineer had broad shoulders, huge muscular arms, and big hands. His
high-speed soliloquies about life, robotics, and the shortcomings of
modern technology—in an accent colored by an English childhood—
made ample use of earthy, self-deprecating humor and an irreverent
attitude toward his employer.

Tilden had been lured away from his job at the University of Wa-
terloo in Canada by Brosl Hasslacher, a researcher with the lab's Center for Nonlinear Studies, who had seen the designer and his robots at
an artificial life show in Santa Fe in 1992. Hasslacher was my escort for
this first visit and, I soon learned, served as the scientist foil for Tilden's
wild-man inventiveness. In fact, Tilden described himself as a sort of
blind watchmaker who knew intuitively how to make the robots work,

while Hasslacher developed the scientific explanations for it all. Tilden's job at Los Alamos was to dream up and build unusual new robotic life-forms. Other researchers are working on robots that mimic simple organisms, but Tilden's use of recycled materials is unique, and he has patented the artificial nervous system that makes his robots work. "This is an example of free, undirected research with the government leaving the scientist alone," Hasslacher said, describing a rarity in this new age of tight budgets and high accountability.

Tilden hustled us into his office and gestured toward a walled platform on the other side of the room. "This is the Robot Jurassic Park," he boomed, pointing down into a pool of sunlight that was populated by a menagerie of motionless widgets. "It's the first of its kind anywhere in the world. These things fight, flock, do all kinds of exotic things," Tilden said. "They're all alive," muttered Hasslacher, a slender, stooped figure with long hair. But nothing seemed to be happening in the pond at the moment, and these wiry creatures looked nothing like our popular image of a robot—neither the dumb mechanical arms that work in factories, nor the anthropomorphic domestic servants and star-traveling androids in science fiction. What they most resembled were insect heads or viruses. Two of them, each equipped with one spindly leg, seemed to be coupled together on some mysterious business of their own. But they really didn't look alive.

People have been trying to build useful intelligent robots for decades, without much to show for it, Tilden said, and that's because they have started with the assumption that you must first build a sophisticated brain for the creature. "They put a powerful computer on a wheelchair, basically. It goes two feet and falls over. Thump. Not good," he shook his finger. "You still can't go out and buy a robot vacuum cleaner, for example. Everybody wants one and nobody has one. And every time anyone, like the Japanese or the Taiwanese, tries to make one, they fail."

Tilden's revolutionary approach has been to build robots that do not have brains at all. He designs autonomous mechanical creatures with silica spinal cords and simple nervous systems that are stimulated by, and react to, information provided by peripheral sensors, while the response is driven by small motors scavenged from cast-off consumer electronics. Their sole purpose is to survive. And they do not bother with the governing laws of robotics, set down by the young Isaac Asimov in his book *I, Robot*, rules that Tilden believes have hampered thus far the development of viable robots. Asimov's rules are:

1. Robots cannot injure humans.
2. Robots will obey all human orders unless they violate law 1.
3. Robots will protect themselves unless this violates laws 1 and 2.

Tilden believes that this construct yields robots that are too paranoid to be useful. His rules for robots are simple: "Feed your ass, protect your ass, and look for better real estate." Such robots will more closely mimic the biological, producing beings that manage to blur the line between what is purely mechanical and what is actually alive. "Parallel life-forms," insisted Hasslacher. The truly useful servant robot may, in fact, turn out to be robot ecologies, similar to the metallic citizens of Tilden's Robot Jurassic Park, or "the pond," as he also called it. Small machines that would have their own jobs and, being solar-powered, would go about their business independently. They could even cooperate, using their combined strength to complete tasks. "And they won't scatter batteries all over the place," Tilden said with a wink. "These things are designed to fight and survive on their way around complex environments, malevolent cats, and stuff like that." This all strikes at the heart of the biggest debate in artificial life, he noted. "What is alive and what isn't? From an engineering point of view, I have my own definition: that which moves for its own purposes."

Tilden wore a look of fatherly pride on his round, mustachioed face as we gazed down at the creatures in the pond. "You'll see everything move eventually," he said. There were over twelve different species and twenty-four different creatures in the pond at the moment. "These robots can't reproduce, they can't think," Tilden said. "But they can live for an obscene amount of time." Some of the pond's occupants had been in continuous operation for thousands of hours. Such longevity is necessary for robot communities to have time to develop. And it leads to something quite startling: unplanned and unexpected behaviors emerge. With this, Tilden believes he is exploring new territory, unknown aspects of artificial life. Since new generations depend upon the actions of the roboticist and not upon natural evolution, he noted, his role is that of a kind of small god, a Lamarckian force of evolution that improves successful features in each generation. "My floor cleaners over there, for example, have gone through seven successive generations, and the eighth is on the way." They are credit-card-size creatures that rove around the floor hunting between sources of light—windows during the day and lamp to lamp at night. In the process, the little brushes on their feet push the dirt to the edges of the room. Tilden has built them to be periodically scared of light, so that they will push the dust into dark corners. "Or if there are any holes in the floor, the dirt gets brushed off it into the apartment below," he said, laughing. "The guy downstairs never complains."

Tilden waved his hand around the office, pointing out the many different life-forms inhabiting it. "I have everything from robot window cleaners, floor cleaners, floppers and walkers, a robotic Venus flytrap, a sixteen-horsepower electric water pistol, good for training dogs. Aggressive glasses that shoot people who smoke," Tilden deadpanned. "I also have the world's first aggressive ashtray." He pointed to an obviously broken thing in what appeared to be a robot cemetery on the shelf. "It was destroyed by a Texan who warn't gonna let no damn machine tell him where he couldn't smoke." Tilden made a silly but recognizable attempt at a Texas drawl.

The rest of the small office was almost entirely taken up by a large, rectangular table neatly filled with the sorts of tools and electronic detritus that you expect of a veteran tinkerer. There was also a video camera and a monitor installed to record the new developments in his robot community. A computer, that Tilden seldom used, he said, except to check his e-mail, sat idle near the back of the room. Along the walls, shelves full of boxes held old tape players and other broken consumer electronic toys that he dissected for parts. And the clock above the door ran backward, a testament, in part, to Tilden's disregard for time.

Meanwhile, on the wall, solar-powered electric wallpaper—made from discarded laptop computers—was busy changing patterns, a process that will continue for up to fifty-six years without repeating itself, Tilden explained. He had built it to find relief from the four windowless concrete walls in his Canadian office. "If there had been a nuclear explosion outside, I would have been the last to know. I'm so glad to have windows now," he said, gazing at the bright New Mexico sunlight streaming into the office. And coursing up and down the glass of the big window over the pond was a spidery metal solar yo-yo. In search of fuel, it coursed over the glass all day. "I'm using the poor creature's self-preservation instinct against itself, like a carrot on a stick," Tilden said. "In the process of trying to get out, it goes over the entire window with its fuzzy little feet and cleans it very well." The seemingly delicate robot had given tireless service through three Canadian winters at Tilden's home, only to be damaged by the movers who brought it to Los Alamos.

Some of Tilden's robots had been created with design input from his cat Ninja. "Cats are usually not dopes," Tilden noted, laughing. "So if a cat responds to something as if it's alive, it's because the cat has basically given it that attribute." Endowed it with life, Hasslacher added reverently. The cat scarer—a spiny creature that could have come from Star Wars—was designed to keep Ninja from eating the black and red plastic-covered wires on Tilden's workbench at home. It stands immobile until it detects the cat's body heat. "Then it starts screaming eeah! eeah!" Tilden said. "Scares the shit out of the cat."

Ninja played a role in the design of the floor cleaners, too. When Tilden first installed them in his apartment, he found upon returning home that they were not doing what he had designed them to do. "They were all on their backs, fuzzy feet in the air, and the cat was licking its paws as if to say, 'Yeah, I killed 'em.'" Tilden's eyes twinkled. The cat had also foiled the designer's earlier attempt to use a conventional robot to help with the housework. He had built a large robotic servant in 1982, and equipped it with a Dustbuster that it would use to vacuum the carpet while he was away. But when he got home he found the robot stalled in the corner of the room. He checked it over thoroughly and couldn't find anything wrong, but later discovered the problem as he lay on the couch one day intending to take a nap. The robot, thinking that its master was out, began to vacuum the rug. Ninja promptly emerged from the bedroom and lay down in front of the device, forcing it to alter its route. Then the cat got up and moved to another position. "Within five minutes my cat had convinced this robot that it was completely surrounded by furniture, causing it to stand there whining until its battery died. Of course, by that time, the cat had already gone back to the bedroom and fallen asleep." The cat had seen through the robot, of course, recognizing it as a stupid presence, something it could not abide, Tilden explained, and so it found the simplest way to eliminate the nuisance. "You can use conventional logic language to teach a robot to recognize a solid object," Tilden said. "But it's impossible to render the concept of a malevolent object." He folded his arms across his chest and chuckled. "Well, if nothing more, robots could be the greatest cat toys in the world."

Finally one of the occupants of the pond moved—a small, ratchety gesture. Tilden pointed to a tiny solar panel on the creature's body. All of the beings in the pond had been fitted with salvaged solar cells that managed to power them, but with such inefficiency that they were forced to sit still for long intervals, building up enough energy to make the next miserly, nearly silent move. "But I call this a feature," beamed Tilden. "Because otherwise, I'd be swapping batteries in them all the time. As it is, they are completely autonomous. Their actions are slow and deliberate, so every time they react to something, it's because they deliberately made that reaction and aren't just bouncing off of walls." Nor is the cat as likely to try and eat them, Tilden added, explaining that this is exactly what had happened to Turbot, now lying in a box in the robot graveyard. "It will never work again because its motors are stuffed full of cat fur," he said, shaking his head. Then he pointed out Turbot II—a four-transistor tetrahedral device that propelled itself around the pond with a single rotating arm. "What a stupid machine," Hasslacher said. "But it could go anywhere." Moreover, Turbot II looked genuinely prickly and menacing. "Actually, this guy's a real *Robotous Rex*," Tilden noted. "He goes wherever the hell he wants, flipping things out of his way. A real nasty little shit."

The obvious application for such aggression would be as a tool of war, and Tilden agreed that his inventions could be used to make terrifying weapons. One Los Alamos scientist mused about such a possibility: an army of tiny robots could creep through tight places unnoticed and assemble themselves into something large and deadly. Reverse Trojan horses, so to speak. Even before Tilden moved to Los Alamos, the U.S. military had approached him about making insectlike hand grenades that would creep up to their target.[1] At Los Alamos, Tilden had turned down cooperative research agreements for robots that could carry bombs across the desert to kill people, as he put it. "It's not easy to turn down your first $3 million, I'll tell ya," he quipped. Both men snickered. "Ethics or obscene quantities of cash?" Tilden crowed, weighing the two choices in outstretched hands. "Do I really need a Porsche? No." He hung his head in mock disappointment and resignation. Hasslacher roared.

Tilden says he wants his inventions to be used only for good. "For example, if you had Turbot II in your sink," he offered with an ornery smile, "you'd never have to worry about a clogged drain again, now, would you?" Then more seriously: "Or if you had one kicking around in your blood, you'd never have to think about clogged arteries." There might be other medical uses for the very smallest of robots, which Tilden had just received clearance to develop. Tiny robotic bugs could be sprinkled on wounds, "and because of their beautiful capillary action, they would become a perfect in-house bandage. Sprinkle, sprinkle, sprinkle, and you would know that you had been healed," Tilden held forth in the style of a revivalist preacher. After they were no longer needed, the creatures would be sloughed off by the body. So-called micro-robots might also be useful in making mechanical repairs in infertile couples, Tilden suggested. And in agriculture, silicon micro-robots could be sent into fields to position themselves on wheat stalks, for example, and bite off the heads of biological pests. Such robots may someday replace chemical pesticides, Tilden enthused, and if any were to make their way into the food supply, not to worry. "If you eat sand, it goes through you; it doesn't get trapped. Your body would reject the robots as if they were grains of sand."

However, truth be told, Tilden doesn't really like the idea of microscale mechanisms, and he has misgivings about really big robots, too. "Tilden's second definition of life," he raised a finger in the air and struck an orator's pose. "That which dies when you stomp on it. I want things that you can see. I really don't want to make robots that go out into space or into our bloodstreams." Lurking at the back of my mind all this time was the question: what if they turned on you? What if all these little parallel life-forms became violent? "They aren't smart enough for that," Tilden said. "They're like gerbils. Are you scared of gerbils?" You might be scared of micro-gerbils, Hasslacher mused. It would be easier to domesticate robots and trick them into doing what we wanted than to train animals, Tilden assured me.

Then he turned abruptly to pick up from his table what he referred to as a more highly evolved creature. It looked like an insect, with four rubber-tipped metal legs, antennae, and a black plastic spine that bore the legend Walkman, having once been part of a tape player. Tilden set it back down on the table, and the four-inch-long mechanical ant immediately began to walk. Reeek, reek, creak. Its legs made small dry metallic sounds as it moved forward. "This little mechanism is obscenely capable," Tilden said. "It's really scary," Hasslacher nodded knowingly, a faint smile on his lips.

Walkman is deceptively trivial; it contains only twelve transistors. "You wouldn't even buy a radio with only twelve transistors," Tilden said. "This thing runs on less energy than a cockroach takes to crack a fart." It had cost forty-five cents to build and had already proved itself capable of using simple stimulus reactions to explore and navigate its environment, adapting its gait, position, direction, and speed to climb over or around the obstacles in its path. "This thing has enough leftover energy not just to move its steely butt around, but to actually do significant quantities of work." The little Walkman could push objects. Furthermore, Tilden could mess with its legs, even tear off a leg or two, and when he put it back down it would sort itself out in a second and move on. "What if it had lasers and glowed in the dark?" Hasslacher wondered.

The day before I visited, a group of people had gathered around Walkman and were laying bets. A psychologist, upon seeing the creature for the first time, backed away and said, "Has it a soul?" An interesting question, Tilden mused. If Walkman and his brethren in the pond were indeed alive, what ethical considerations must be made when using them for human purposes? Should they be put into harm's way, as in one of Tilden's favorite ideas, the creation of robotic teams that could ferret out land mines and blow them up. "We could throw them out of airplanes, the way land mines are seeded, and when they hit the ground they would team up in chains with the heaviest and least intelligent of them in last position, ready to sacrifice itself by detonating the mine. "Another reason not to make them too intelligent," Tilden added. "If you put a robot into a minefield, and it knows it's in a minefield, it's going to be scared of getting blown up. So it's going to be careful." The survivors could be captured and domesticated by native residents of the area, Tilden brainstormed, sending them into their fields to clear out more land mines.

He suggested we take Walkman out into the hallway and see what it could do. He bent down, put it on the floor, and gave it a little nudge with one of his thick fingers, and off it went, feeling its way around corners and backing away from baseboards. Interestingly, this version of Walkman had fewer transistors than its predecessors. "This is one thing that I'm very excited about," Tilden said, explaining that the evolution of this species seemed to necessitate actually moving backward, simplifying instead of becoming more complex. The process seems counterintuitive, he noted, but it proved to increase the robot's ability to survive in complex environments. Walkman could successfully traverse a pile of coat hangers, for example.

Hasslacher stressed that while the structure of Walkman had become simpler in some ways, it was based upon chaos theory, in which a simple beginning could result in surprisingly complex dynamics. By interacting with its environment and surviving, Walkman manages to develop a kind of subcognitive intelligence. Its artificial nervous system was designed such that stimuli changed an internal landscape, creating and destroying links between neurons in a parallel system. In effect, Walkman learns. Furthermore, the advantage of not having a central processor driving everything is that if one part of the robot is damaged, it can still carry on. "We want machines that can take massive damages and say, 'I'm hurt, but I'll do the job.' It's a real Gunga Din," Tilden said. "This is actually really cool." Eventually Tilden would add the solar technology of his pond species to his walking robots. Then he would be able to set Walkman free to see how well he could survive. "Once we have a machine that can look after itself, avoid your dog, stay away from your cat, and avoid getting run over, then you can have it do things like cut the grass or clean the windows," Tilden said. Perhaps someday people will be able to buy a dozen credit-card-size robots that can be tossed down in the house to quietly keep the floor clean or assassinate cockroaches.

Since walking robots have long been considered the most complex challenge, Tilden decided that this would be the best demonstration to take to the artificial life show. He and his creatures ended up being a big hit. "But at first, people came up to me and said, 'Where are your papers? where are your grants? Blah, blah, blah,'" Tilden boomed. "And I said, 'I don't know, but here is the little robot,' and when they feel it struggle in their hands, all of a sudden these stuffy scientists remember what it was like to be eight years old and to want shit like this. Then they started making suggestions: 'Why don't you make it this long, or why don't you give it visual heads and so on, and so on.' That's the thing, you know. Something has to spark people's imaginations first, because, after all, that's really how science moves forward," he said.

Tilden had felt out of place at the artificial life show. "For starters, everyone had a Ph.D. When it came time for me to talk, I really felt like a Johnny-come-lately." He had developed his robots in his spare time without the benefit of an advanced degree, research grants, or even a sympathetic employer. He was told that he had to use vacation time to attend conferences and give talks. When he began to get noticed for his innovations, it was deeply resented by the mathematics faculty, he said. "They had been working unnoticed for twenty years on all their calculations, and there I was in *Scientific American*. Well, duh!" he said, smacking his head, knowing full well that what he was doing was a lot more interesting. "But it turns out that I was the only roboticist who bothered to bring anything to show." He took along a walking robot called the Tally Ho Automatic Bed Wetter, an assassin device that waits beside your bed until you fall asleep. "Then it leaps onto you, piddles and jumps off, going HA, HA, HA!" Tilden boomed. "It was really funny, but robotics is serious stuff," he made a prissy face. "Instead of coming down here and saying, 'This is what I hope to do, send me twenty thousand dollars and I'll give you a paper and a software package,' I *showed* them something."

Meanwhile, Hasslacher was down on the floor of the hallway, watching Walkman explore. The robot was going in circles. Tilden figured out that he had reattached one of the legs backwards. Both men had a good laugh over that. They reminded me of a breed of brainy kids who will spend hours in the basement, tinkering and inventing weird things. And it's just that sort of youthful curiosity that's needed to open doors into new worlds, Tilden explained. His robots often resurrect such long-lost feelings in even the crustiest of scientists when they first lay eyes on them. Indeed, while we were playing with Walkman in the hallway, a physicist who was taking a shortcut through the building did a quick double take and asked, "What the hell is that?" Then he crouched down to watch the bug with Hasslacher, who began to talk about complex systems and chaos theory. "Yeah, yeah, yeah, . . . but what's important," Tilden said in a low voice, leaning toward me, "is that my creatures are reality-reviewed. We can use an oscilloscope to watch the nerve impulses go around, but the great thing is we don't have to look through a microscope and hope that we can figure out by visual perception what's going on. You know what they are because you can feel them struggle in your hand." After the physicist left, Hasslacher explained that the man had been stunned by what he had seen and demanded to know just how the robot worked.

"God! It is so frustrating being a sole prophet," Tilden bellowed, raising his arms in mock exasperation. It isn't as though he is trying to keep the technology a secret. For years now he has preached the principles of his robotics philosophy, labeling them BEAM, an acronym for biology, electronics, aesthetics, and mechanics. Since 1991 he and other like-minded roboticists put on the BEAM Robot Olympics, in which builders from all walks of life enter their inventions in competition. It's an opportunity to compare notes and ultimately to improve the state of robotics technology, but it's also a chance for budding young roboticists to excel. "Seven-year-old girls routinely beat out MIT professors," Tilden proudly explained. The competition includes the high jump, drag races, sumo wrestling, and micro-mouse, a race through a maze. The entries are judged according to the BEAM principles, and the novelty of their design, their power efficiency, the quality of their hardware, and the sophistication of their behavior. Most of all, the event must be fun.

One of the great things about building biological robots, Tilden said, is these creatures exhibit behaviors that are comfortable for humans to live with. The walkers, for example, exhibit useful body language. You can understand and predict their next move by looking at them. That's not the case with the clunky wheeled robots, for example, that were designed to wheel up and down corridors delivering mail, Tilden said. "Everybody hated them, and they didn't work very well." And the solar-powered robots bear a touching similarity to the wake/ sleep cycle of biological creatures, he continued. "Like when the sun comes up on my Robot Jurassic Park," he said. "All you hear is 'psst, psst, zzzt zzzt zzzt.' You'd think it would very distracting, but it isn't. It's like waking up in the forest, where things are moving all the time. I listen to these things, and they're not even as stupid or as predictable as the ticking of a clock. You can get used to it."

Unlike his little robots, Tilden's mind has a hard time standing still at all; he's always thinking of new ideas for his growing menagerie. Each time I went back to visit, his creatures had made stunning evolutionary leaps, a rate of progress made possible not only by his fertile imagination but also by his work ethic. He puts in long days and nights—"Office hours are ten 'til ten," he said, with a deep chuckle. He had recently learned that in his early thirties he was suffering from high blood pressure and might have to think about slowing down. It pissed him off, he said. "If I never get married, if I never have kids, these little robots will go on without me for a while. At least I hope so." He was suddenly embarrassed by his candor and shouted, "Oh, my God! Waxing philosophic, we are!"

The price for being such an oddball, though, was that Tilden seemed lonely. He didn't like the Los Alamos women he'd met and hadn't taken time to explore New Mexico. When he looked around at the spectacular landscapes surrounding Los Alamos, he got the names of the mountains wrong. And he was having trouble adjusting to Los Alamos culture. One time at dinner in a Los Alamos restaurant filled with other researchers he complained loudly about the typical lab personality—dry, boring, and obsessed with work. In fact, Tilden believed they had all sold their souls. He leaned across the table and said, "You know, Los Alamos actually means lost souls." A couple nearby, still wearing their security badges, glared at us. Tilden especially liked this restaurant; he was friendly with the waitress, who teased him about his voracious appetite. His best friends, so far, he said, were the secretaries in his office building. In fact, he has invented a five-foot-tall walker named Bigman that can walk down the hall to fetch his secretary. It had been Tilden's youthful dream to create a robot that could march into the village and abduct women, he said. However, he had wisely compromised and created a Bigman that politely summoned the secretary. Tilden liked to think of himself as the world's first robobiologist, and the final line of his résumé said it all: I wish to be the world's first robot scientist who means it when he says, "Go my creature and destroy the unbelievers in the village." He was just joking, he said, waving his hands in the air. "If you can't have a laugh, what the hell are you doing?"

8

The Black Hole

The tolerance in Los Alamos for wildly eccentric personalities extends well beyond the laboratory's walls into the neighborhoods and hearts of the greater community. "We've had some real nuts around here," as Manhattan Project physicist J. Carson Mark once put it.[1] Clearly one of the nuts the community tolerates is Ed Grothus, who likes to call himself Eduardo de Los Alamos and has lived in the town since 1949, when he arrived there to work as a machinist in the weapons program. During an intense personal crisis in the late 1960s Grothus left the laboratory; he had come to oppose the Vietnam War and would soon develop deep misgivings about the mission of the laboratory. He emerged from this time as a vocal and lonely protester against the powerful company in this company town. Many residents described him as a pain in the ass, akin to the troublesome uncle whose quirks are tolerated only because he's part of the family. Grothus writes prickly letters to the editor of the local newspaper, discussing a variety of topics, ranging from nuclear weapons to sexuality. On October 31 in 1991 and 1992, he nailed a parchment manifesto to the door of St. Francis Cathedral in Santa Fe, demanding of Pope John Paul II that the Catholic Church reform its teachings on human sexuality. Later he published the manifesto in *Playboy*.

But above all, Ed Grothus is a peace activist, speaking out against the laboratory where he had happily worked for twenty years. "God, we had fun! And then, throughout the fifties we were building the H-bomb. We were all cold warriors."[2] But, while other lab employees who grew uncomfortable with the mission usually moved away, Ed

Grothus stuck with the place that had become his home, albeit suggesting in a 1980 statement to the county council that the town be renamed Buchenwald II. A local history teacher once asked in a quiz what Baltimore journalist of the 1920s had "ridiculed all of the institutions held dear by the average American," and got back from one student the answer "Ed Grothus." The boy got credit for the answer. Outsiders often ask Grothus why he doesn't move away; some town residents wish he would. "But where would I go?" he replies, mystified by the question. "All of my friends are here, and all of my enemies." So, whenever I asked people in town who I should meet, they often sighed and grudgingly said, "Ed Grothus."

Besides being the self-appointed conscience of Los Alamos, the robust, ruddy-faced grandfather—now in his seventies with a thick shock of unruly white hair—makes a living from a quirky salvage business called the Los Alamos Sales Company. Ironically, it is built upon the excesses of the very laboratory Grothus opposes, trading in vast quantities of discarded technical equipment that has been sold at auction for a fraction of the price originally charged to the American taxpayer. "I refer to it as nuclear waste," Grothus said. "In a different sense than you would normally think of it, of course." His enemies will say, "How well and good for Eduardo de Los Alamos to now be a peacenik after he's made a bloody fortune off of all the things that he was recycling from the laboratory," and "All of the things that he had in his business were the direct result of the work of the laboratory and his participation in it." Millions of dollars worth of vacuum tubes, test equipment, cryogenic tanks, laser components, fiber optics, faucets, phones, racks, desks, and spaghetti tangles of black cables and hair-fine wire are piled to the rafters of an old Shop 'N' Cart grocery store and an abandoned A-frame Evangelical Lutheran church building. There are laboratory clamps, ring supports, pH meters, files for glass slides, rubber stoppers, fine mesh sieves, and a small mountain of typewriters. "When I worked at the lab I thought, 'Jeez, if I could only have one of these nice typewriters.' Now I've got a hundred of them, and I can't give 'em away." The flood of techno-trash spills out onto the parking lot, prompting neighbors and local government to label the establishment an eyesore and demand its removal.

Grothus isn't the only person in town who amasses huge quantities of technical flotsam, though. "Other people have their garages filled with this stuff," he said. "They've got it under their beds and every-where else." Mark Tilden laughingly called this a sex-linked disorder, with males overwhelmingly the victims of the technical hoarding disor-der. "There's a guy in White Rock who has totally filled his house and garage with the stuff. It's amazing," Tilden said. However, Grothus is the undisputed king of Los Alamos techno-trash.

He prefers to call his stockpile "the artifacts of the nuclear age." He has lent items to movie and television production companies for use in *Silkwood*, *The Manhattan Project*, and *White Sands*, for example. "And they sent it all back to me!" Grothus moaned, as though the castoffs were adult children who refused to leave home. The equipment also finds its way to money-strapped science departments at universities and has been shipped by the truckloads to such small countries as Taiwan and Costa Rica. "My dream was that I would find a few Third World countries that could take advantage of all this," he said, making a grand sweeping gesture toward the racks, tubes, and tanks moldering in the shadows of the Ponderosa pines that ring the parking lot. "I'd love to sell it all to them. Los Alamos is so damned rich, and maybe there should be a few places like it in the world, places that have such lavish funding and cutting-edge technology," he allowed. "But it begets this kind of waste."

Much of the surplus at the Los Alamos Sales Company had been jettisoned by the laboratory after the devastating Tiger Team visit in 1991. Things were thrown away so fast, and Grothus snapped up so much of it, that it quickly accumulated on his properties. Some of the stuff is timeless basic hardware that has never been used. "Brand new in their boxes," Grothus said, affronted. He held up a handful of parts from a bin. "Here, look at these. The finer ones can cost fifty dollars and I gave a hundred for all of them. There's no reason why they shouldn't put some of this stuff back into stock; it's not obsolete, you know."

Grothus is a natural showman, who answers his phone with a flour-ish, "Good afternoon, Los Alamos Sales Company. This is the Black Hole," another name he applies to his business. He has erected a sign on the front of the Shop 'N' Cart with an artist's idea of a black hole, a swirling vortex dotted with chunks of technical equipment. "By the way, I get more publicity than anyone else in this town," claimed Grothus, who keeps careful track of the articles and books in which he appears and is ready to pass out photocopies to writers who show any interest at all. He asked me to sign his guest book. "Did you see me on CNN or TBS? The CNN piece wasn't that good, but Turner Broadcasting did a half-hour show that, at least from my point of view, was better. There was more of me," Grothus said. "I've got copies of this stuff if you're interested." One local minister said it as kindly as he could: "Ed's a narcissist, an egomaniac who lives off the media, feeding off the attention he gets. If people ignored him he would die from heartbreak in a couple of months."

Grothus had unearthed for me a *Scientific American* article that had been written about him, but then laid it down somewhere while we were walking around. "You put things down in here and they're lost forever," he said, shaking his head. While much of the salvage had been organized by type, the unheated Shop 'N' Cart looked like a jumble. The place had the sharp odor of an old machine shed—brass, aging rubber, plastic, insulation, machine oil, solvents, and dust. But what it really amounted to was a kind of loony technical history of Los Alamos National Laboratory. And, indeed, for years Grothus had dreamed of creating such a museum, housing it in a fourteen-story building that he quixotically imagined media mogul Ted Turner could be persuaded to build for him. With Radio Free Truchas on the top, Grothus added, his eyes twinkling. Truchas refers to a mountain peak that shimmers in the hazy distance beyond the Rio Grande Valley. "We could set up a real nice nuclear museum here." He wrote letters to Turner and even tried to make his case in person when the Atlanta businessman and his wife, Jane Fonda, attended an environmental conference in Albuquerque. He had thrust copies of all the letters he had sent them into Fonda's hands, but to no avail.

Another Grothus dream was the establishment of the Omega Peace Institute, to be housed in the abandoned church. According to a 1973 brochure, it would be "a scientific community . . . dedicated to projects that will benefit mankind." Grothus hoped to attract radical young scientists who would work on problems related to energy, food production, pollution, and waste reclamation. At the time, he told a Santa Fe reporter that odds were "a thousand to one against us," and, as it turned out, he was right. The A-frame church is now filled with junk. Ed Grothus is for all the right things, said that same local minister, but nobody wants him on their side.

As we toured the Black Hole, Grothus poked through layers of debris, pulling objects from what seemed to be a geological time scale of technical progress in which the smoothly finished mahogany cases of outdated test equipment might just as well have been dinosaur fossils from some Mesozoic rock bed. A large periodic table of the elements hung from the ceiling. There was a DANGER sign nailed to the wall, and it seemed appropriate. A misstep or injudicious digging could yield an avalanche.

We came to a luminous grouping of metals and Plexiglas at the back of the store; Grothus called it his "sculpture section," having thoughtfully stocked it with objects that might appeal to the Santa Fe artists who frequent the warehouse in search of baubles to incorporate into their work. Freelance tinkerers also pop in to find deals on equipment they need for their home-brew experiments, while a fair number of tourists show up, too—all part of the strange parade that is drawn into the vortex of the Black Hole.

On one normal day at the Los Alamos Sales Company a local woman stopped in to buy scientific equipment for experiments she was doing at home. Santa Fe artist Ericka Wanenmacher arrived to hunt for materials, bringing with her Tom Jennings, a computer specialist from San Francisco who is known for having written the software for FidoNet, a bulletin board intended to provide inexpensive public access to e-mail and e-news. He showed me his tattoos—a graphic bullet hole peeking through the close-shorn pale hair on the back of his head; there was a snake tattoo twined around his leg. Meanwhile, an engineer stopped by to borrow something from Grothus and struck up a conversation. He was a gentle, soft-spoken man who bowed over my hand when we met, and he gave me the phone number of someone who could fill me in on the activities of witches and devil worshipers in Los Alamos, an old rumor about the town that no one ever seems to pin down. And another tinkerer walked in looking for sheet metal. "This is great," said Grothus. "The whole town's going to be here by the end of the day."

Wanenmacher wanted to go over to the church and look around, so Grothus suggested we all go. "I'll say mass," he said. The artist explained that this is kind of what Grothus does. He worships technology, just as the town does, and it was the sad irony at the heart of the aging technician's existence that technology was being used for all the wrong reasons. There is a strong streak of the evangelist in Ed Grothus, and the old A-frame church was as much a shrine to technology as it was a warehouse, with Grothus as the high-tech priest. He had dropped out of traditional religion, calling it a curse. "More people get killed by religious wars than any other thing." He, the oldest child in a large family, blamed the church for his mother's sufferings, hence the sexual reformation statement, in which he declared that "artificial contraception is neither evil nor sinful and that it is wrong for the church to make even a married couple feel guilty if they use any form of artificial birth control." He testified at the World Uranium Hearing in Salzburg, Austria, in September 1992, protesting the use of nuclear energy. "I point to the sun, the hollering sun, and say, 'That is the only good nuclear reaction around. The site is ideal, ninety-three million miles away, and its operation is infinite as far as we are concerned. Man will survive if he can learn to live within the parameters of that power generation station.'"[3] Of course, this is heresy in Los Alamos, Grothus noted.

The man's inclination to take on such big enemies—the Catholic Church, the military-industrial complex, the nuclear power industry, Los Alamos National Laboratory—seemed to be an integral part of his personality. His David-and-Goliath style may be what so endears him to outsiders. He surely must know what he's up against, and yet he stays on, trying to be at least a faint excoriation on the thick skin of the institution that dominates his town. At the same time, he keeps monuments to technical achievement. In his home, the first modern adobe structure in Los Alamos, he displays a picture of himself standing next to Glenn Seaborg, the man who discovered plutonium and later became the chairman of the Atomic Energy Commission. Also on the wall hangs a picture of the mesa taken from space by *Skylab 2*. Grothus traced the lines of the canyons with his finger, pointed to Omega Bridge, which crosses a deep gorge between the town site and the laboratory. "And here's my house, and the water tower, . . ." Grothus said softly. Unlike some of the antilab, antinuclear protesters who make their way to the town, march in front of the buildings, wage protests next to Ashley Pond, and deny their own reliance upon modern technology, Grothus still believes it can make life better. He isn't afraid of low-level radiation, for example, and believes that the laboratory is careful about what it releases into the environment. "I have never been wild-eyed about it," he said. "Perhaps because of my twenty years in the lab, working with depleted U-238. We really don't know what kind of nuclear particle triggers cancer in you or me." He agrees with many lab scientists that chemical pollution is more worrisome than low-level radiation. He is not unsympathetic to some of the challenges the lab has been facing. "They have just been crippled by all of the health, safety, and environmental rules and regulations. They can't mix two chemicals without getting permission to do it and all kinds of paper-work. It's really awful." However, he is dead set against the high-level nuclear waste that results from nuclear power and weapons production.

Grothus pointed out an object on a shelf near a window—a prickly-looking device of the type used to measure the hydrodynamics of im-plosions during the 1950s. Grothus had built it himself during his time at the lab. It was one of the tools they used to determine what would happen during a one-point failure. The device looked somewhat like an old broadcast microphone, with wire spikes of various lengths sticking out of it—weird sculpture. During an implosion, the wires, connected to capacitors and resistors, would send blips of information to oscillo-scopes and be recorded for later study. "You could calculate the speed of the implosion and the kinds of pressures involved," Grothus said. "Sometimes you'd get a flood of debris flying ahead, but what you wanted was a nice smooth, clean implosion to maximize the effect of the bomb." Eventually, this technology would be replaced. The infor-mation would be fed directly into computers, Grothus said. The oscil-loscopes are part of the laboratory waste piled up in his warehouses.

Grothus had used his technical knowledge to build his home—a highly energy-efficient structure that still retained the character of the Southwest architectural style. The house stood out from the other structures that Los Alamos residents built when the federal govern-ment allowed them to finally own property and build their own homes. Most of the homes looked like they had been imported from the mid-western towns many of the lab's employees had come from. The Grothus house has sixteen-inch walls, a sloping roof with heated *canales*, the drainage canals in the roof of a traditional adobe home that often freeze up in winter. The tile floor design is inlaid with adapted traditional Indian symbols—the roadrunner, the zia or sun sign, moun-tains, and lightning and thunder, while near the fireplace, a magnetic fish mobile drifts into alignment with the earth's own magnetic force lines. The logs and branches that formed the woven ceiling were peeled and prepared by Grothus's wife Margaret, a dignified, white-haired woman who runs another of the family's businesses, the Shalako Shop, a gift store offering traditional Indian crafts and a smattering of Grothus's antinuclear postcards and other materials. The couple raised five children in Los Alamos.

During our tour of the A-frame church, Grothus stepped over coils of black electrical cord to get to the pulpit, where he turned and raised his arms, addressing the chapel: "All of these things are my congregation," he intoned. "I charge them to go home . . . but none of them go away?" He shrugged and walked down to where Wanenmacher and Jennings were picking through the parishioners—piles of equipment in the place where pews should have been. Grothus had recently tried, under pressure from local government, to get rid of large quantities of his inventory, having signed a contract with a man who was going to liquidate it for him, but the deal had gone wrong. The contractor had failed to sell more than $750 worth of equipment. The contract was bought out by another person, who ended up calling in the Environmental Protection Agency (EPA), claiming that the site was terribly polluted with hazardous chemicals. There were pathetic pictures of Ed Grothus standing near his cordoned-off warehouses in the local newspapers. For a time, yellow tape was stretched around the Black Hole, the church, the apartments where Grothus had some things stashed, and two other warehouses in town. The EPA finally concluded that while there were dangerous chemicals on-site—PCBs in capacitors, asbestos on the pipes in the Shop 'N' Cart, and ferric cyanide stored in one of the warehouses—nothing was leaking into the environment or posing any hazard. The whole affair served to get a color picture of Grothus on the front page of the *Albuquerque Journal*, but it also induced the second contractor to walk off the job and sue Grothus for breach of contract. Meanwhile, the cream of Grothus's collection had been skimmed away, he said. He seemed to mourn most the loss of the Antares tubes, huge cylinders of quarter-inch-thick highly polished steel that had been part of the dismantled Star Wars project at the lab. He'd bought them from the laboratory when the Antares project was dismantled, and later sold some of them back, "saving them a million dollars in the process," he claimed. The salvagers had cut the tubes apart with plasma torches and sold them as scrap, a stunning waste, as far as Grothus was concerned. Most recently, a Grothus stunt yielded more press coverage and a visit from the Secret Service. Two agents from Albuquerque paid a visit to the Black Hole after Grothus mailed cans of "organic plutonium" to President Clinton for Christmas 1996. The cans didn't really contain plutonium, of course, but rather canned corn or beans that Grothus had bought on sale and relabeled. Grothus, who sells the cans for five dollars, made sure to ask reporters to show up on the occasion of the hourlong visit by the Secret Service agents, whom he described as "very nice people."[4]

The local woman had come to Grothus looking for a dewar, a vacuum bottle that is used in laboratories to contain liquefied gases. Preparing to return to the Black Hole where these were stored, Grothus turned and asked Wanenmacher to pull the door shut behind her as she left. "But I tell people that mine is the only place in the world where shoplifting is encouraged."

As we walked back across the parking lot, past the semi-truck trailers that were also stuffed with hardware, I tried to get the woman to tell me why she needed to buy a dewar. "I want to keep some biological samples in it," she said, giggling. "I'm just a housewife that happens to be married to one of those crazy scientists, and I guess it must have rubbed off on me." She'd had some science in college, she said, but hadn't wanted to pursue a career because it would mean leaving her home and family. But at some point she had realized she knew enough to strike out on her own with research projects. "I'm interested in biology and physics, but I can't tell you any more, because it's top secret," she leaned toward me as her words trailed off into a whisper. Grothus showed her a variety of dewars, noting that out in the parking lot there was a huge fiberglass dewar—nine feet in diameter and twelve feet deep—that had cost the laboratory $180,000, he said. It wasn't what the woman needed, of course, but he just wanted to mention it to her. She tilted her head to the side and thought for a moment, then replied that what she really needed was something that she could carry around on her own. He showed her an assortment of aluminum and steel vessels of different sizes and finally pointed to a fifty-liter stainless-steel dewar that he thought might be too big, actually, but it certainly was a nice one. "This is a sperm or semen dewar that they use for artificial insemination of cows or horses," Grothus said. "You don't want that." She gave it a whack with her fist, making a deep, muffled booming sound. "Well, why not?" she asked. "I guess it depends on what you're trying to do?" Grothus probed. The woman giggled again, and said she'd take the big stainless-steel job because it came with sperm holders. "I want a hundred and fifty dollars for it," Grothus said, eyebrows raised. The housewife pulled a roll of hundred dollar bills out of her purse. "I'll put it in a bag for you, ma'am," Grothus quipped. "Paper or plastic?" By this time I was just dying to know what she was working on and asked her again to tell me. She laughed hard this time, a snorting, gasping laugh, and said, "I knew I shouldn't have started talking to you." Her relatives no longer wished to hear about her experiments, she said. "I guess they consider it unusual." I went along as Grothus carried the dewar to the woman's car, and as she drove away, he shook his head and said, "I don't know about that lady. She buys some weird stuff. But then, this is the place to come for that."

Wanenmacher and Jennings had found a few things to buy, including a small bottle of luciferin for the artist. Luciferin is a pigment that emits light when it oxidizes. It's what makes fireflies glow. Wanenmacher had already incorporated a small bottle of luciferin from Los Alamos National Laboratory into a work that was currently on exhibit at a gallery on Canyon Road in Santa Fe. She had decided that the laboratory used this substance from bioluminescent beings in the making of nuclear weapons. Grothus pointed out that this wasn't really true, but the artist said her work was a metaphor for the work of Los Alamos. Wanenmacher's luciferin piece consisted of a polished wooden box, opened to reveal in one half a lens, a diagram of a bomb, and a diagram of a lightning bug, while in the other half a copper Lucifer, the archangel who fell from heaven, was twined around a glass cube containing the tiny bottle of luciferin.

At the end of the afternoon, Wanenmacher left with Jennings in his 1963 Rambler Classic; it was fueled by a propane tank fastened to the roof and had the words THE SPERM MOBILE painted on the side. We were all leaving, and Grothus, for the moment, was left standing alone in the parking lot.

9

Too Many
Ph.D.'s

Los Alamos has always been a community of odd
ducks, with skewed demographics going back
to the Manhattan Project, when many of the world's brightest engineers and physicists found themselves holed up on a remote plateau behind high fences that were guarded by armed military police. This was
unnerving for some of the Europeans, who found it too much like a
concentration camp. Today the guard tower sits empty, the military police are gone, and there are no longer locked gates across the roads into
town, but the skewed demographics still remain. "Too many Ph.D.'s,"
according to people in town, even Ph.D.'s themselves. And, indeed, the
town boasts the highest number of Ph.D.'s per capita in the world, and
the lab has a higher concentration of physicists than at any other institution in the United States. Furthermore, the overall education level in
the populace is high, with fully 53.4 percent of Los Alamos adults college-educated, the highest of any city or town in the nation. But, even .
though education is extremely important to the community, it is considered crass to address someone as "Doctor" unless he or she is a
physician. The practice began during the Manhattan Project when the
purpose of the laboratory and the identities of the researchers were
carefully guarded. It's one of the factors contributing to the studied informality that pervades the town.

The homogeneity of the community is both a strength and a weak-
ness, said Dale Arnink, pastor of the Unitarian Church of Los Alamos
since 1976, who is disturbed by the fact that there are so few minorities
living in the community. He blames the filtration system of the educa-

tional process for the absence of cultural diversity. However, the town is surrounded by other cultures, who are increasingly vocal about the disparities Los Alamos represents. The community and the laboratory were accused of racism, particularly when the recent waves of layoffs focused on the large numbers of minority workers who made up support staff at the laboratory. At the high school, controversy erupted over a mural depicting the school mascot, Topper Man, who was making what Hispanics considered a racist gesture with his hand. And when thirty-eight teachers were hired in Los Alamos County during the 1994–1995 school year, only one was a minority member. The previous academic year had been similar. After decades of simmering silence, the cultural diversity that lapped at the edges of the mesa was now boiling with discontent. "We up here, including myself, often don't have a real grasp of what people who aren't like us are going through, or how it looks to them. And so I think there is a naiveté about the world we live in because of our homogeneity. We don't hear those other voices as much as we ought to. Not often enough and forceful enough to change us," Arnink said.

There are some positive aspects to the community's homogeneous makeup in terms of education and temperament, however, Arnink said. People tend to speak the same language and approach problems in the same way, resulting in a kind of intellectual clarity and efficiency that can be very useful, he said. However, it also made for some peculiar local government. For example, he noted with a chuckle, "when the county council addresses an issue, there are minds that are ready to analyze it to the nth degree and figure out exactly what the options are and what the game plan should be for solving the problem." This same approach didn't work well when it came to solving family problems, however. When he counsels families he occasionally finds that at least one member thinks that this same strategy can be applied to matters of the heart. "And so often you can't sort out emotions that way and come up with a game plan to fix what's wrong in the family," Arnink explained.

Los Alamos is also a community in which education is considered very important. Many of the professionals here have risen to their positions from lower-middle-class rural or urban backgrounds, Arnink said, "and they are proud of their educations, their positions, their incomes, and their comfortable lifestyles," he said. But they worry a lot about their children being able to achieve in the way that they did. "So, by God, their kids are going to go to college," Arnink laughed. Their children may not have to be scientists, but they have to be educated persons. Education is a kind of idol in this community, he noted. "And yet, we can't get parents to come to PTA," said laboratory archivist Roger Meade. "There's very little involvement by parents. They see the importance of investing in a Ph.D., but not in elementary education."

All of this makes for an unusual environment in which to live, most especially for the children. Joe Martz and his wife, Virginia, both grew up in Los Alamos, children of lab employees—Joe's father a statistician and Virginia's an electrical engineer. They enjoy the safe and easygoing atmosphere of a small town that happens to have an unusual number of cultural benefits for a community of fewer than twenty thousand people. Art exhibits, orchestra concerts, plays, and lecture series find their way to the top of the mesa with pleasing regularity, Joe said. And within the community, an avid interest in music, art, and theater accounts for some lively local entertainment. Joe liked to describe it as the small-town American dream, and it irked him that the rest of the world didn't always see it that way.

We were sitting in a booth at the Hilltop Diner, its decor a cozy interpretation of the Manhattan Project era, with knotty pine walls adorned with old skates, coffee tins, bottles of 7UP and Choco-cola, a wooden milk box from the Hillside Dairy—"Right from Moo to You!"—and above each wooden booth a framed photograph from the 1940s. Near the door, group shots of the Atomic Energy Commission watch over the cash register with Cold War intensity. The little restaurant was crowded with noisy lab employees, as it is every weekday at noon.

"Here's what you should have," Joe said, pointing out what he considered the best things on the menu, and turned to get the attention of a waitress. He muttered that we would have to talk very slowly to her. "Contrary to what you might have read, Los Alamos was a nice place to grow up," said Virginia, a petite, gentle woman with russet hair. She had grown up a few houses away from Ed and Margaret Grothus. "I don't know how many times Margaret picked me up and patched my scrapes when I fell down on my skates in front of her house," Virginia said. Joe had played bridge with Ed. "A smart boy," said Grothus, who thought highly of Joe.

The Martzes resented the way the outside world portrayed their tight-knit community and pointed to an article that had appeared in *Time* magazine over fifteen years ago. Virginia was still upset about it. "I really am, because it was so unfair," she said earnestly. The article had painted Los Alamos as a community of remote, overachieving male scientists whose educated wives had become alcoholics out of sheer boredom and whose children were subjected to tremendous pressure to succeed in school. "A supercharged college-bound boy shocked his demanding father by announcing that if he had to live his life over again, he would like to try it as a Teddy bear—so he could be hugged," the story concluded.[1] A headline in the *New Mexican*, a Santa Fe newspaper that isn't always friendly to the laboratory and Los Alamos, read, "Time Magazine Does a Hatchet Job on Los Alamos." And that is the prevailing opinion in the town. Several residents of Los Alamos mentioned the article when I spoke with them, and in the minds of many younger residents, it served as a symbol for all the wrongheaded ideas the outside world had about their little town. Paula Dransfield, whose father was a Manhattan Project scientist, said that she had canceled her subscription to *Time* that day and never looked at the magazine again.

Of course, this wasn't the first time an unflattering article had been written about Los Alamos. The Historical Society keeps fat file drawers full of them, some so far off the mark that they're funny. The most egregious error of all is found in a piece titled "Terror Town Is Working for Peace," written for the *London Telegraph* in 1979. It described Los Alamos as an eerie ghost town "with sagebrush blowing between the shacks," and suggests that Trinity Site—where the first atomic bomb was tested—lies just over the horizon. The radiation is "still so intense that twenty minutes is the maximum safe stay." Trinity Site is located two hundred miles to the south near Alamogordo, New Mexico. The story claimed that "when workers get into their cars at the end of the day and speed out of Los Alamos, they seem glad to leave behind the deadly place."

The reference librarians at Mesa Public Library also keep a file at hand with a bibliography of such articles collected over the decades. There seem to exist in the town both the need to keep secret and safe and also the desire to be understood and validated. This creates a palpable tension in a small society to whom it seems to matter very much what the world writes about it. Nevertheless, it's a chore sometimes to get people to talk to you. "What sort of book are you writing?" asked local newspaper writer Karen Brandt, a weary suspicion in her voice. "Frankly, people in Los Alamos are tired of writers breezing into town and doing hatchet jobs on the laboratory and the community. You'd better figure out some way to convince them up front that you want to write the truth, or no one is going to talk to you," she warned.

Joe and Virginia wanted to talk. They invited me to their home, a modern-looking structure a couple of blocks from downtown. It was built by a physicist, "and it shows," Martz said with admiration. The house used solar energy to heat water for the household, and an expanse of glass along the back looked out at the beginnings of a deep canyon that is the tributary of Los Alamos Canyon, the breathtaking view that you see when you drive up the side of the mesa on the main road, New Mexico Highway 502. The house is nearly hidden from view on the street side, being at the bottom of a short, steep drive and surrounded by trees. While it's right in the middle of everything, it has a secluded feeling, too, Joe pointed out.

The couple's three dogs greeted us at the door, jumping and barking. Joe quickly steered me down the stairs to a lower level, to get out of the hubbub, but also to show me some of his photos, taken underwater during diving expeditions. He and Virginia, a software designer for a laboratory contractor, are serious hobbyists. They share an avid interest in model building, deep-sea diving, and racing cars, while Joe loves underwater photography. He wanted to show me a picture of Virginia taken against the backdrop of a coral wall. She was holding a sponge, and a small fish had just darted out to nip at her hat, so that the picture Joe snapped was of a startled Virginia, wide-eyed and looking sideways at the fish; in surprise, she had just exhaled a luminescent bubble of air. This is one of Joe's favorite pictures.

We went upstairs and out onto the deck overlooking the canyon. Fog was wrapped around the tops of the pine trees below, and in the far distance were the peaks of the Sangre de Cristo Mountains. The view dramatically contradicts the notion that this is a closed, intolerant, and secretive community. You can see for many miles through clear mountain air. "Although, I used to think it was a very close-minded place with a narrow set of opinions and ideas," Joe said. "But then I got out into the world a bit, spending two years living in San Francisco and four years in Texas; I came to realize that our town is one of the most open in this country." Joe had gone to graduate school in Berkeley, a place that has a reputation for accepting all ideas, he noted wryly. "But I found them the most closed-minded community of all. If you didn't have their particular set of ideas and didn't agree or conform with those ideas, you were very much an outcast." Joe's ideas about plutonium and nuclear weaponry provoked a protest on the occasion of his first graduate seminar in 1987. "I had the word *plutonium* in the title. They were not at all happy about the idea of a Berkeley graduate working at Los Alamos on plutonium, of all things!" The incident had had a profound effect on Joe. "I think one understanding and knowledgeable person working inside the laboratory can make more of a difference than tens of thousands of activists on the outside holding signs," he said. The Berkeley incident also forced him to see his hometown in a completely new light. "Take someone like me. My ideas about reducing nuclear weapons and our reliance on them might seem pretty radical for a community that's had their livelihood based for fifty years on the design and production of those devices. And yet I feel very accepted and receive a lot of support from friends and casual acquaintances."

Joe believes that such acceptance exists because the laboratory draws people from all over the world—"the best and the brightest," he called them—with the common bond that they are intellectuals who are self-starting achievers. "It's not the staid, conservative, white-collar Caucasian male community that people think it is," he said. Although, I thought it was understandable that people might get that impression when they visit the laboratory and the town. The face that the community presents to outsiders is still mainly white.

But the resentment of surrounding communities encloses the highly educated and well-paid Los Alamos enclave like a dark sea. For years protesters of various stripes have spray-painted insults on the highways and the signs leading into town. One favorite graffiti read, MORMONS RUN LANL!—a reference to the time when several of the lab's upper administrators were members of the Mormon Church. "There was this false perception that there was some sinister takeover plot," Joe said. "But the best part is that somebody went around about a week after the signs appeared and erased all the second M's in the word, so that the signs now read, MORONS RUN LANL!" The community loved it. In recent years, the graffiti—such as DOE KILLS—had disappeared from the roadways. "And maybe that's a measure of the progress we're making in opening up communications?" Joe wondered. "Maybe people are beginning to understand?"

Growing up in an environment where condemnations of your parents' work are spray-painted on the highways, and where protesters accused them of being warmongers and killers, is only part of the unusual pressure that is placed upon the children of Los Alamos, and that comes from outside of the community. The greatest pressure comes from within—from the community, from within families, and within individuals themselves. The thing that is most difficult for Los Alamos to accept is mediocrity.

"Yeah, there are pressures here," Virginia said, "but it's partly because you've got a whole community of parents who have succeeded, and so they want their children to succeed and they expect a lot of them." The high school is challenging and the competition can be brutal, Joe explained. "Going away to college is actually a kind of decompression, a relief. In many ways it's much easier, once you've managed to survive our high school. I don't know whether that's good or bad." Virginia had decided that overall this was a good thing. "At least it was for me," she said. "I wasn't one of the top students here and I had to work very hard. At college I suddenly became one of the top students and my ego went up like that," she said, zooming her hand into the air like a rocket. But that's because Virginia is naturally gifted with high self-esteem, Joe said, smiling slightly as he looked across at his wife. "You will probably find this surprising, but I have an exceptionally low self-esteem," said Joe, who had experienced unusual success for one so young. During our long conversations he had unblushingly described the honors he'd won, his recognition as an expert on various aspects of plutonium science and nuclear weapons. I had grown accustomed to the ferocious egos of so many of the people I met at the laboratory, and it actually surprised me to hear this from Joe.

"Everybody is always surprised by this, but I think I understand why," Virginia offered in a soft voice. "When you're the kind of person who doesn't always succeed, everybody makes a big deal about it whenever you do something well. People want you to feel good about your-self. But when you're somebody who seems to succeed at everything you tackle, then everybody thinks that if they make a big deal out of it, well, he's just going to get a big head. And so, throughout his life, Joe's never really gotten the praise that most people get for doing things." This is true, Joe said, thoughtfully, looking beyond us through the window. "Even my father has said that he never took much interest in what I was doing in high school, or in any of my accomplishments in college. It was just accepted, and my fulfillment has come through external signs—newspaper articles and stuff like that. I didn't get that closer to home." Not surprisingly, at the laboratory the reward for good work is more work, Joe said. "A bit of a negative reinforcement, I guess. A catch-22." But that happens anywhere in life, Virginia said in soothing tones, noting that you often get feedback only when you've made a mistake. It's human nature. But in management situations, Joe worked hard at reinforcing positive self-esteem in others, Virginia said as she rose to go back to work.

One of the dogs was standing next to the table, wagging her tail and panting. Joe absentmindedly reached down and patted her head. Then the phone rang and he went to answer it. In that clipped, precise manner, he said, "Thank you for your help, but I do not accept unsolicited offers on the telephone." Click. He came back to the table and asked me if I would like to see his newspaper clippings. He rushed off and brought back a stack of paper that included articles back to his high school days. As a sophomore at Los Alamos High School he had devised an experiment that flew on the space shuttle. Two years later he withdrew an experiment—"Low Temperature Ultra Purification of Common Metals by Electrotransport"—from the International Science Fair in Albuquerque because the judges had questioned his data collection techniques. A scientist at the laboratory said to him, "Oh, Joe, why don't you just go, anyway." But Martz thought that the most honorable thing to do was withdraw, so he did. Another boy went in his place, and Martz said he was surprised when the entire incident made the papers. "I had scientific integrity even then," he said. At the age of twenty-two, newly married to his high school sweetheart, Martz received an all-expenses-paid trip to Washington, D.C., to play in the National Monopoly Tournament. He set a record for bankrupting an opponent faster than anyone else in history. Too soon, though, he theorized, thinking that that was the reason he lost. Besides, he said, "winning is really ninety percent luck and only ten percent strategy." He sorted through the stack and carefully pulled out a more recent article, asking me to read it on the spot. "For reasons that are beyond my comprehension, I have been in the media on a continuing basis for many years. It embarrasses me to think that the Albuquerque newspaper has such a thing as a file photo of me."

Ironically, while kids like Joe Martz felt insecure and unappreciated for their accomplishments, they were the ones who made people like Karen Brandt feel hopelessly inadequate. "I just knew I wasn't going to be anybody until I had a Ph.D.," she said when we had our first conversation over a long lunch at Montoya's, a restaurant on Central Avenue in Los Alamos. Rain was pounding on the street outside that day because Los Alamos was in the midst of the monsoon season, as they call it there, when rain falls on the mesa in lavish amounts during July and August. It is a luscious reward for living through the dryness that dominates the weather most of the year. Montoya's was a small, simple place, like most Los Alamos restaurants, serving northern New Mexico cuisine. On clear days it was awash with sunlight streaming through the big windows that wrapped around two sides of the building. One of the servers was named Leila; she'd been waiting tables on the hill since the 1940s and could tell many good stories, Brandt said, if you can get her to talk, and I tried. She looked me up and down and in her rolling, rich Spanish accent refused, saying, "I have told it all."

It had already started to rain when I arrived at the strip mall where the restaurant was located; hail bounced on the asphalt around me as I ran from the car. I took refuge momentarily in a shop, as I worked my way down to the restaurant. A huge thunderclap pounded the town, shaking the walls of the building I was in. Other people who had had the same idea looked out at the downpour and oohed at the thunder with uncomplicated curiosity and even pride. "There's more energy in a lightning strike than there is in a nuclear explosion," James Mercer-Smith had once told me. Now, of course, this made sense. Surprisingly, the sun was shining a few blocks away, although twisted ropes of lightning made inroads into the patch of blue sky. During the monsoons there are brief, frequent thunderstorms and many lightning strikes.

Los Alamos is used to it, and often people don't even look up. That day Los Alamos residents seemed giddy with the sight and the smell of the rain. There had been a record-setting heat wave during June, with highs in the upper nineties on the hill where normally they are in the eighties. I overheard a woman say to her companion that she felt like dancing in the streets.

Karen Brandt was casually dressed, in keeping with the comfortable town style that is an amalgam of college campus and ski resort. It harks back to the early days of the laboratory when the new town's residents adopted casual dress because it was practical—for the difficult conditions and constant hard work as well as the secrecy of the wartime project. Enrico Fermi, arguably one the world's greatest physicists, walked around Los Alamos "looking like a farmer, in rumpled clothes," noted one of the soldiers assigned to guard the secret community. "One time we were playing baseball, and he came up and asked if he could play, too," the former army man said. "It was only later that we found out who he really was." Then during the fifties, it was the highest fashion for prominent scientists to wear ratty jeans and caps and drive beat-up old pickups they'd bought from the Zia Company, the entity that until 1986 was responsible for construction and maintenance at the laboratory.

Brandt's personal style also was a throwback to the 1960s; she peppered her speech with verbal mannerisms of that time—"Outa sight"—and wore her graying hair long and straight. "I am a child of the sixties, that's for sure," she said. "And I hate the music now, so I listen to the oldies all the time." One of the local oldies stations, with studios in Santa Fe and a joint license with Los Alamos, is called K-BOM—"We're radio-active!" At the same time, Brandt is clearly a child of Los Alamos, born to a draftsman at the laboratory and a teacher in the Los Alamos school system. She had been working at the *Los Alamos Monitor* for two years, already having learned the extent to which Los Alamos distrusts people who would write about them, even when the writer was one of their own. "They believe that they will be misquoted and, consequently, they will comb through stories for sinister meaning," Brandt said. But that's just the way scientists are, she added. Writing for the local newspaper in a town full of Ph.D.'s is challenging. "We live in a town of highly educated experts who absolutely will let you know if you're wrong. In one of my historical articles, I misspelled the name of

Dorothy McKibbin. Believe me, I heard about that one right away," she said. McKibbin was the beloved Santa Fe hostess whose job it was to greet every newcomer to the secret wartime project, helping with housing problems, handing out security passes, and generally acting as a housemother to the predominantly young scientists and their families as they arrived at her office on East Palace Avenue in Santa Fe. She continued to work for the laboratory until 1963 and remained good friends with many of the people she had helped. In 1982, on the occasion of an Albuquerque TV special about her, she recalled Robert Oppenheimer as a natural, active person who "made the best martinis you've ever had." He walked lightly on the balls of his feet, she said, so that he seemed not to touch the ground.[2] Legends like Oppenheimer and McKibbin are not to be messed with, Brandt knew, and misspelling such an important name was a stupid mistake that was not likely to happen again.

"We get interesting letters to the editor, too," Brandt said. "People here have opinions and they are not afraid to express them. But then, that's part of what makes this an interesting place to live," Brandt said with eyebrows raised, a wry smile on her face. After a year at the paper she received what she considered a plum assignment—to write profiles of Manhattan Project pioneers for a special section published on the occasion of the fiftieth-anniversary reunion. She brought along a copy of the special section for me to see and opened it to the story about Jean and Winston Dabney, a WAC and army master sergeant who met and married in Los Alamos during the Manhattan Project. "We worked long hours," Brandt lovingly read Jean Dabney's words. "We just worked and worked. On Sundays we would go on picnics. . . . Smokey and Julius (the mess sergeants) would fix us a picnic basket. For two years we just worked and worked and worked."

The chance to interview the people who beat the rest of the world to this technical achievement was meaningful to Brandt because of its historical importance, but it was also personally gratifying, she said. "For one thing, it was an opportunity to meet face to face people who until then had been no more than names on Christmas cards. And to have them tell their stories about my father, who died in 1983, was a gift, an unimaginable gift." Brandt's father, an army soldier from northern Michigan, had been stationed at Los Alamos during the laboratory's early days. He had helped to build the first rope tow on the Los

Alamos ski hill and championed the first ice-skating rink in town, she said. Working on these stories had been valuable for another important reason, she said. It had helped her to better understand her birthplace and to be proud of its heritage. Brandt served on the board of directors of the Los Alamos Historical Society.

Nevertheless, in 1969, when she graduated from Los Alamos High School, Brandt couldn't wait to leave town. She'd realized that to be considered valid there, you had to be a researcher or some other highly educated person. While Brandt said she didn't get this kind of pressure from her parents, neither of whom were scientists, it was everywhere else in her environment. As a teenager she assumed that everyone went to college, because, of course, nearly everyone in Los Alamos did. "At the time I thought that the only people who didn't go to college were girls who got into trouble and had babies. It never occurred to me that you might actually make the choice not to go. It just was not an option here." Brandt wrote a novel to try and work through her feelings about growing up in "this strange place," she said. She called it *Catharsis*. "And what I found in writing this book is that I had never really felt adequate, in terms of career expectations, goals, or anything. I think that came from the fact that many of my classmates went to exclusive, expensive Ivy League schools and other places that would be considered the nation's finest. They were all pursuing careers as geneticists and economists. I went to college in the Midwest, in Hays, Kansas, to become a social worker."

Los Alamos managed to establish itself as an outpost of the counterculture despite its remote location and tendency to shut out the world, Brandt explained. People joined communes; drugs were plentiful. It was no different from the rest of the country, she stressed. One of the heavily polluted canyons near the laboratory was called Acid Canyon, Joe Martz had said, chuckling. "And it wasn't all because of things the lab did." Brandt's high school class was deeply affected by the drug culture of the sixties, and a number of her classmates had been burnt out by it, she said, carefully adding that there were also Vietnam vets whose lives had been irredeemably changed as well. (The high school's gymnasium had been named after a graduate who died in combat in Vietnam.) Nevertheless, her class produced a record number of National Merit Scholars, and many successful and prestigious graduates. "What the majority of us are doing with our lives today would blow your mind," enthused Brandt, who brought a yearbook to one of our meetings. "I would say that we have a minimum of twenty-five physicians in my class. We have people in the State Department, professors of medicine at leading universities, inventors, millionaires." There are some twenty-five of the class of '69 still living in Los Alamos, Brandt said. "Actually, I am seriously thinking of writing my own book: *The Children of the Bomb.*"

Brandt managed to stay away from Los Alamos for ten years before she realized that it really was where she wanted and needed to be. After getting a degree in social work, she'd married, moved to Texas and spent several years as a social worker, "dealing with really heavy stuff, like abused children," she said. But when her marriage failed, she moved back to Los Alamos in November 1979 to live with her parents and start all over again. "You want to know what I was really thinking? Los Alamos used to be a town with walls and gates and no one could penetrate them. Those walls were still up when I was a child. It sounds extreme, I know, but there's something quite wonderful about knowing that you can go for a walk any time of the day or night and you'll be okay. I'd had some hard experiences out in the world. I wanted to be back in a place where I could feel safe again. I also wanted to live in a place where I could do my own security clearance on men," she said. "I knew that if I came back here, I would have a far easier time learning the truth about people."

Even so, after ten years away, she had forgotten a few things about the personality of her hometown. She often cites the following incident to prove her point. She had gone out on a dinner date at a local restaurant soon after moving back. "When it came time to pay the bill, three of the men at the table whipped out their calculators to figure out to the penny what each person owed. And I mean, man, they had singing calculators, high-tech stuff, and I thought, wow, what have I done to myself coming back here? Then I remembered, yeah, this is what it's like. I'd forgotten. I'd moved here from Dallas, where that sort of thing never happened."

Los Alamos men are frequently portrayed as socially inept, at best, an image Brandt dismissed as humorous folktale. "Of course, some of these guys were so intense going through school that they didn't necessarily develop what people in the outside world would call social graces," she admitted. "People joke about that all the time. And there certainly are eccentrics, people who look like they just got out of bed and forgot to comb their hair. I mean, that's all here, too. But it's part of the charm of the place." She smiled serenely.

Brandt has never regretted returning to Los Alamos, even though it didn't make much sense in terms of her career. "I mean, what is a social worker going to do in Los Alamos? People up here certainly will not admit that they have any problems!"

That doesn't mean there isn't a very real need for that kind of help, said Tom Ribe, who also was born and grew up in Los Alamos, the son of a lab physicist. "I think a lot of these families in Los Alamos were very dysfunctional and continue to be so today," he said. The most recent stresses the community was feeling over reduced budgets, staff reductions, and a changing mission for the laboratory had only exacerbated existing tensions in the community and in families. "We are definitely a community under siege right now," said Paula Dransfield, noting that under such circumstances there are always tensions within families. But the town had always been oppressive in many ways, Ribe said. "I thought the adults were all so disciplined and straight. The fathers—and it was mostly the fathers when I was a kid—were so ambitious and were working so hard. My father would come home, eat dinner, sort of push us around a little bit, and then go right back to work. He did this for years. I wouldn't see him in the evenings at all, and then on the weekends he would come home and say, 'Okay, here's what we're going to do, we're going to go off up here and we're going to play real hard.'" In many Los Alamos families, the fathers were very detached because they were so into their work, Ribe said. "And I understand that this happens a lot today, too. Families are sort of fragmented because of it. Perhaps kids were a little neglected because of this push to work, work, work."

After years away from the mesa, Ribe had returned to Los Alamos to work at the laboratory for many of the same reasons that his father had first moved there in 1955. "My dad was very clear on why he came here. He could do good science and also go camping on the weekends. He grew up in Texas, and he wanted to be in a western place where he could fish and hunt and all that stuff." As it turned out, all of the Ribe boys were eager to leave Los Alamos when they finished high school; Tom is the only one who ever came back, and even then not because he missed the community. He missed the mountains and forests of northern New Mexico, where he had spent his youth camping and exploring with his friends. "I used the outdoors as an escape, to get away from the things about my family and the town that I didn't like," Ribe said. He and his friends spent their weekends camping, drinking beer, "and smoking illegal things around the campfire." But the emphasis was on spending time out in the woods. It meant getting away from the pressures that made high school in Los Alamos particularly difficult, he said. The message from home was that children should aspire to great intellectual achievement. The high school became the competitive field upon which these hopes and desires were played out. "We all got scarred by it. A lot of my own neuroses and low self-esteem came from that rather poorly managed drive by my father to make us into successful, ambitious, upper-middle-class intellectuals." Each of the Ribe boys is successful by those standards, however. One is a lawyer, one an economist in Washington, and another is a professor of landscape architecture. Tom was the last of the Ribe brothers to fall in line with the pattern outlined by his father and his community. "I was a real a rebel for a long time, a total hippy drug-head. That's just the way I approached life," he said. "I didn't really care whether I was an advanced placement kind of kid in school, although I did manage to get into advanced placement English," he quickly added. "I did have a very low self-esteem, but I seemed to be sure about what I was doing at the time." His lack of focus and drive, however, resulted in years of drifting and wandering around professionally, as he described it. During years in borderline working-class jobs, he got bored and longed for someone to talk to about politics and ethics. "I realized that I just needed to do something where I could use my head more and that if I didn't do something like that I was just going to be a nothing," Ribe said. His dad had finally won.

Ribe's love of the woods led him to study botany and forest ecology at the University of California at Santa Cruz. He worked in California as a park ranger for the California park system. He spent time at Yosemite and Kings Canyon, "a massive, beautiful granite wilderness with giant sequoias," Ribe lovingly described it. Then he returned to

Santa Cruz to get a graduate certificate in science journalism; he went on to earn a master's degree in environmental studies at the University of Oregon in Eugene, writing his thesis on logging practices in Bandelier National Monument near Los Alamos, managing to shake up the forest service and get some people fired. Finally, in need of a good job and longing for the forests of northern New Mexico, he came back to Los Alamos to work in environmental restoration. "When I heard about this opportunity, I thought, 'Ah, I can do something environmental and I can go back there,'" he said. And he was surprised by the way the community embraced him, even though he has been active in local, non-lab-related environmental issues, writing letters to the editor of the local newspaper and speaking out. He was sure he would become a pariah, he said, and eventually lose his job over his activism. "But, instead, I find they are very glad for my perspective and are really eager to know me. It's gratifying and, in a way, almost better than living in leftist towns on the West Coast where I sort of blended in. Here people seem really intrigued by what I represent, what I do, and where I put my energies." He had always loved this place, he said. "Especially Bandelier and the mountains around here. I used to dream about it; it's home to me, and I expect I'll stay here on and off for the rest of my life." Ribe credited a teacher at Los Alamos High School with stimulating his interest in environmental issues, noting that his and his classmates' concerns had more to do with the dangers of coal-burning power plants and mining practices than with anything the laboratory was doing.

Los Alamos is a strange place for kids to grow up, though, Ribe said. "I think kids would really rather be in a more normal town. It's very confusing for them because this is such a white town, while just down the hill, you're suddenly among Indian pueblos; in Santa Fe it's at least fifty percent Hispanic, and the culture is very different right away." The resentment that these surrounding communities feel for Los Alamos is very isolating, especially for the kids, Ribe said. "You didn't just go and have a pleasant rivalry in a nearby high school, because you were dealing with schools that were mostly Hispanic," he noted. Competition took on other deeper meanings. "This town has a sense of detachment from the rest of the state, and especially the local communities, even though there are thousands of people from those communities that work up here," Ribe explained.

A legendary and controversial Los Alamos problem, which has been cited often in magazine and newspaper articles about the community, is the quality of life for women on the mesa. Now, of course, there are many more women working as researchers at the laboratory, but during the early days, when Ribe was growing up, during the community's *Leave It to Beaver* period, as he called it, there were not a lot of options available for the educated wives of scientists. "I think it was very tough for women to be here. Let's say you're a female at some university and you fall in love with a guy who is a physicist. He gets a job at Los Alamos, and here you are working on a degree, like my mom, who was working on a French major, or let's say you're working on a master's in art history or something. You marry some guy, especially in the fifties, and off you go to Los Alamos. You end up in this completely sleepy little town and all you have is a bunch of other college-educated women around you; not many opportunities for work in the lab, although a lot of women did end up working there." Most of them worked in support roles, not as scientists. "There were very few women scientists," said Paula Dransfield, who grew up in the community and now serves in a management role at the laboratory. "Those women who were scientists were for the most part considered to be very odd people because here they were being very scientific and focused, and not particularly interested in makeup or hair or clothes."

So basically the dads brought home enough money to support that *Leave It to Beaver* lifestyle, said Ribe. "And, as you can imagine, the baby boom really boomed here. In fact, we had a baby explosion. But I think life was extremely difficult for the women, because they were bright and bored to death. It caused a lot of frustration, and as a result, there was a lot of alcoholism and I understand that there was a lot of infidelity, stuff that I didn't know about or see, but that I understand happened."

The women used their good minds as well as they could and did a lot of good for this community, said Paula Dransfield. They served on the school board and in county government, and worked to benefit the hospital, the library, the schools, and other important community institutions, she said. "There were a lot of very well-educated, intelligent women up here who were not being allowed to use their intelligence because it was the 1940s and '50s, when you were expected to take care of your family first." That was traditional culture everywhere else, she noted, not just in Los Alamos. "They did for themselves what needed to be done," she said.

Today the Cold War–era *Leave It to Beaver* lifestyle that Tom Ribe described is largely inaccessible to today's young Los Alamos families because the cost of living on the mesa is extraordinarily high. Real estate is very expensive, and given the geographic limitations of the Pajarito Plateau, housing is scarce. A cost-of-living study by the Los Alamos Economic Development Corporation in 1994 found that housing costs for middle-management households in the city were 70 percent above average. The study also compared the costs of utilities, transportation, food, health care, and other needs in Los Alamos to three hundred other communities in New Mexico and around the nation. While housing was by far the most expensive item, the other categories were high as well, making the cost of living in Los Alamos higher than Santa Fe, Chicago, or Los Angeles. But salary comparisons found Los Alamos middle-manager incomes to be higher than those in Los Angeles and Chicago, as well.

"We're not all just living in little middle-class houses, either," Ribe said. "I met a guy the other day that I think is living in his office, which is actually a very university type of thing to do." Students and postdocs often find themselves living in crumbling old apartment buildings like the stained concrete "Cave" located down the street from Montoya's. Housing is a big problem in Los Alamos, and it always has been. When the scientific community was founded in 1943, the burgeoning population overwhelmed the limited resources and expansion room of the rocky plateau. The plan had been to employ a small staff of one hundred research scientists to do the final design and assembly of the atomic bomb, but instead, the number of scientific personnel doubled every nine months into a large industrial laboratory. Furthermore, after a year, the builders of the atomic bomb, whose average age was twenty-five, had already created a baby boom, exacerbating the housing crunch and producing a generation of people whose birth certificates showed only "P.O. Box 1663" as a birthplace.

Ribe was living in a converted school bus in Poquaque, a pueblo-based community in the valley. He had refashioned the interior so that it could serve as a cheap and portable home. He raised the roof four and a half feet to make a sleeping loft, put in carpeting, and installed wood paneling, a full kitchen, and a bathroom. "It's pretty comfortable. I've got my computer, a huge stereo, and a big woodstove that is the sole heat source in the wintertime." He knows of another lab employee who lives in a bus, a housing solution that he referred to as a relic of the West Coast, where it is easier to manage because of the milder climate. "And there's another guy that lives in a tent up in the woods, and he's going to spend the winter out there. That's really harsh."

The first time I talked to him, during the summer monsoons, Ribe was getting restless and anxious to do something else with his life. "I can't do this forever," he said quietly. "It's a very interesting experience working here, almost an honor to be here, really, because this has got to be one of the more bizarre human organizations and stranger aspects of human history." But by the time winter had arrived, he was feeling hopeless about being there. It wasn't his culture, too entrenched and antiprogressive, he said. The weapons culture was against everything he believed in, and he knew in his heart that he couldn't do much good there, spending endless years trying to convince the lab to be more progressive and open. His friends were worrying about him, too, he said. "The people that I went to graduate school with—hard core environmental activists, peace activists, people who feel you have to live your life fully in an ethical way. They ask me what I'm doing here, and they're concerned mostly that I'm doing something that goes against my conscience or against my better judgment. My Karma, you know?"

It was late in the afternoon on an unusually cold December day. Winter had arrived in earnest on the mesa that past week, Ribe said. All he wanted to do was go home to his bus and get the fire going.

10

A Thousand
Cranes

By the middle of that winter of 1995, plans for commemorating the upcoming fiftieth anniversary of the bombing of Hiroshima were well under way in the United States as well as in Japan. It was soon obvious, though, that the psychic wounds from that world-changing event had never fully healed and that the moral questions it presented were far from being resolved. This was vividly demonstrated by the controversy surrounding a proposed Smithsonian Institution exhibit of the *Enola Gay*—the B-29 Super Fortress that carried "Little Boy" to Hiroshima. Veterans were outraged over the wording of the exhibit, claiming that it was far too generous toward the Japanese and did not hold them accountable for starting the terrible war in the first place. It was pointedly noted in the passionate public debate over the exhibit that Japan had never apologized for its actions in the war, so why should an exhibit in an American government institution be apologetic for the way in which the war was concluded?

Meanwhile, commentators on both sides of the Pacific urged American and Japanese citizens to bind up their wounds and look forward instead of back. And, as it turned out, Japan did make an awkward apology, while the *Enola Gay* exhibit was reduced to a minimalist presentation that sought to offend no one. Nevertheless, by August 1995, a *New York Times*–CBS News poll found that a majority of Americans, especially those who had lived through the war, still supported the bombings of Hiroshima and Nagasaki. And 76 percent of those queried did not believe that the United States owed Japan any apologies, while

58 percent said there was nothing morally wrong with the bombings.[1] Those citizens who remembered World War II recognized "Fat Man" and "Little Boy" as technical miracles that had saved many lives. Estimates at the time reckoned that some 500,000 to 1 million American soldiers would have been killed in an invasion of Japan—men like weapons designer Merri Wood's father. "I wouldn't have existed," Wood said. "My dad was on the main line to ship out to Japan." An estimated 100,000 American prisoners of war in Japan may also have been saved by the bomb, as archived Japanese military records show, because, in the event of an Allied invasion, the American prisoners were to be quickly put to death. Analysts claim that by preventing an invasion, the near annihilation of Hiroshima and Nagasaki had actually saved many other Japanese lives. However, historians have also uncovered evidence that Japan was ready to surrender, anyway.

President Truman had described the August 6, 1945, bombing of Hiroshima as an attack on a military base, even though the majority of the victims were not soldiers at all, but overwhelmingly civilian. Merri Wood and Jas Mercer-Smith were quick to point out that many more civilians were killed by the firebombings of Japanese cities that preceded the attacks on Hiroshima and Nagasaki. "How many people died in the great raid on Tokyo?" Wood asked rhetorically. "A hundred and fifty thousand. And how many died in Hiroshima? Eighty thousand. And which one do people yell about?" she asked in disgust. In truth, the estimates of numbers killed in either bombing vary considerably. The firebombing of Tokyo on March 9, 1945, accelerated by especially high winds that day, destroyed some sixteen square miles of the city and killed an estimated 34,000 to 100,000 people. It also marked a distinct departure from the American practice in Europe of making strategic bombing strikes against targets of military importance. Nagoya, Kobe, Osaka, Yokohama, and Kawasaki were also incinerated in an urban area bombing plan that killed as many as 400,000 people before the atomic bombs were dropped on Hiroshima and Nagasaki.[2] By the end of 1945, the Hiroshima death count rose to 145,000, or 54 percent of the city's population. After five years, deaths counted against the bomb were estimated at 200,000. By contrast, the deadly firebombing of Tokyo killed about 10 percent of that city's population. The difference between the two came down to the dense efficiency with which the atomic bomb did its killing.[3] In the most pragmatic terms, the new bomb brought warfare to an unprecedented level of efficiency, with one atomic bomb carried by one airplane doing the destructive duty of many hardworking bombardiers in many airplanes. Manhattan Project physicist Philip Morrison suggested that this is the true military meaning of Hiroshima and Nagasaki.

> At the height of its mobilization in World War Two, the United States could manage to make six or eight hundred big bombers. They could visit a city and do big damage in one night. If these eight hundred came to a city several nights, they could do the damage of an atomic bomb. So, you could manage to knock off, with all your forces, a city a week. But now, a thousand cities a night! It's the numbers. It's the cheapness.[4]

That, Morrison declared, is why we are in this big trouble, as he described the so-called genie that is out of the bottle. "War is lousy," said a grim Merri Wood. "And we don't condone killing people with nuclear weapons or anything else. But you're dead from a nuke, you're dead from a bullet, you're dead from a nuclear-induced fire, you're dead from an incendiary-induced fire. The effects are the same." She and Mercer-Smith referred frequently to "a handy book," as Wood put it. "A book you can read if you really want to scare yourself," Mercer-Smith added, chuckling. It is *The Effects of Nuclear Weapons* by Samuel Glasstone and Philip J. Dolan, published by the United States Department of Defense and the Energy Research and Development Administration. Mercer-Smith leafed through his copy of Glasstone to find a picture of ground zero after the Nagasaki explosion. "This building was only a tenth of a mile from ground zero," Mercer-Smith said, holding out the book for me to see. "There's a lot of that building still left," he offered. "However, the fire killed a lot of people." It's called a fireball for a reason, Wood noted, laughing. Packaged with the Glasstone book is a surprisingly low-tech tool called the Nuclear Bomb Effects Computer—a circular sandwich of plastic wheels "designed to make effects data easily available," according to the thin leaflet that accompanies it. "You can get all this from the Government Printing Office for about seventeen bucks," Wood said. Mercer-Smith manipulated the disks to calculate what happens to a city unfortunate enough to be bombed by a one-megaton nuclear weapon. The fireball radius for an airburst would be about 0.65 miles, Wood guessed. Exposures leading to radiation illness were limited to two miles from the epicenter, although those people receiving a prompt radiation dose had other things to worry about, anyway, she noted. "You're gone in the blast or you're gone in the fire," she said, shrugging. "Let me remind you that far more people are going to die from the burns, from the fires," she said. "Oh, I don't know," Mercer-Smith countered mischievously. "We could do it right, Merri?" Wood laughed heartily and said, "Oh, Jas! But seriously, how many people died in Dresden of burns?" They went on like this, making grim jokes, balancing the types and time frames of death in war, juggling statistics, and making arguments much in the way that historians, commentators, and ordinary citizens were now doing during the fiftieth-anniversary year of Hiroshima.

"I suppose I could get into trouble for saying this," said chemist Matthew Monagle. "But I think weapons people practice a kind of compartmentalized thinking that probably protects them from the reality of what they do." One could study the science of nuclear weaponry, consider the physical and political consequences of its use, weigh lives and sovereignty lost or saved, and find justification. But there was always that nagging worry, "I hope I'm right about this?" Mercer-Smith had said. "If we are wrong, we are responsible for killing millions of people." It was true, acknowledged Unitarian pastor Dale Arnink, that weapons designers, like many other humans, were prone to a kind of compartmentalized thinking in which they assumed responsibility for only their part of the problem. As Mercer-Smith had put it when he described the search for peaceful solutions to world affairs: "Frankly, I hope there's somebody out there smarter than I am who can figure out how to do that. It's not our job," he said. "We are here to maintain technical options."

There is very little guilt in Los Alamos over the mission of the laboratory, observed Pastor Arnink. "You're either for or against it, and if you're against it, you don't come to work at Los Alamos in the first place," he said, an opinion Mercer-Smith had also expressed. "I think most of our people came to that conclusion before they came here."

Over ten years earlier, when the Roman Catholic bishops were preparing their letter on peace in which they denounced nuclear weapons, Arnink decided to prepare a series of talks for his own flock in which he sought to address the moral questions associated with the laboratory's work. He decided to study 'Just War' theory, and found that one of the most easily grasped aspects was that noncombatants should be exempt from suffering. "They particularly ought not to be killed," he said emphatically. "There is such a thing as innocence, even in warfare, and that is the virtue of the 'Just War' theory. War is not hell and must not be made into hell! Otherwise, you have no right to fight for anything," he continued. "So if you follow out that logic, you realize that this is what makes nuclear weapons so atrocious, so immoral. Because you kill the innocent." It was an increasingly commonplace occurrence of twentieth-century warfare, anyway, he noted. It was reaffirmed by the atomic bomb.

He had hoped that by preaching on these issues and writing letters to the editor of the *Los Alamos Monitor,* he could stimulate discussion in the community. But it just didn't happen. People responded to the philosophical conundrum by insisting that they had never intended to actually use the bombs. "But that's not true," Arnink declared. The Cold War had been built upon the intention to use the bomb if it became necessary. So, does that then render the intention itself immoral? It was a pretty heady philosophical discussion, which Los Alamos residents seemed unwilling to take up, Arnink said, wondering if, in fact, it was his own fault. Perhaps he wasn't a good enough teacher. Nevertheless, he continued to try to address the ambiguity of these moral issues, telling his parishioners that there were no easy answers. "One is involved in doing something that is morally ambiguous and doing work that perhaps is evil," he said, but it is an evil that is part of a bigger picture in which justification could be reasoned. They had to make these weapons of destruction because the Russians were doing it; it was a matter of national security. "It then becomes what I call a necessary evil," Arnink explained. But if you recognize that you are doing an evil, even though it is necessary, then you have some moral responsibility to try to reduce the necessity. "You can't just do the evil without working on the larger problem," he had told his parishioners, admonishing them to at the very least write to their congressmen and the president, urging them to somehow get Los Alamos off the hook. "You see, I think it's a quagmire, and I don't think there are any saints or demons, that we're all sinners and have to carry the responsibility for the sin we do. A necessary evil perhaps to prevent a larger evil, but it's still evil. There is no righteousness in what we do." Arnink is still puzzled by his congregation's unwillingness to respond to his message. "You could argue that these people should be more sensitive, that they should have a better ethical system and should not have bought into the Cold War rhetoric," he speculated. "But they seemed to have examined the issues and had decided that they were okay with them." Of course, the cynic would point out that, of course, they're okay with it because the money is so good in weapons work, he added. "But that's part of it, too, isn't it? That's always been part of the ethical system. There are always these kinds of trade-offs," he shrugged, admitting that he, too, had bought into the system. "I'm a parasite on government funds. I really am," he admitted laughingly. "Over the years I occasionally try to remind us in our self-righteousness that, to the outside world, we're one of the worst welfare programs that the government has. And I'm a part of it." But he has vowed to his parishioners that he will stand by them through everything, although, in truth, he would like to see the intellect of the laboratory turned away from supporting the military and toward solving societal and environmental problems.

In his years at Los Alamos he had known only one person who had left Los Alamos for ethical reasons. "He was an astronomer who knew that his research was going to be used for weapons guidance systems and it bothered him so much that he had to quit and go somewhere else," said Arnink. Truthfully, people in Los Alamos felt more guilt about filling their free time, Arnink said, than they ever felt worrying about nuclear weapons. They were driven people who needed to always be busy. They worried about the same things that people in suburban professional communities everywhere worried about: Will I keep my job? Will I get a raise? Can I trust management to keep the laboratory alive? "This is a huge bureaucracy and people just don't trust it," Arnink noted, adding that Los Alamos scientists also worry that they won't be able to continue doing science in the way that they always have. Until the most recent troubles, their major concerns had been over their families. "Would their kids get into the college of their choice? Or would they get into the drug scene in Los Alamos and lose their souls? Why doesn't my spouse love me more? Everyday human American problems," Arnink concluded. "You know, people want to believe that this is a sick place, doing sick work, and so it's got to be full of sick people. But I just don't see it that way."

During the weekend of the fiftieth anniversary of Hiroshima, parishioners at Arnink's church, during a part of the service when they are encouraged to share their thoughts, listened as Kaye Manley, the widow of Manhattan Project scientist John Manley, vented her frustrations with all the news reports that talked about guilt over the use of nuclear weapons in Japan. "She came into church with a lot of anger over all of this," Arnink said, adding that perhaps she had jumped on his use of the word *guilt* in relation to Hiroshima. She was fed up, she said, and talked passionately for ten minutes about how Los Alamos had worked to end Japanese atrocities and to bring a horrible war to an end. There was no reason to feel guilty for that. For his part, Arnink suggested to his congregation that no one was without guilt in this affair. "In twentiety-century warfare there have been no clean hands," he concluded, abruptly ending the discussion that could otherwise have dominated the day's service. "Can we not get into a long discussion about this," Arnink said wearily. He spent the balance of the time talking about the poetry of Rainer Maria Rilke.

The community had already made it clear that they would not assume a public mantle of guilt over what happened to Hiroshima and Nagasaki when a group of Albuquerque schoolchildren approached the Los Alamos County Council for permission to erect a Children's Peace Statue in the town. The group had gathered over forty thousand signatures of children from the fifty states and fifty-three nations and had raised twenty thousand dollars to invest in building the statue, and the Los Alamos County Council seriously considered the merit of the children's vision of peace. But they also responded to the views of their community, many of whose residents believed that it was because of the work of the laboratory that peace had prevailed for decades and that a global nuclear holocaust had been avoided. It was thought that such a peace statue would be a slap at the laboratory and the town, and that it would attract even more protesters to the community. Furthermore, some of the parents worried about how such a monument would affect their own children. One young boy declared to the council that he did not want to grow up with that kind of guilt. A councilwoman said she had never been ashamed of what Los Alamos stood for, while another resident suggested that the town erect a statue of its own design, honoring the Los Alamos–designed Vela satellite, part of the first space-based nuclear explosion detection system that had so successfully supported the test ban treaty. Residents also spoke in favor of the children and the statue, but the room erupted in cheers and applause when a teenager, Joel Younger, the son of weapons designer Steve Younger, pointed to the American flag and said, "We don't need peace statues because we have the flag over there."[5] With a 3–3 tie vote, the Los Alamos County Council refused the Children's Peace Statue, which was finally given a place in Albuquerque. Privately some residents said that the Japanese got just what they deserved, and that no one should feel sorry about the bombings.

Also during this time, a small group of Japanese citizens, survivors of the bombings of Hiroshima and Nagasaki and members of the Tokyo Federation of Atomic Bomb Sufferers, visited the sites that were being proposed for the Children's Peace Statue. They visited Fuller Lodge, the Historical Museum, and the Bradbury Science Museum, wishing to see for themselves the place where the atomic bomb that had ravaged their cities was built. During their visit, someone shouted to them that the bomb had ended the war, to which a spokesman for the group responded that Americans still did not comprehend the suffering the weapon's use had caused; the visitors wished somehow to explain this to Americans, to explain what it had been like.[6]

At the Bradbury Science Museum, the Japanese visitors were able to look upon shell casings identical to those used for Fat Man and Little Boy. Unlike the bombs that were dropped on their own cities, however, these were painted white, as were the life-size statues of Oppenheimer and General Leslie Groves that stand in front of a history wall with a time line and artifacts from the Manhattan Project. The rest of the museum is given over to exhibits, many of them hands-on, that explain in broad terms the unclassified aspects of the laboratory's work in weapons development and other areas of research, as well as vague information about underground nuclear tests. The exhibit includes an instrument rack, like those that had been lowered into the earth to gather data during underground nuclear explosions at the Nevada test site. Suspended overhead in the museum are a cruise missile and two satellites.

Each year some 130,000 people from all over the world visit the museum that Ed Grothus and other peace activists refer to as merely a public relations tool and not a real science museum at all. At the request of the Los Alamos Study Group—a Santa Fe–based activist organization that opposes the mission of the laboratory and works to bring nuclear weapons policy decisions to public debate—an area was established in the museum for such opposing viewpoints. In contrast to the rest of the museum, where the effects of nuclear weapons are carefully sanitized, activists say, the public forum wall should show the human impact of the laboratory's work with grisly pictures of Japanese victims of the bomb, for example. To counter this, however, the Los Alamos Education Group—a coalition of Navajo Code Talkers, the Bataan Death March Organization, the Veterans of Foreign Wars, the American Legion, and the Laboratory Retiree Group—created an exhibit, as well. "We mourn the lives lost and celebrate the lives of those who survived because of the decision to use the atomic bomb to end the war," they wrote. The display addressed the notion of whether or not the Japanese were ready to surrender and asserted that the bomb did save civilian and military lives. By the end of 1996, the Bradbury Science Museum developed a policy whereby different organizations could have a turn occupying a 150-square-foot area of the Public Forum Wall for a six-month period, giving everyone fair access. In the event of more than one applicant, there would be a drawing. In December 1996, the Los Alamos Study Group and the Los Alamos Education Group both applied for the space, but the Study Group withdrew, leaving the display to the Education Group for the period January 15 to July 15, 1997.

Next to the Public Forum Wall there is a large book provided so that visitors to the museum can write down their thoughts about the laboratory, nuclear weapons, and the bombings of Hiroshima and Nagasaki.

"People should all get along," wrote one visitor, who had also sketched a peace sign on the page.

Others wrote:

"I feel it was necessary that President Truman order that the bombs be dropped on Japan in order to stop the killing of innocent men and women in the world."

"This is pure Japanese propaganda. As an infantry soldier at the Bulge, scheduled to go to China, I am grateful the bomb was dropped. It may have saved my life. The Japanese deserved the two bombs. Too bad we did not have 100 to drop before the war was over."

"As the bride of an American lieutenant, I welcomed the surrender of Japan in mid-August '45. But when I learned the extent of the horrible deaths my fellow Americans had inflicted on Japanese civilians, I felt for the first time a loss of complete patriotic belief in the moral core of my country. I still believe we lost the ability to be man's best hope for freedom and democracy the day Harry Truman authorized the dropping of the bombs. The crime and violence which plague our cities and homes today reflect the same indifference we showed to the suffering of the Japanese on August 6 and 9, 1945."

"War isn't pretty, but there's no substitute for winning."

"As usual innocent citizens must pay the price for political hubris! At the time, there must have seemed to be no other solution. But we must not continue to glorify war or to *revel* in this kind of victory."

"The fact that I am writing this note is very probably because my life was saved by the dropping of the bomb. My battalion was scheduled to be involved in the invasion of Honshu Island."

"39 million deaths in a war the U.S. didn't start!"

"All I have to say is that I visited the museum in Nagasaki when I was 12 and cried for 2 days."

"And when my best friend learned her father had died at Pearl Harbor, she cried for weeks and spent the rest of her life, from age 12 on, fatherless. (His body was never recovered.)"

"One bomb is too many.—Eduardo de los Alamos"

"Get real you hand wringing, whining, knee jerk, airhead liberals. Without the bomb we would all be eating raw fish."

"Remember Pearl Harbor, the Bataan Death March, the Rape of Nanking, the biological experiments and other blessings of Japanese culture! They bloody well deserved it!"

Joe Martz makes a point of visiting the Bradbury Science Museum every few weeks in order to read the comments in the big book.

✦

While the 509th Bomber Group, that had included the crew of the *Enola Gay*, was marking the August 6, 1995, anniversary at a convention in Albuquerque, the day arrived in Los Alamos with very little public fanfare. A few people in town hoped the 509th would drive up to Los Alamos, and they kept an eye out for the group's red overseas caps and insignia. But the 509th didn't show up for the only visible public event in town—a peace vigil at Ashley Pond, sponsored by the Los Alamos Study Group. The laboratory had commemorated the event earlier with a series of lectures, but, in truth, the bigger and more purely celebratory event for the community had been in 1993, on the occasion of the fiftieth anniversary of the founding of the laboratory, with a symposium, of course, and a nostalgic reunion of Manhattan Project veterans. There had been a dance, and Edward Teller had given a piano concert. One of the few sour notes had been the extreme measures the organizers of the event had been forced to take in order to keep Teller and Hans Bethe from running into each other, such was their bitterness toward each other.

But on August 6, 1995, the laboratory and the town seemed to be keeping a low profile. In fact, it could have been any other sunny, quiet

Saturday in Los Alamos, the kind of day when Joe Martz might be found sitting on the grassy bank of Ashley Pond testing his radio-controlled boats in the tiny body of water. But on this day a small group of activists had drifted into the park, settling down to sit for peace a few yards away from the area where the world's first nuclear weapon had been constructed. They sat rigidly straight, their legs crossed and their backs turned to the other people lounging on benches, waiting for something interesting to happen. An old Volkswagen van was parked nearby on the street. It looked markedly out of place in Los Alamos, hand-painted as it was with the bright blue of the New Mexico sky and dotted with fluffy white clouds. There was a "Save the Earth" sticker in the back window.

A family walked around the edges of the pond, the children feeding chunks of bread to the ducks. And a little boy raced around the park stabbing at the air with his makeshift weapon, a turkey baster. He opened and slammed the row of car doors that had been set up in the park as part of the sculpture show—doors to nothing, rusty, graffiti-damaged symbols of American technology. A few people in Los Alamos had thought the sculpture laughable. Finally, onlookers were gratified by the appearance of a disheveled man in a black chiffon cocktail dress. His hairy legs showed beneath a crooked hem, as did his sensible men's socks and sandals. He had set up shop on a picnic table where he hurriedly folded sloppy, origami paper cranes that he later would give out to anyone who would take them. He fluttered his hands in the air and rolled his eyes to the heavens as he tried to explain what he was doing. A nattily dressed TV reporter smoothed his hair and strode up to the man in the dress to snag an interview. There actually were more reporters in the park than there were protesters; they had to wait their turn to talk to Dress Man. "Do you know the story of the thousand cranes?" he asked anyone who would listen, urging them to recite the tale if they knew it and handing them a five-dollar bill if they said it to his satisfaction. It's a widely known, true story about a little girl named Sadako who survived the initial blast of Hiroshima only to succumb ten years later to leukemia. As she lay sick in the hospital, she was reminded of the Japanese legend that if a sick person folds a thousand cranes, she will get well. The girl managed to fold over six hundred cranes before she died at age twelve, inspiring her school friends to finish the task and also to collect money from other Japanese schoolchildren to honor Sadako and all the children who had suffered from the bomb. A statue of the little girl stands in Hiroshima's Peace Park. "This is our cry, this is our prayer, peace in the world," reads the legend on the base of the monument.

The only person not watching the quiet drama unfold next to Ashley Pond was a gray-haired man who appeared to be sleeping on a bench. His arms were folded under his head and he had casually crossed one leg over the other. His black baseball cap—bearing a mushroom cloud design and the words "Trinity Site, 16 July, 1945. Fifty Years of Peace"—was pulled down to shade his face.

I leaned down and asked him, "Why are you here?" Captain Dean Merot pulled the cap aside and grinned, "Because I haven't died yet," he said, sitting up to look around at the odd assortment of people in the park. "What can you say about a man wearing a skirt," he said, tipping his head in the direction of Dress Man. "I just came down here to satisfy my curiosity," he explained, looking at me from the corners of his eyes. He was a retired Los Alamos police captain who had seen a lot of demonstrations in Los Alamos over the years, he said, especially during the Vietnam War when they were at their weirdest and most worrisome. Like the one in 1970, when a much larger group than today's came and gathered around the pond, Merot remembered. "They lit little candles and expounded on peace. And they also threatened to shut down the laboratory, so, we got the police force down here, some auxiliary police, state police, and mounted patrols." But the laboratory stayed open, of course. None of the demonstrations had ever really been any trouble, Merot explained, leaning back to watch the goings-on in the park, his arms crossed over his chest. Merot had lived in Los Alamos since 1956, when he arrived as a member of the army protective force. "People like to be close to something unusual," Merot said. "I've sure been able to do that."

Ed Grothus had shown up and was erecting a large display at the other end of the park. It included a huge American flag and a sign with a mushroom cloud, as well as a banner that read, "We are sorry about Hiroshima and Nagasaki." At the same time, a teenaged boy was tying a bed sheet to a sculpture near the center of the park. On it were written the words "Japan started WWII to ensure Tyranny. America ended

WWII to ensure Freedom." His homemade banner asked the question "How many died before the A-bomb guarenteed [*sic*] our freedom?" and listed the number of Chinese, British, and American soldiers and civilians who had died in World War II. The boy was seventeen-year-old Joel Younger, who said he felt his viewpoint should be represented at the event, too. "Those who forget history are doomed to repeat it," declared the fresh-faced, muscular kid who hoped to join the marines when he graduated from high school. "The price of peace is eternal vigilance."

Steve Younger had stopped by the park to see what was going on and take a look at his son's efforts. Within the coming year he would leave his position with the Center for International Security Affairs, the lab organization that worked to reduce the worldwide threat of nuclear war, and accept the directorship of the Nuclear Weapons Technology Program at Los Alamos. And Energy Secretary Hazel O'Leary, after engineering a profound transformation of the unwieldy DOE complex and making more than a few enemies in the process, would be hounded by what she referred to as pronuclear conservatives who accused her of taking too many extravagant trips. She would submit her resignation after the reelection of Bill Clinton, who chose Federico Peña to replace her. Meanwhile, the government would pay millions of dollars in reparations to citizens who successfully claimed that they had been unwittingly experimented upon with radioactive substances. And Sig Hecker would announce his resignation in 1997 as laboratory director, after a difficult year of heavy layoffs that also brought down upon lab management an uncharacteristically stern disapproval from the perennially loyal New Mexico congressional delegation. It was a year in which an unusual number of accidents had forced the first ever stand-down of the laboratory. A twenty-two-year-old graduate student had suffered a serious electric shock, and Hecker received "a call that all managers (or parents) fear," he wrote in his July 19, 1996, "Inside Story" column in the *Newsbulletin*. "When I got to the hospital, I watched as one of our students was struggling with all his might to regain consciousness. It was a frightening and sobering sight. It was one that we could have done more to avoid and must avoid in the future." When he announced his resignation, Hecker noted that his wife had been reminding him for a while now that he had promised to stay in the post for only ten years. It had now been twelve years, and under his watch the lab had celebrated its fiftieth anniversary, the Cold War had come to a surprising conclusion, throwing the mission of the institution into doubt, while lab scientists began what had seemed unthinkable not long ago—a collaborative relationship with Russian weapons scientists. Nuclear testing had ended, the DOE's openness policy had forced the laboratory to open itself to closer inspection by a suspicious public, and the institution had been forced to adjust to unprecedented budget shortfalls. Hecker had made massive organizational changes in the laboratory management structure. "We have gone through this very difficult and trying time of self-examination and public examination," said Hecker. The important thing is to be stronger for it, to emerge on the other side of the experience with not only an understanding of what had gone wrong during the Cold War and the conduct of federally funded research, but also an appreciation for the good things that had come about because of it. For his part, he would dedicate his last year as director of Los Alamos National Laboratory to striving to improve worker safety at the laboratory and develop a more functional relationship with the Department of Energy.

By 1997 the laboratory would resume underground testing at the Nevada test site, conducting subcritical experiments in which small amounts of plutonium were subjected to extreme forces from chemical explosions, yielding pressures that came usefully close to those found in a real nuclear explosion. While the stated purpose was to better understand the effects of aging on weapons in the stockpile and not to develop new ones, activists insisted such tests violated the spirit of the Comprehensive Test Ban. A federal judge refused to grand an injunction that would stop these and other tests designed to maintain the U.S. nuclear stockpile.

"To be truthful, this isn't much of a protest, is it?" said young Joel, as he looked disdainfully at the sparse crowd of activists being questioned and photographed by the press. A cold, sharp rain had begun to fall, the sunny summer day gone in the fickle way of mountain weather. And then a big wind roared down from the Jemez Mountains, billowing the flag and banners that Ed Grothus had raised on a timber frame.

He put his strong back into holding it up as it threatened to fold around him, while the Los Alamos Study Group remained sitting under a tree, ignoring everything. The television reporter had already scurried away to get out of the weather, and Dean Merot got into his pickup and drove away, while the paper cranes that Dress Man had heaped onto a table were captured by the wind and took flight.

Notes

Introduction

1. From an address given by Richard Rhodes on June 10, 1993, in Los Alamos at the fiftieth reunion of the Manhattan District.

2. Richard Rhodes, *The Making of the Atomic Bomb* (New York: Simon & Schuster, 1986), 572.

3. Lawrence Badash, Joseph O. Hirschfelder, Herbert P. Broida, eds., *Reminiscences of Los Alamos 1943–45* (Boston: D. Reidel Publishing Company, 1980), 100.

4. John Fleck, "Selling Government to Taxpayers," *Albuquerque Journal*, March 23, 1997, B1.

Chapter 1

1. Richard Rhodes, *Dark Sun: The Making of the Hydrogen Bomb* (New York: Simon & Schuster, 1995), 342.

2. Henry Kissinger, *American Foreign Policy: Three Essays by Henry A. Kissinger* (New York: W. W. Norton, 1969), 61.

3. Gar Alperovitz and Kai Bird, "The Centrality of the Bomb," *Foreign Policy* (Spring 1994).

4. Ibid.

5. J. Carson Mark, "Do We Need Nuclear Testing," *Arms Control Today* (November 1990), 13.

6. Larry Bernard, "Atomic Bomb Saved Lives in WWII, Bethe Says," *Cornell Chronicle*, April 14, 1994.

7. Mark, "Do We Need Nuclear Testing?" 13.

8. Nicholas Metropolis, "Random Reminiscences," in *Behind Tall Fences: Stories and Experiences about Los Alamos and Its Beginnings* (Los Alamos: Los Alamos Historical Society, 1996).

9. Stephen M. Younger, "AGEX II: the High-Energy-Density Regime of Weapons Physics," *Los Alamos Science*, no. 21 (1993), 63.

10. Younger, "AGEX II," 63–69.

11. Steve Watkins, "Horner: Let's 'Go to Zero,'" *Air Force Times*, August 1, 1994.

12. William M. Arkin, "Nuclear Junkies: Those Lovable Little Bombs," *Bulletin of Atomic Scientists* (July/August 1993).

13. "U.S. Nuclear Weapons Stockpile, July 1994," *Bulletin of Atomic Scientists* (July/August 1994), 61–62.

14. John Fleck, "Sensors Can Track Bombs' Health," *Albuquerque Journal*, December 26, 1995.

15. Watkins, "Horner: Let's 'Go to Zero.'"

16. Ibid.

Chapter 2

1. David Fulghum, "Small Clustered Munitions May Carry Nuclear Wastes," *Aviation Week and Space Technology* (October 11, 1993), 61.

2. Phil Williams and Paul N. Woessner, "The Real Threat of Nuclear Smuggling," *Scientific American* 274, no. 1 (January 1996), 40–44.

3. Stephen M. Younger, "Russian-American Collaboration," *Los Alamos Science*, no. 21 (1993), 81.

4. "U.S. Paid Russians for Nuclear Details," *Washington Post*, October 27, 1996.

Chapter 3

1. John McPhee, *The Curve of Binding Energy* (New York: Noonday Press, 1974), 118–19.

2. Reuters, *Philadelphia Daily News*, July 18, 1983: 44.

3. Terry Atlas, "Terrorist Threat in U.S. a Matter of When, Not If, Senators Told," *Chicago Tribune*, March 28, 1996.

4. McPhee, *The Curve of Binding Energy*, 153–54.

5. Robert Wright, "Nukes, Nerve Gas and Anthrax Spores: Be Very Afraid," *New Republic* (May 1, 1995).

6. Hal K. Rothman, *On Rims and Ridges: The Los Alamos Area since 1880* (Lincoln: University of Nebraska Press, 1992), 278–79.

7. "Taking on the Future: Harold Agnew and Los Alamos Scientists Discuss the Potential of the Laboratory," *Los Alamos Science*, no. 21 (1993), 22.

8. Ferenc Morton Szasz, *British Scientists and the Manhattan Project: The Los Alamos Years* (New York: St. Martin's Press, 1992), 92.

9. Ibid., 94.

10. "British Documents Indicate Soviet Spies Infiltrated U.S. A-Bomb Program," Associated Press, October 3, 1996.

11. Priscilla Johnson McMillan, "Flimsy Memories," *Bulletin of Atomic Scientists* (July/August 1994), 32.

12. Hans A. Bethe, Kurt Gottfried, and Roald Z. Sagdeev, "Did Bohr Share Nuclear Secrets?" *Scientific American* 272, no. 5 (May 1995), 84–90.

13. Ibid.

14. Margie Szaroleta, "FBI Refutes Retired KGB Officer's Charge of Atomic Scientist Espionage," Associated Press, May 2, 1995.

15. "Colleagues Say Oppenheimer Was Not a Spy," *Philadelphia Inquirer,* April 19, 1994, A11.

16. "Secrets Radiate from Nuclear Labs," *Philadelphia Daily News,* October 11, 1988, 13.

17. Theodore B. Taylor, "Putting the Nuclear Genie Back in the Bottle," Nuclear Control Institute, http://www.nci.org/nci/ib5196.htm.

Chapter 4

1. Rhodes, *Making of the Atomic Bomb*, 326–27.

2. Ibid., 346.

3. Eileen Welsome, "The Plutonium Experiment," *Albuquerque Tribune,* November 15, 1993.

4. "Plutonium," Nuclear Issues Briefing Paper 18, Uranium Information Centre, Melbourne, Australia, May 1996.

5. John Jagger, *The Nuclear Lion: What Every Citizen Should Know about Nuclear Power and Nuclear War* (New York: Plenum Press, 1991), 98.

6. David N. Schramm, "The Age of the Elements," in *The World Treasury of Physics, Astronomy, and Mathematics,* Timothy Ferris ed. (Boston: Little, Brown, 1994), 177.

7. Catherine Caufield, *Multiple Exposures: Chronicles of the Radiation Age* (Chicago: University of Chicago Press, 1989), 23–28.

8. Ibid., 52.

9. Ibid., 40.

10. Jeff Wheelwright, "Atomic Overreaction," *Atlantic Monthly* (April 1995), 38.

11. "Human Radiation Studies: Remembering the Early Years: Oral History of Dr. George Voelz, M.D.," Department of Energy Openness: Human Radiation Experimentation, http://www.ohre.doe.gov/roadmap/histories/0454/0454toc.html, May 9, 1996.

12. Ibid.

13. Wheelwright, "Atomic Overreaction," 38.

14. "Plutonium," Nuclear Issues Briefing Paper 18.

15. Rhodes, *Making of the Atomic Bomb*, 741–42.

16. Ibid., 740.

17. "The Study of Long-Term Health Effects in the Survivors of the Atomic Bombings of Hiroshima and Nagasaki," Radiation Effects Research Foundation, http://www.rerf.or.jp/eigo/radefx/toc.htm.

18. L. H. Hempelmann, C. C. Lushbaugh, and G. L. Voelz, "What Has Happened to the Survivors of the Early Los Alamos Nuclear Accidents?" Conference for Radiation Accident Preparedness, Oak Ridge, Tennessee, October 19–20, 1979, 4–16.

19. Ibid.

20. Karen Nilsson Brandt, "WAC, SED Build Life Together in Los Alamos," *Los Alamos Monitor*, Special Section, June 6, 1993, 11.

21. David Hawkins, *Project Y: The Los Alamos Story* (Los Angeles: Tomash Publishers, 1983), 198–99.

22. Ibid., 270.

23. Thomas L. Shipman, "Acute Radiation Death Resulting from an Accidental Nuclear Critical Excursion: Description of the Accident and Subsequent Events," *Journal of Occupation Medicine* (March 1961), 147–49.

24. Human Radiation Studies: Remembering the Early Years, Department of Energy.

25. Memorandum to J. R. Oppenheimer from L. H. Hempelmann, re: Health Hazards related to Plutonium, August 16, 1944, Los Alamos National Laboratory.

26. "Human Radiation Studies: Remembering the Early Years," Department of Energy.

27. Ibid.

28. Debra D. Durocher, "Radiation Redux," *American Journalism Review* (November 12–18), 1996.

29. Final Report of the Advisory Committee on Human Radiation Experiments, Department of Energy, http://www.ohre.doe.gov/roadmap/achre/report.html.

30. Ibid.

31. M. A. Van Dilla and M. J. Fulwyler, "Radioactive Metabolism in Children and Adults after the Ingestion of Very Small Doses," *Science* 144(1964), 178–79.

32. "Cartoon Time in the Laboratory, Nothing Makes Children Sit Still Quite So Well as a TV Set," *The Atom*, Los Alamos Scientific Laboratory (March 1964), 10.

33. "Human Radiation Studies."

34. Ibid.

35. "Research Articles, Health Reports Released by Human Studies Project Team," Los Alamos National Laboratory, May 23, 1994.

36. "Twenty-seven Radiation Experiments Done at LANL," *The New Mexican*, February 10, 1995.

37. "Hillerman, Health Reports Form Human Studies Release," Los Alamos National Laboratory, May 9, 1994.

38. Final Report . . . Human Radiation Experiments.

39. Bayo Canyon/The Rala Program, Human Studies Project Team Factsheet, LALP-94-6, Los Alamos National Laboratory, January 10, 1994.

40. "Human Studies Project Team Ends Phase One," *Los Alamos National Laboratory Newsbulletin* (October 14, 1994), 2.

Chapter 5

1. "Meeting President Clinton's State of the Union Challenges," Department of Energy, June 17, 1996.

2. Frank von Hippel et al., "Eliminating Nuclear Warheads," *Scientific American* (August 1993), 47.

3. "Nuclear Leftovers Stored Waste-to-Glass Plant Designed to Transform Liquid into Cylinders," Associated Press, March 24, 1996.

4. "High-Level Nuclear Waste," The National Energy Institute— an organization representing the nuclear energy industry, December 1995.

5. Gregory H. Canavan, Stirling A. Colgate, O'Dean P. Judd, Albert G. Petschek, and Thomas F. Stratton, "Comments on 'Nuclear Excursions' and 'Criticality Issues,'" Los Alamos National Laboratory, March 7, 1995, 1.

6. Ibid., 5.

7. "Director Sig Hecker: The Laboratory's Position on the Underground Supercriticality Controversy," LANL *NewsBulletin* (March 17, 1995), 2.

8. "Accelerator Based Conversion of Surplus Plutonium," *Los Alamos Science*, no. 21 (1993), 106.

9. William Broad, "Deadly Nuclear Waste Piles Up with No Clear Solution at Hand," *New York Times*, March 14, 1995.

10. Nuclear Control Institute Homepage, http://www.nci.org/nci/index.htm.

11. Greg Gordon, "Nevada Town Does End-Around," *Minneapolis Star Tribune*, March 30, 1995, 4A.

12. Glenn Zorpette, "Confronting the Nuclear Legacy," *Scientific American* 274 (May 1996), 88–97.

13. Vicki Allen, "Senators Want New Hanford Nuclear Cleanup Law," Reuters, March 15, 1995.

14. Zorpette, "Confronting the Nuclear Legacy."

15. Byron Spice, "Gophers Could Pose Risk at Waste Site, Study Says," *Albuquerque Journal*, July 16, 1982, A2.

Chapter 6

1. Lawrence Lack, "DOE Investigators Study Los Alamos Nuclear Waste," *Christian Science Monitor*, October 3, 1993, 7.

2. Ibid.

3. Sig Hecker, "The Inside Story—Five Years Later," LANL *News-Bulletin* (October 31, 1996).

4. Ibid.

5. "Taking on the Future: Harold Agnew and Los Alamos Scientists Discuss the Potential of the Laboratory," *Los Alamos Science*, no. 21 (1993), 20.

6. "Human Radiation Studies: Remembering the Early Years: Oral History of Don Francis Petersen, Ph.D.," Department of Energy Openness: Human Radiation Experiments, http://www.ohre.doe.gov/roadmap/histories/0460/0460toc.html, May 9, 1996.

7. Elizabeth Corcoran, "National Conundrums," *Scientific American* (January 1993).

8. Ibid.

9. Scott McCartney, "Lab Partners: With Cold War Over, Los Alamos Seeks New Way of Doing Business," *Wall Street Journal*, July 15, 1993.

10. "Weapons Labs: After the Cold War," *Science* (November 22, 1991), 254.

11. "Taking on the Future," 13.

12. John Fleck, "Small Firms Lack Means to Wait Out Red Tape," *Albuquerque Journal*, August 6, 1995.

Chapter 7

1. Stephen Strauss, "Don't Throw Out That Old Calculator," *Toronto Globe and Mail*, January 9, 1993: A4.

Chapter 8

1. McPhee, *The Curve of Binding Energy*, 112.

2. Vivian Gornick, "Town Without Pity," *Mother Jones* (August/September 1985), 20.

3. Statement of Edward B. Grothus, World Uranium Hearing, Salzburg, Austria, September 1992.

4. Tom Sharpe, "Secret Service Not Amused Over Joke Gift Can of 'Plutonium' Sent to Clinton," *Albuquerque Journal*, February 26, 1997.

Chapter 9

1. Joseph Kane, "Los Alamos: A City Upon a Hill," *Time* (December 10, 1979), 14.

2. Elizabeth Staley, "'Gatekeeper' Kept Secret for 40 Years," *Albuquerque Journal*, April 9, 1982.

Chapter 10

1. "50 Years after Hiroshima, U.S. Still Supports the Bombing," Associated Press, August 1, 1995.

2. Stewart Udall, *The Myths of August: A Personal Exploration of Our Tragic Cold War Affair with the Atom* (New York: Pantheon Books, 1994), 57–60.

3. Rhodes, *Making of the Atomic Bomb*, 734.

4. Studs Terkel, *The Good War: An Oral History of World War Two* (New York: Pantheon Books, 1984), 514–15.

5. Chairman Schaller, "What Was Said about the Statue . . . ," *Los Alamos Monitor*, February 14, 1995.

6. Stephen T. Shankland, "Atom Bomb Survivors Visit Los Alamos," *Los Alamos Monitor*, October 14, 1994, 1.

Index